Monstrous Imagination

D0861266

Monstrous Imagination

—

M A R I E - H É L È N E   H U E T

H A R V A R D   U N I V E R S I T Y   P R E S S

Cambridge, Massachusetts

London, England

1993

This book is printed on acid-free paper, and its binding materials
have been chosen for strength and durability.

Library of Congress Cataloging-in-Publication Data

Huet, Marie Hélène.
    Monstrous imagination / Marie-Hélène Huet.
        p.   cm.
    Includes index.
    ISBN 0-674-58651-4 (cloth)
    ISBN 0-674-58649-2 (paper)
    1. Mimesis in literature. 2. Abnormalities, Human, in literature.
3. Monsters in literature. 4. Imagination in literature.
I. Title.
PN56.M536H84   1993
    809'.912—dc20   92-29384
                                                              CIP

Acknowledgments

I started working on this book in 1982. During the following years, I received considerable help, advice, and moral support from my friends and colleagues. I am particularly indebted to Scott Bryson, who did the initial translation of Chapters 1 through 5, 7, 8, and 10 from the French and gave me stylistic advice on the chapters written in English. Jay Caplan, Thomas Dumm, Henri Dutour, Andrew Parker, Avital Ronell, and Debra Zaller read all or parts of the manuscript and made important suggestions and criticisms. John Farley shared with me his considerable knowledge of the history of embryology, and a great part of my research would have been impossible without Margaret Groesbeck and Michael Kasper, reference librarians *extraordinaires*. To all of them, to Gianna Celli and the late Roberto Celli, who made the Villa Serbelloni in Bellagio such a wonderful place to think and study, this book is dedicated with gratitude.

I wish to thank the University of California at Berkeley for a Humanities Research Fellowship I received in 1983, when the project started to take shape. Amherst College gave me two Faculty Research Grants in 1986 and 1990, as well as research funds that helped me travel to France and England, where most of the initial research was conducted. I am grateful to the Guggenheim Foundation, which made it possible to take a year of leave in 1987–88, and to the Rockefeller Foundation for a residency in Bellagio in July 1989.

Excerpts from Part I of this book were published in *Critical Inquiry* (1991) under the title "Monstrous Imagination: Progeny as Art in French Classicism"; an early version of Chapter 9, entitled "Living Images: Monstrosity and Representation," appeared in *Representations* (1983). I thank the editors of these journals for their permission to use this material.

Contents

Illustrations

Monstrous Imagination

Introduction

Where do monsters come from, and what do they really look like? In the Renaissance, answers to these puzzles were as numerous and varied as the physiological prodigies they sought to elucidate. Monsters came from God and the Devil, they were caused by stars and comets, they resulted from copulation with other species and from flaws in their parents' anatomies. The cosmic range of speculations also tried to account for the physical aspect of the marvelous beings observed in nature. Some monsters lacked an essential part of the body, others claimed an extra member, some looked like mythical animals, and a few were born with hermetic symbols imprinted on their strange physiology. Thus the much-discussed Ravenna monster was born without arms, but with a beautiful pair of wings, a fish tail, and mysterious markings on his chest: an epsilon, a cross, and, in some accounts, a half-moon as well.[1] But a remarkably persistent line of thought argued that monstrous progeny resulted from the disorder of the maternal imagination. Instead of reproducing the father's image, as nature commands, the monstrous child bore witness to the violent desires that moved the mother at the time of conception or during pregnancy. The resulting offspring carried the marks of her whims and fancy rather than the recognizable features of its legitimate genitor. The monster thus erased paternity and proclaimed the dangerous power of the female imagination. The theory that credited imagination with a deceiving but dominant role in procreation continued to be the object of heated discussions until the beginning of the nineteenth century.

Around the same time, literature reappropriated the complex

1

The Ravenna monster, after Boaistuau, from Ambroise Paré, *Des monstres et prodiges*, 1573.

relationship between imagination and resemblances, between unfulfilled desires and the act of generation. By assigning to the artist as monstrous father the power once attributed to the mother to create singular progeny, the Romantic metaphor of procreation restaged in its own terms the ideology of misguided desires that spawned aberrant offspring. Imagination, already rehabilitated in the 1777 Supplement to Diderot's *Encyclopédie* as a powerful creative agent that "belongs to genius" and spurs poetic "fecundity,"[2] played a privileged role in the conception of the Romantic *oeuvre*. The first part of this book thus examines the role of the maternal imagination as it was debated in Western Europe from the Renaissance to the end of the Enlightenment. The second part of the book considers the Romantic claim that artistic creation was a monstrous genesis and the work of art a form of teratological disclosure.

In the fourth book of *Generation of Animals,* Aristotle wrote: "Anyone who does not take after his parents is really in a way a monstrosity, since in these cases Nature has in a way strayed from the generic type. The first beginning of this deviation is when a female is formed instead of a male, though this indeed is a necessity required by Nature, since the race of creatures which are separated into male and female has got to be kept in being; . . . As for monstrosities, they are not necessary so far as the purposive or final cause is concerned, yet *per accidens.*"[3] These lines make a decisive association between the monstrous and the female as two departures from the norm, as two exceptions to another tenet of Aristotelian doctrine, namely, that "like produces like." The monster and the woman thus find themselves on the same side, the side of *dissimilarity*. "The female is as it were a deformed male," Aristotle also pointed out (II, iii, p. 175). Since she herself is on the side of the dissimilar, it was argued, the female appears to be destined by nature to contribute more figures of dissimilarity, if not creatures even more monstrous.[4]

But the female is a necessary departure from the norm, noted Aristotle, a useful deformity; the monster is gratuitous and useless for future generations. Aristotle's thoughts on generation offered a definition of monstrosity that was primarily linked not to physical imperfections but rather to a deficiency in the natural and visible

link between genitors and their progeny. "Monstrosities," he repeated, "come under the class of offspring which is unlike its parents" (IV, iv, p. 425). But the monster is also monstrous in another
important way, one that Aristotle described as a "false resemblance" to another species.

> It is not easy, by stating a single mode of cause, to explain . . . why
> sometimes the offspring is a human being yet bears no resem-
> blance to any ancestor, sometimes it has reached such a point that
> in the end it no longer has the appearance of a human being at
> all, but that of an animal only—it belongs to the class of mon-
> strosities, as they are called. And indeed this is what comes next
> to be treated . . . the causes of monstrosities, for in the end, when
> the movements (that came from the male) relapse and the mate-
> rial (that came from the female) does not get mastered, what re-
> mains is that which is most 'general,' and this is the (merely) 'ani-
> mal.' People say that the offspring which is formed has the head
> of a ram or an ox; and similarly with other creatures, that one
> has the head of another, e.g., a calf has a child's head or a sheep
> an ox's head. The occurrence of all these things is due to the
> causes I have named; at the same time, *in no case are they what they
> are alleged to be, but resemblances only,* and this of course comes
> about even when there is no deformation involved. (IV, iii,
> pp. 417–419, emphasis added)

Monstrosities are thus doubly deceptive. Their strange appearance—a misleading likeness to another species, for example—belies the otherwise rigorous law that offspring should resemble their
parents. By presenting similarities to categories of beings to which
they are not related, monsters blur the differences between genres
and disrupt the strict order of Nature. Thus, though the monster
was first defined as that which did not resemble him who engendered it, it nevertheless displayed some sort of resemblance, albeit
a *false* resemblance, to an object external to its conception.

   The genesis of that false resemblance played a crucial role in one
of the most ancient and enduring theories of generation, namely,
the tradition that credited the mother's imagination with the shape
of her progeny. A lost text, attributed to Empedocles, first suggested what was to become one of the most popular beliefs in the
study of procreation. Empedocles was said to have stated that
"progeny can be modified by the statues and paintings that the

mother gazes upon during her pregnancy."[5] Far from being discarded by medical thought when discoveries on generation redefined the respective roles of the father and mother in procreation, the view that the maternal imagination was responsible for the shape of progeny gained a growing number of followers in seventeenth- and eighteenth-century Europe. In 1621, Maître André du Laurens, the chancellor at the University of Montpellier as well as first physician to the king of France, expanded on Empedocles' suggestion as follows:

> Empedocles the Pythagorician links [resemblance] to imagination alone, whose power is so great that, just as it often changes the body of one who has some deep thought, so it inscribes its form on the fertilized seed. The Arabs granted imagination so much power that, through it, they thought the soul could act not only on its own body, but on that of another. It seems that Aristotle recognized the imagination's power in the act of conception, when he asked why individuals of the human species are so different from each other, and answered that the quickness and activity of human thought and the variety of the human mind leave different marks of several kinds upon the seed.[6]

As late as 1788, Benjamin Bablot reminded his readers that "the philosopher Empedocles, from Agrigenta in Sicily, who, according to received opinion, died at a very old age when he fell into the sea and drowned in 440 B.C., acknowledged no other cause for dissemblance between children and their parents than the imagination of pregnant women. According to Amyot, Plutarch's naive translator, Empedocles held that it was through the woman's imagination during conception that children were formed, for often women have been in love with images and statues and have given birth to children resembling them."[7] Thus, following Empedocles' theory, it was long believed that monsters, inasmuch as they did not resemble their parents, could well be the result of a mother's fevered and passionate consideration of images. More specifically, monsters were the offspring of an imagination that literally imprinted on progeny a deformed, misshapen resemblance to an object that had not participated in their creation. They were products of art rather than nature, as it were. Of course, during the Middle Ages and the Renaissance, the mother's imagination was only one of several elements believed to cause monstrous births: others included sex with the devil or animals, as well as defective sperm or a deformed womb. Yet no theory was more debated, more passionately attacked or defended, than the power of the maternal imagination over the formation of the fetus.[8]

Several traditions linked the word *monster* to the idea of showing or warning. One belief, following Augustine's *City of God*, held that the word *monster* derived from the Latin *monstrare:* to show, to display (*montrer* in French). *Monster*, then, belongs to the etymological family that spawned the word *demonstrate* as well.[9] For Renaissance readers, this tradition confirmed the idea that monsters were signs sent by God, messages showing his will or his wrath, though Fortunio Liceti gave it a simpler meaning in 1616: "Monsters are thus named, not because they are signs of things to come, as Cicero and the Vulgate believed . . . but because they are such that their new and incredible appearance stirs admiration and surprise in the beholders, and startles them so much that everyone wants to show them to others [se les *monstre* réciproquement]."[10] Another tradition, the one adopted by current etymological dictionaries, derived the word *monster* from *monere*, to warn, associating even more closely the abnormal birth with the prophetic vision of impending disasters. These etymologies gave monstrosity a pre-inscribed interpretation. They also justified its existence by including the monster within the larger order of things. Monstrous births were understood as warnings and public testimony; they were thought to be "demonstrations" of the mother's unfulfilled desires. The monster was then seen as a visible image of the mother's hidden passions. This theory gained a greater audience in the seventeenth century and culminated in the hotly debated Quarrel of Imaginationism, which lasted through the eighteenth century.

Although the mother's imagination was never considered the *only* possible cause of monstrosity, and did not receive exclusive medical attention at any time in the history of thought on the process of generation, it nevertheless haunted centuries of medical research. In fact, the theory that the mother could be responsible for monstrous births persisted despite all possible evidence to the contrary. In the nineteenth century, discoveries in the fields of embryology and heredity provided scientists with new ways of explaining resemblances. But if the mother's imagination was no longer perceived by the medical field to be a factor in resemblances, its role as the shaper of progeny was never totally forgotten. The idea that imagination could give life and form to passive matter became a central theme of Romantic aesthetics, and to this day popular beliefs still attribute birthmarks to maternal desires during pregnancy.

The theory that confers on the maternal imagination the power to shape progeny also suggests a complex relationship between procreation and art, for imagination is moved by passion and works in a mimetic way. "Nature," wrote Claude de Tesserant in 1567 in *Histoires prodigieuses*, "portrays after a living model, just as a painter would, and tries to make children resemble their parents as much as possible."[11] For Paracelsus, "By virtue of her imagination the woman is the artist and the child the canvas on which to raise the work."[12] In 1731, François-Marie-Pompée Colonna noted: "It is true that the semen is the visible agent, but we can also say that like the Painter, the Sculptor, and other Artisans who use certain instruments to fashion their materials into desired shape, similarly this invisible workman uses the male's seminal matter as the instrument that leads the female to generate an animal."[13] In 1812 in *Tableau de l'amour conjugal,* Dubuisson added, "The semen is to generation what the sculptor is to marble; the male semen is the sculptor who gives shape, the female liquor is the marble or matter, and the sculpture is the fetus or the product of generation."[14] From this point of view, the mother could be said to have taken over the male role of the artist when, overwhelmed by gazing at images or by unchecked desires, she let her imagination interfere with the creative process and reproduce strange figures, or monstrosities. If Art must imitate Nature, in cases of monstrous procreation Nature imitates Art. Treatises on the role of the mother's imagination received very little attention after the theory was set aside by the medical world in the early 1800's. Yet these texts offer a striking reassessment of the maternal role in procreation and at the same time elucidate the relationship between imagination and art, nature and mimesis.

Thus when the thesis that the maternal imagination played an important role in the formation of monstrosities was finally abandoned toward the beginning of the nineteenth century, it remained an important part of literary aesthetics. In many texts, we find explicit reference to the power of imagination in procreation. In *Elective Affinities,* for example, Goethe describes the birth of a child who displayed the effects of his parents' imagination, thereby betraying their moral adultery. Charlotte and Edward's son is the striking image not of his parents, but of those they love secretly: "People saw in it a wonderful, indeed a miraculous child . . . what surprised them more . . . [was] the double resemblance, which became more and more conspicuous. In figure and in the features of the face, it was like the Captain; the eyes every day it was less easy to distinguish from the eyes of Ottilie."[15] E. T. A. Hoffmann's Cardillac, the monster of his short story "Mademoiselle de Scudéry," attributes his fateful passion for jewels to "the strange impressions which afflict pregnant women, and . . . the strange influence these impressions from outside can have on the child."[16] "What vision of a tiger haunted my mother when she was carrying me?" asks Musset's dramatic hero Lorenzaccio.[17] Oliver Wendell Holmes, in his best-known novel, *Elsie Venner* (1859), describes his heroine as the monstrous result of her mother's imagination, the mother having been terrorized by an encounter with a deadly snake, "an antenatal impression which had mingled an alien element in her nature."[18]

But if many nineteenth-century writers explicitly referred to this all-but-discarded theory of monstrosity, their implicit reappropriation of the idea of the monstrous imagination was more striking still. In theories of monstrosity the maternal element repressed the legitimate father. The maternal imagination erased the legitimate father's image from his offspring and thus created a monster. In the constitution of the modern *episteme,* the silent father regains his place. Romantic aesthetic theory sketched out a model genealogy for the work of art and the procreative role of the artist.[19] In so doing, Romanticism reassigned the *vis imaginativa* to the father alone. Romantic aesthetics reaffirmed the seductive power of the monstrous as aberration, and the creative role of the scientist, or the artist, as visible father. Imagination was reclaimed as a masculine attribute, and just as theories of generation had long been theories of Art, Romantic Art became a theory of generation. For the Romantics, imagination was no longer the faculty to reproduce images, but the power to create them. Imagination did not imitate, it generated, and in doing so, it also produced monstrous art. The notion of monstrosity that emerged shifted its emphasis from the maternal to the paternal but kept intact the key elements of singular progeny. The act of artistic creation thus appeared as an imitation of a monstrous genetic process: as painted models, fatal passions, striking resemblances, and creatures that were as frightening for their deformities as for their perfection. The erasure of the maternal role in procreation and new forms of mechanical engendering were also echoed in the myth of the Romantic artist as lone genitor in awe of his own creation. If the theory that credited the maternal imagination with the birth of unnatural progeny implied a theory of art as imitation, Romanticism, in turn, reinterpreted art as teratology. The vision of the Romantic artist as creator borrowed a metaphor of creation from the theory that long ascribed the birth of monstrous progeny to the maternal imagination.

This reappropriation in literature of an idea associated primarily with medical beliefs was anticipated in treatises of the Renaissance which quoted with equal regard poets, physicians of Antiquity, hearsay, and personal testimonials. Tales of monstrous births caused by the maternal imagination could be found in legends, philosophy, and medical essays. For this reason, my exploration of the belief that the mother's imagination was to be held responsible for monstrous births could not be confined to a discussion of embryology, though the notion was, at one time, a topic of passionate debate among embryologists. Nor are my examples drawn only from the history of medicine, since this tradition reappropriated nonmedical materials such as legends and myths as acceptable evidence. Moreover, the belief in the power of the maternal imagination was also relevant to literature and art, inasmuch as it was primarily defined and understood in terms of imitation and resemblances. This book will thus examine the idea of the monstrous imagination in areas as diverse as those from which it first emanated. In the Renaissance, this theory was an intrinsic part of the literature on prodigies; at other times it was debated in courts of law or by ecclesiastical authorities. It appears intermittently in scientific speculations, philosophical reflections, and texts of medical observations. No doubt contemporary medical history could provide the reader with many insights into the individual pathologies sometimes discernible in testimony from scientists and physicians of the past. But although the development of the theory of the monstrous imagination may have been affected by specific considerations at different times in history, the theory itself never belonged to a single corpus or to a particular medical belief. The texts considered here are varied and represent both canonical views on imagination and popular reevaluations of monstrosity. In this perspective, Ambroise Paré, Malebranche, Spallanzani, Camille Dareste, and Nathaniel Hawthorne all contributed equally to the expression of an enduring idea that reflected in various ways the belief that progeny was art and art a monstrous progeny.

Part I

The Mother's Fancy

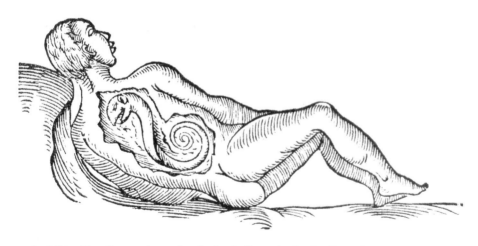

A child with a live snake eating its back, from Ambroise Paré, *Des monstres et prodiges,* 1573. This drawing was reproduced in *Anomalies and Curiosities of Medicine* (1896) by George M. Gould and Walter L. Pyle with the following legend: serpent in a fetus.

1

The Renaissance Monster

In his *Essays,* Montaigne relates the following story: "We know by experience that women transmit marks of their fancies to the bodies of the children they carry in their womb . . . There was presented to Charles, King of Bohemia and Emperor, a girl from near Pisa, all hairy and bristly, who her mother said had been thus conceived because of a picture of Saint John the Baptist hanging by her bed."[1] In this account of a famous case of monstrosity, Montaigne attributes the child's deformity to the double influence of the mother's imagination and the contemplation of images. Although Renaissance thought did not single out the mother's fancy as the only reason for monstrous births, it nevertheless credited both imagination and images with the power to form odd and unnatural progeny.

The Renaissance belief in the power of the maternal imagination was inherited from Antiquity. In *Des monstres et prodiges,* published in 1573, Ambroise Paré, physician to the kings of France, noted: "The ancients who sought out the secrets of Nature (i.e., Aristotle, Hippocrates, Empedocles), have taught of other causes for monstrous children and have referred them to the ardent and obstinate imagination that the mother might receive at the moment of conception—through some object, or fantastic dream—of certain nocturnal visions that the man or woman have during conception."[2] Renaissance theories on generation were influenced by different models. Although Aristotle's views were often misinterpreted, they were the most influential, particularly the belief that, in generation, "the female, *qua* female, is passive, and the male, *qua* male, is active."[3] The efficient male semen initiated the movement

13

of generation, while the female contributed nourishing matter—
menstrual blood—to the fetus. Followers of Galen and Hippocrates believed in a female semen. In *De Animalibus,* Albertus Magnus
(1206–1280) spoke of a female seed that combined with the male
semen and the menstrual blood to form and develop the fetus. But
the female contribution to generation was never considered equal
to that of the male. In cases of monstrous births, though, particularly those caused by the power of the maternal imagination, the
mother's role gained considerable importance. Just as monstrosities challenged the general laws of procreation, imagination challenged the respective roles of males and females in generation.

As Katharine Park notes, the debate over the force of imagination "was complicated by the fact that the most ardent defenders
of the powers of the imagination included both the most credulous—writers like Paracelsus who would believe any story—as well
as the least superstitious—writers like Pomponazzi and Montaigne
for whom the imagination provided a credible and natural explanation for some of the more far-fetched claims of popular magic
and religion."[4]

In "Of the Power of the Imagination," Montaigne gave a detailed
account of the many powers of imagination, of its capacity to make
a person healthy or diseased, and even to kill: "There are some
who through fear anticipate the hand of the executioner. And one
man who was being unbound to have his pardon read him
dropped stone dead on the scaffold, struck down by his mere imagination" (I, 21, pp. 68–69). Through this mysterious faculty one
can affect others as well as oneself, noted Montaigne, just as a contagion transfers the disease from one body to another: he cited
Pliny's claim that women of Scythia could kill simply by looking in
anger. For Montaigne, however, imagination was particularly influential in sexual matters, as in the much-discussed example of a
young woman who became a man through the force of her desiring imagination. If imagination has such power in the area of sex,
it is not surprising that it should endow pregnant women with the
active, otherwise male, power to give shape to their progeny.

These views were challenged by several scholars, among them
Thomas Fienus, professor of medicine at the University of Louvain. In *De Viribus Imaginationis,* he argued that the power of imagination, though real, was restricted by the very fact that, as L. J.

Rather puts it: "The imagination is a cognitive, immanent and immaterial faculty or power. Therefore imaginative *species* and *phantasmata* cannot act directly on matter, the bodies in which they occur included."[5] But if imagination did not affect the body directly it nevertheless played a role per accidens "by exciting the emotions."[6] And most of all, imagination played a role in the formation of the fetus.[7]

For several thinkers, imagination alone made it possible to understand how the female herself could be the agent of resemblances between parents and offspring. In a treatise on generation, Paré estimated that imagination contributed as much as the father's seed to the resemblance between fathers and their children: "One more commonly sees children who resemble their father than their mother because of the mother's great ardor and imagination during carnal copulation! So much so that the child takes on the form and the color of what she knows and imagines so strongly in her mind."[8] Although imagination could play a formative role, and one that, for Paré, ultimately followed the natural order of things by reproducing the father's form and face, its unpredictable character, especially in women, could render it dangerous as well. As Montaigne had emphasized, fear and desire trigger the power of imagination; Pietro Pomponazzi, professor of natural philosophy at Padua, commented: "Sometimes, the powers of imagination and desire attach themselves to an object so much so that *they are no longer natural dispositions* but set and permanent habits controlling the mind and the blood: in this case, then, the imagined and desired object may be truly produced by the powers of the imagination and desire."[9] Thus were monstrous children born. In 1616, Fortunii Liceti remarked: "Now, if the imagination of either the father or the mother can provoke a monstrous birth, nevertheless the cause must be assigned to the mother's imagination rather than the father's, because though the father's imagination can affect him during the sexual act, the woman's is always at work, after copulation and during conception, when the fetus is formed. In any case, women's imaginations are stronger and more ardent and, according to what is normally stated with as much truth as grace, what women love, they love passionately and without limits, just as what they hate, they hate cruelly, and never in half-measure."[10]

Multiple causes were cited for the heightening of the maternal imagination's power and its resulting usurpation of the father's role. They could be accidental, or derive from longtime habits; they could reflect a fright, a desire, or bear the mark of a particular trauma. Paré contributed the following anecdote to a series of popular tales of monstrous births during the Renaissance:

> In the year 1517, in the parish of Bois-le-Roy, in the Forest of Bièvre, on the road to Fontainebleau, a child was born having the face of a frog. He was seen and visited by Maistre Jean Bellanger, surgeon to the King's artillery, in the presence of gentlemen from the Court of Harmois . . . The aforementioned Bellanger, a man of good sense, wanting to know the cause of this monster, inquired of the father what could have been the cause of it. The father replied that he thought it was because his wife, who was suffering from fever, had followed a neighbor's advice that she should hold a live frog in her hand until it was dead. That night, she went to bed with her husband, still having the frog in her hand; her husband and she embraced and she conceived; and by the power of imagination, this monster had thus been produced.[11]

The story was accompanied by an illustration captioned "Prodigious Aspect of a Child with the Face of a Frog."[12] Most Renaissance texts on monsters were similarly illustrated, and just as their authors borrowed freely from earlier tales, they also felt free to reproduce their accompanying illustrations. These drawings had a twofold importance: they provided concrete evidence for tales of extraordinary births, and they possessed a tangibility that was more striking than words. But, most of all, they duplicated in frightening detail the workings of the maternal imagination, whose nature consisted in reproducing images indiscriminately chosen by force of desire or terror.

Desire and Imagination

Since Antiquity, even the most innocuous deformities, birthmarks, had been thought to be caused by the mother's imagination and her capacity to imprint on her child's body the mark of a cherished or desired object. The birthmark's origin came to be illustrated by the French word *envie,* which literally means *desire.* The word ap-

Prodigious figure of a child with the face of a frog, from Ambroise Paré, *Des monstres et prodiges*, 1573.

peared at the end of the seventeenth century to designate birthmarks, and was used along with the traditional word *tâche* in both medical and popular texts. For the power of imagination is first of all the power invested in the very force of desire. Conversely, the monster appears as the public display of all secret, and at times illegitimate, yearnings. There are no desires, shameful or innocent, that one's progeny does not publicly disclose. Pomponazzi noted, "If a pregnant woman greatly desires a chickpea, she will deliver a child bearing the image of a chickpea. That is how Cicero's family got its name" (p. 139). Moreover, "when a woman imagines something during the sexual act, she indeed imprints its image on the fetus. If, during pregnancy, she desires a pomegranate, she marks her child with a pomegranate or something that resembles it" (p. 229). In a treatise on birthmarks, Paracelsus argued that "such intolerable ulcers have been cured, but also some animals have been removed by using their living equivalent, for example, when a man bears some signs from his birth, which resulted from his mother's imagination when she either craved something, or was afraid or had a fright—the principal causes of such blemishes."[13] The cure proposed by Paracelsus for the removal of birthmarks was similar to the process that caused them to appear in the first place:

> Let us suppose that you have before you the visible and colored image of a worm of perfect likeness in every aspect of its body; first, the mother should be questioned as to the type, the size, the color, and the form of the worm, along with the weather, the day, the hour, and the minute in which such imagining took place and was accomplished . . . If the blemish is the result of some fear or terror that the mother experienced, you must give a similar experience to the child while the worm is attached to him . . . In this way, you can erase all signs of all sorts, not only of animals, but also of fruits and other scars by using the living equivalents of what the mother had imagined. (pp. 159–162)

Paracelsus goes further than other physicians of the time, who were more interested in causes than in the therapeutics of signs, marks, and monstrosities. In his view, not only does like engender like, but when an accident caused by the mother's imagination occurs, like can only be cured by like. Paracelsus' remedy implied a rigorous principle of analogy, whose epistemological impact has been described at length by Michel Foucault.[14]

The idea of erasing birthmarks was soon abandoned, but the medical discourse on birthmarks continued to argue that they were caused by the woman's passionate imagination and unsatisfied desires. Two hundred years after Paracelsus, Nicolas Andry de Boisregard, dean of the Faculté de médecine of Paris, would state that "*envies* (desires), so called because they are attributed to the various desires that mothers have had during their pregnancies, are strange marks to be found at birth . . . If the pregnant woman's passionate desire [*envie*] for certain things she cannot obtain right away is sometimes capable of producing deformities in the child she is carrying, the sight of an object that causes her revulsion and horror is even more capable of doing so."[15] Desire and repulsion, craving and horror come together, exciting the imagination, which is capable of marking the progeny with the proof, for all to see, of an unsatisfied desire or a shameful fascination. Many troubling secrets are made public by women the day they give birth, when the monster reveals what has remained hidden since conception. The ability of women to feel desires so violently that they mark their progeny with the signs of their unsatisfied cravings thus illustrates the role of imagination as the faculty, both mental and physical, that produces deformities in the child. But more troubling still for many thinkers, and more mysterious, was women's fascination with images.

Above all, women's imaginations were thought to be strongly affected by images. Following Empedocles' suggestion that the shape of progeny could be modified by the statues and paintings that the mother gazed upon during her pregnancy,[16] many believed that artistic representations made a particularly deep impression on pregnant women. If imagination was thought to be the power to produce or retain images in the brain, a weakened imagination was characterized by its inability to differentiate between a living model and its representation.[17] Several stories of monstrosities caused by a mother's troubled contemplation of images became extremely popular in the Renaissance. They appeared, with few variations, in the great treatises of the period, including Konrad Lycosthenes' *Prodigiorum Liber,* Jacob Rueff's *De Conceptu et Generatione Hominis,* Pierre Boaistuau's *Histoires prodigieuses,* Ambroise Paré's *Des monstres et prodiges,* Fortunii Liceti's *De Monstrorum Caussis, Natura et Differentiis,* and Ulysses Aldrovandus' *Monstrorum Historia.*[18]

The best-known example of the power attributed to images is that of the so-called hairy virgin, mentioned by Paré, Montaigne, and previously discussed by Pierre Boaistuau: "The respected author, Damascenes, affirms that Charles IV, the emperor and king of Bohemia, was shown a virgin completely covered with hair like a bear; she was born thus deformed and hideous because her mother had gazed too intensely upon an effigy of St. John dressed in animal skins which hung at the foot of her bed when she conceived."[19] This story remained, in its simplicity, the prototype, the perfect example of a monstrous birth brought about by a woman's *vis imaginativa* at the moment of conception. It also demonstrates how a series of transgressions led to the birth of a monster. The

A hairy virgin conceived by the force of imagination, from Pierre Boaistuau, *Histoires prodigieuses*, 1560.

mother's imagination reproduces what it sees without discrimination, without understanding—thus, the furs covering John the Baptist are "translated" into a hair-covered body. A similar fallacy seems to have decided the sex of the offspring (as Paracelsus noted, "A child's sex is determined by which of the two parents' imaginations is the stronger").[20] John the Baptist, traditionally portrayed with long hair, might be said to resemble a woman; thus, the offspring would be a girl. There was also something blasphemous in considering too intently the image of a saint and martyr at the time of conception and "reproducing" this image in the form of monstrous progeny.

But the story also suggests the mother's unspoken bestial desire, one of the most scandalous deviations from nature's laws, which is exposed and punished by the birth of a hairy monster. The question of bestiality generated much debate during the Renaissance, in particular over whether having sex with an animal could actually result in offspring. According to Aristotle, such a coupling would be necessarily sterile. But the author of *Secreta Mulierum* (widely thought to be Albertus Magnus) attributed the birth of monsters either to contempt for nature's laws, that is, human copulation with animals, or to the mother's delinquent imagination at the time of conception. The idea of moral fault, though not essential, is also linked to many theories of monstrosity: bestiality is so morally repulsive that it is only fitting that it should result in the birth of a monster. And even the mother's "moral" bestiality, that is, her imagining herself copulating with an animal, should be punished just as severely by the birth of a monstrous child. This is made explicit by Boaistuau in his *Histoires prodigieuses:* "It is certain that these monstrous creatures most often are the consequence of divine judgment, justice, punishment, and curse; horrified by their sin, God allows [women] to produce such abominations because they hurl themselves forward indifferently, like savage beasts that only follow their appetites, with no consideration of age, place, time, and the other laws established by Nature" (p. 23). In the Renaissance, the monstrous birth is cause for wonder rather than scandal. But it is also seen as divine punishment, and in this case, a punishment that strikes indiscriminately both those who actually copulate with a beast (which "naturally" produces a monster) and those whose deranged imaginations may visualize such copulation during conception.[21] The same authors who deny that an act of bestiality can generate offspring argue, like Aldrovandus,[22] that the woman's imagination is so powerful that if she imagines intercourse with an animal, her progeny will bear the marks of those images. Although bestiality cannot produce living beings, women's *vis imaginativa* can imitate bestiality. The maternal imagination mocks the taboo of mixing and confounding species; it brings about what Nature will not allow. It alone can bring to life "a girl covered with hair, like a bear."

Other stories attributing an offspring's unexpected appearance to the contemplation of an image widen the scope of the debate on the question of resemblance and reproduction. Two recurring tales, made more respectable because of their sources, are thus retold by Paré: "That it was true, wrote Heliodorus, that Persina, the queen of Ethiopia, conceived with King Hydustes, himself an Ethiopian, a daughter who was white, and this by means of her imagination [having been] drawn to a likeness of the beautiful Andromeda, whose painting she had before her eyes during the caresses from which she became pregnant." Conversely, "Hippocrates saved a princess accused of adultery because she had given birth to a child black like a Moor, when both she and her husband were white; she was absolved upon Hippocrates' persuasion that it was [caused by] a portrait of a Moor, similar to the child, which was customarily attached to her bed."[23]

The offspring in question are monsters not in the common sense of the term, but only in the narrower Aristotelian definition, that is, in their lack of resemblance to their parents. The obvious suspicion arising from such stories, that of adultery, is explicitly dismissed. The noble nature of the characters involved and the authority of Antiquity's most famous physician suggest, rather, that an unexpected appearance, an unnatural progeny, can be explained as the result of a general, if not strictly natural, phenomenon: the power of images over the mother's imagination and the power of the mother's imagination over the fetus. On a certain level, these stories "naturalize" the maternal imagination's intervention in the formation of the progeny. However, when a woman's imagination becomes obsessed with gazing at images, nature is circumvented, and like produces unlike.

Fortunii Liceti wrote the first critical evaluation of the Andromeda story attributed to Heliodorus. In *De Monstrorum Caussis* (1616) he remarked: "The story attributed to Heliodorus is indeed just a story, a poetic fiction . . . he poeticizes everything and what he conveys are poetic fictions rather than facts" (p. 165). He added: "To a natural philosopher's eyes, since Andromeda was born to Cepheus and Cassiopeia, the king and queen of Ethiopia, she was black" (p. 167). But while Liceti questioned both the accuracy of the source and the likelihood of the story, he expressed no doubt of the principle that contemplation of a portrait could mark an unborn child through the power of the mother's feverish imagination. His inquiry was instead intended to revise the definition of monstrosity. Thus Liceti argued—and in this he differs markedly from Aristotle—that if the offspring were well formed, albeit different in color from their parents, they could not be classified as monsters:

> I concede to [Hippocrates] that, through the power of imagination, white parents can produce a black offspring, and black parents can have white children, and, as Plato noted, such births are monstrous and such progeny comparable to monstrosities. Nevertheless, we will not classify a white female born to black parents, or a black female born to white parents, among monstrosities, because they do not cause any surprise among those who see them, and their bodies possess nothing monstrous when considered in themselves and without comparison to their parents. For the monster is substance and something absolute *(de parfait en soi-même)*. The monster exists in itself and not by comparison. The rarity of their origin is not enough to classify these females in the category of monsters, for there are many things that are rare without being monstrous. (p. 164)

Liceti makes an essential point: If these stories have traditionally been included in the corpus of monstrosities caused by the imaginative power of women, it is because the *process* of engendering, rather than its *product,* is monstrous. He emphasizes that for the authors of the Renaissance, the monstrous was not an absolute state, an essence in itself, but rather—and here Renaissance thought was strictly Aristotelian—a state of dissemblance in regard to the creation's parents and more specifically, in regard to the legitimate father. Although Liceti accepts without question the account of the "hairy virgin" and classifies her in the category of monstrosities because she is so visibly different, he also attempts to show that, in fact, the Renaissance combined two elements of monstrosity: the deformed child and the aberrant mother. That the mother's imagination could defy the laws of nature and produce a false resemblance is monstrous as well. But these tales of monstrous births that are caused by the contemplation of images also suggest a series of important transgressions that call into question the role of the legitimate father as well as the natural hierarchy whereby the maternal imagination reproduces the father's image and art imitates nature.

Progeny and Art

When the mother takes art, rather than nature, as the model for the child she is carrying, she not only subverts an important hierarchy, but also shows herself to be an undiscerning and misguided artist. The desiring imagination that leads her to usurp the father's formative role in procreation drives her to a series of fateful confusions: confusions between art and nature, between *physis* and *technè*, and between imitation and reproduction. Whereas the artist imitates with discernment, the mother's imagination artlessly reproduces a model that is already an imitation of nature.

When the mother's imagination substitutes the lines of a portrait for the father's features, it inverts yet another hierarchy, that of the primacy of nature over art. The father's image is erased and the resulting disorder in fact reemphasizes the respective places of models and imitations. Every transgression of this hierarchy will result in monstrosity. As noted earlier, the specific character of the mother's imagination is most precisely defined as plastic art. It is because the mother's imagination has been led astray that it gives shape to a monstrous child; and it is because imagination shapes only the exterior part of the child's body that the monster is human.[24] Moreover, since the progeny imitates a model that belongs to art rather than nature, it can be seen as the most illegitimate of offspring.

In the *Sophist,* Plato makes a distinction between two forms of imitation in art: likenesses produced by *eikastiken* art, exact in all dimensions, devoid of interpretation, and semblances produced by *phantastiken* art, in which the artist selects the best possible proportions to produce a beautiful work of art:

> *Theaetetus.* Will you tell me first what are the two divisions of which you are speaking?
>
> *Socrates.* One is the art of likeness-making—generally a likeness of anything is made by producing a copy which is executed according to the proportions of the original, similar in length and breadth and depth, each thing receiving also its appropriate colour.
>
> *Theaetetus.* Is not this always the aim of imitation?
>
> *Socrates.* Not always; in works either of sculpture or of painting, which are of any magnitude, there is a certain degree of deception; for if artists were to give the true proportions of their fair works, the upper part, which is farther off, would appear to be out of proportion in comparison with the lower, which is nearer; and so they give up the truth in their images and make only the proportions which appear to be beautiful, disregarding the real ones.[25]

In the Platonic sense, the monster is only eikastiken art, that is, a reproduction without interpretation. But paradoxically, it could be said that the mother escapes Plato's mistrust of artists and painters in that she does not distort what she sees, but duplicates literally, if disastrously, what she beholds, without the form of interpretation that renders art at once beautiful and unfaithful. If, according to Plato, the artist is powerless to grasp the ideality of things, and contents himself with grasping only their appearance, then, superficially at least, the mother would be the consummate artist, mastering an art that has no model other than art, a misguided aesthetic whose model would always be itself an imitation. But whereas painting is a matter of appearances *(phantasies)* rather than reality, the mother seems to confuse appearances *with* reality. As maker and artist, she reproduces the very distortions that art has already imposed upon reality. Thus, in the case of the hair-covered girl, animal skins that literally cover the image of St. John's body are reproduced as animal-like skin. We could say that, in this manner, the monstrous creation also betrays the unfaithfulness of art to its model; it exposes all of art's lies, what Plato describes as "a certain degree of deception."

The maternal *vis imaginativa* is concerned not with "appearance" but rather with "likeness." By choosing an image *(eidolon)* for its model, the mother's imagination produces another image (eikastiken) rather than the artistic resemblance posited by phantasies, which are the creative images possessing a certain degree of invention and interpretation. Unlike the painter and the sculptor, who choose and adapt the proportions of their works in function of their overall beauty, the mother is the artist of blind resemblances, incapable of choice, adaptation, or discrimination. The objective of the artist is to create beauty—the mother produces a monster. The artist undertakes a series of critical and reasoned choices; he proceeds by selecting, with a full mastery of techniques adapted to his art. Carried away by her unsatisfied desires, the mother abandons herself blindly to an image she does not recognize as *technè*.

Thus, the plastic nature of monstrosity might be said to lie in the difference between "likeness" and "appearance," eikastiken and phantastiken. But at the same time that monstrosity takes art as its model, its mimesis is devoid of aesthetic intention. Far from dissimulating its artificial nature, that is, its own artistic origin, the monster reveals its genesis. There is no *faux-semblant* in monstrosity. On the contrary, the monstrous creation does not mislead, it reveals; it does not hide its nature, it exposes the shameful source of its deformity, its useless and inappropriate model. As art, the monstrous creation could be said to be the most straightforward of all artistic pretenses. It makes images from images; it is the art of reproducing oblivious to taste and judgment, a *disproportionate* art of gratuitous resemblances that repeatedly reveals its origins, or reveals that its origins are merely appearances.

The Platonic artist both uses nature and corrects it by imposing beautiful proportions on what he perceives. The artist's work is inexact on several levels, but the liberties he takes in relation to the viewer's gaze are also proof of his superior talent. His work is made to be seen and admired. If this be art's "lie," then the monster is its terrible truth. The monster is art without interpretation or signature, since the father, the only one who has the right to leave his mark (as he gives his name to the child he engenders), has been erased and supplanted by the image produced by the mother's imagination. Whereas European languages have long hesitated between the Latin *imaginatio*—the ability to form images—and the Greek phantasia, which Plato defined as the power to make images *while interpreting them,* it may be said that the maternal *vis imagina-tiva* falls within the scope of imaginatio, also described as the capacity to produce images similar to "wax imprints," reproductions without interpretations.[26] Roger Bacon compared the working of imagination to wax: "Wax . . . retains the impression in good style because its humidity is tempered by dryness. Whence it is said that the one receives, the other retains. This goes on in the organ of common sense and imagination."[27] The term "fantastic" was to become widespread in the nineteenth century, when imagination itself was rehabilitated as a distinctive masculine quality. The literature of the fantastic would become the privileged realm of fantasy, terrifying and always creative. Thus the monsters of nineteenth-century tales would be the progeny of masculine phantasia; those born to the unhappy mothers of the Renaissance and the European Classical Age were primarily products of maternal imaginatio.

Iconoclasm and Monstrosity

The monstrous birth, frequently attributed during the Renaissance to a fascination with images, also testified to the strange power of icons. Simultaneously, it illustrated an epistemological concern with the role and danger of idols. Although the tradition associating the possibility of a monstrous birth with the contemplation of images preceded the Reformation, it was also fed by the Reformation's own iconoclastic values.[28] We know that the Reformation's criticism of images amplified an explicit concern, already present in the late Middle Ages, that image worship had become too extreme in religious practices. Thomas Aquinas had earlier called attention to the role played by the senses in the difficult path to the spiritual, and Carlos M. N. Eire notes that by the late fifteenth century "the Augustinian Gottschalk Hollen could actually claim that people were led to piety more effectively 'through a picture than through a sermon.' Moreover, the common worshiper found it extremely difficult to apply the theological distinctions proposed by the Church, and popular piety sunk far below the level proposed by the theologians. The image and the prototype often became indistinguishable in the mind of the supplicant."[29]

Although many scholars have noted the link between the Reformation and the sudden increase in writings about monstrosities, as well as the polemical use of monstrous births in various debates, the more specific connection between the idea of the monstrous mother and the Reformation's war against images has received no critical attention. It is significant that the war against icons targeted from early on images of the Virgin Mary, the pregnant mother, represented at times by statues that opened to reveal the Holy Trinity in the womb. Criticism of images, expressed simultaneously by poets, writers, and theologians, intensified in France, Germany, and Bohemia. Jurgis Baltrusaitis has shown how theories on the birth of monsters spread from Switzerland and the German principalities to France,[30] following closely the path of the Reformation itself. Konrad Lycosthenes' edition of *Prodigiorum Liber* appeared in Basel in 1552. It contained the first engraving, often reproduced, of the "hairy virgin" modeled after the painting of John the Baptist. Jacob Rueff's *De Conceptu et Generatione Hominis* (to which Paré is greatly indebted) was published in Zurich in 1554; Pomponazzi's posthumous *De Naturalium Effectuum Admirandorum Causis, sive de Incantationibus* was printed in Basel in 1556. It was followed four years later by Boaistuau's Paris publication of *Histoires prodigieuses* (another of Paré's sources) and, finally, by what was to become Paré's immensely popular book, *Des monstres et prodiges*, printed in 1573 in Paris. During the same period, Paracelsus' earlier writings, in particular *De Virtute Imaginativa*, were widely read across Europe.

For Reformation theologians, image worship was closely tied to the cult of the Virgin Mary. As Martin Bucer pointed out, all pious images are dangerous in that they grant the Virgin Mary and, to a lesser degree the saints, a power that belongs to God alone.[31] Worship of images encourages a form of usurpation. As has often been remarked, the iconoclastic revolution which devastated the European churches of the sixteenth century primarily consisted in the destruction of Catholic *feminine* iconography. This destruction was simultaneously accompanied by the establishment of a masculinized religion: "Another cultural change effected by iconoclasm," notes Eire, "was an increased masculinization of piety. If, as recent studies have shown, nearly fifty percent of late medieval church art was devoted to Mary and the saints, the removal of these feminine representations marks a definite shift away from a gender-balanced, feminized piety to a more strictly masculine one . . . The richly symbolic feminine aspects represented by the Virgin Mary as 'Mother of God,' and by other female saints, were suddenly replaced by those of a transcendent, but overtly masculine God."[32]

The various treatises on monstrosity—more specifically those pointing to the maternal imagination as the cause of fetal deformity and attributing the monster's shape to an external cause, the contemplation of images—intersect on several points with iconoclastic ideology. For example, they illustrate the dangerous power of images, which distract attention from God in church and from the legitimate father in procreation. In bearing a monstrous infant, the mother reproduces the sin of idolatry, which Calvin condemned when he wrote, "As often as Scripture asserts that there is one God, it is not contending over the bare name, but also prescribing that nothing belonging to his divinity be transferred to another."[33] When the monstrous mother substitutes a painting for her husband, she thus transfers the creative power of generation from her legitimate spouse to the idolatrous image. Just as the idolater believes that part of a divine power resides within its representation, or in that of its saints, so woman bestows on images the mimetic power that should belong to the father alone.

In his chapter on Calvin, Eire also points out that for the great Reformer, idolatry was linked to the image of fertility. "Idolatry is certainly so very fertile," Calvin wrote, "that of one feigned god there should quickly be begotten a hundred" (p. 225). The metaphor of a "fertile" idolatry that hideously perpetuates itself recalls the monstrous imagination, fulfilling Calvin's prophecy that such idolatry carries with it its own punishment. It is also worth noting that from the perspective of the Reformation, the Renaissance accounts of monsters caused by the mother's consideration of images rule out any possibility of the monster's being a miracle or a divine prophecy. Indeed, what disastrous miracle could account for the transformation of one of the Church's greatest saints, John the Baptist, into a hirsute virgin? In fact, the account of the "hairy virgin" and its accompanying illustration attack both idolatry and the cult of the Virgin Mary. The monstrous birth is traced first and foremost to the dangerous contemplation of a sacred image; it is caused by a woman, and the result of her crime, so like idolatry, is a monster made to look like a caricature of the Virgin Mary. There is no miracle here, but rather a sense of divine punishment. The mother is easily identified as the cause of monstrosity, while the monster itself proclaims by its physical deformities the genesis of its (mis)conception. For the Reformation, such births are the closest thing to a human sin against God and Nature.

Renaissance treatises on monstrosity offer no single, coherent perspective on theology, nor do they present a unified theory of deformities. While certain chapters admit that miracles may be caused by demons, others, within the same book, deny this categorically. Certain authors wrote in fear of arousing the ire of Protestants and Catholics alike; as physician to the Catholic king of France, Paré was particularly vulnerable to retribution for his writing, while others were never threatened. Yet the iconoclastic movement that shook sixteenth-century Europe certainly contributed to the popularity of stories attributing to images the power to engender monsters. It could well be argued that Malebranche's later account of a monstrous birth externally caused by the image of a pope—the symbol of the Church itself—reflects, as Voltaire later remarked, the influence of Protestant thought on the most iconoclastic of priests.[34]

Finally, the idea of the monstrous mother becomes a blasphemous parody of the cult of the Virgin Mary. In erasing all traces of the progeny's legitimate father, the monstrous mother replicates, and derides, the Immaculate Conception. She also demonstrates that such births are not miracles.[35] Even those authors most predisposed to believe in wonders and marvels, who admit, for example, the possibility of insemination by an incubus, unanimously declare that in the case of a monstrous birth resulting from an idolatrous imagination there has been no adultery, no miraculous impregnation, but the simple obliteration of the husband's mark, of his signature.

For Paré and others, the birth of a monster may reflect the glory or the wrath of God, it may foretell disasters and wars, it is a prophetic sign; considered a miracle and a wonder, it testifies to the infinite variety of things. But in the category of monstrosities caused by the misled maternal imagination, the offspring is nothing more than the sad reflection of another image, an unfulfilled desire, the twofold sin of idolatry and moral adultery. The progeny conceals no state of grace, no mystery, no Immaculate Conception.

On the contrary, it shamelessly reveals its shameful origins. Renaissance authors called on the authorities of Antiquity to support their views and to lend credibility to many of their own theories or accounts. But, except in the case of Heliodorus of Emesus, nothing remains in the writings of most sources, such as Empedocles or Hippocrates, that would confirm the stories attributed to them. The "respected author" Damascenes, who is credited with the first modern account of a monstrosity caused by a painting—the story of the hair-covered virgin—is also untraceable.

In his essay entitled *Les iconoclastes,* Jean-Joseph Goux connects the worship of images with the prohibition of incest:

> Freud states it himself in his last book, *Moses and Monotheism:* The prohibition against making an image of God implies that sensory perception takes a back seat to the abstract idea. It consecrates the triumph of the spirit over the senses, or more specifically, the renunciation of instincts. Now Freud explicitly links this religious innovation to a passage from matriarchy to patriarchy, but his lack of insistence on this point is noteworthy. It is odd that he does not explicitly establish what we find to be the particularly illuminating relationship *between the Judaic prohibition against image adoration and the incest taboo with the mother.* By carving images of gods, one is making a material image of the mother, and adoring the maternal figure through the senses. By tearing oneself away from the seduction of the senses and elevating one's thoughts toward an unrepresentable god, one turns away from desire for the mother, ascends to the sublime father and respects his law.[36]

The Reformation explicitly relegated the maternal image and its adoration to the background by forbidding both the worship of idols and the cult of the Virgin Mary.[37] In this perspective, the theories on the maternal imagination's power over the unborn child, on women's fascination with images, and on the resulting teratological disasters illustrate the indissoluble and fateful association among the image, the feminine, and the monstrous.

Progeny and Legitimacy

In 1619, a trial took place in France, and the text of the defense was published in Paris under the title *Plea on the question of whether*

a child alleged to have been a monster, and who, for this reason, was denied
the Holy Sacrament of Baptism, had been capable of receiving his father's
succession on the strength of his testament; and whether upon his death he
had allowed his mother to inherit by virtue of the pupilage substitution.[38]
The child in question had been born with a cloven foot, a severely
deformed body, and a face that was described as resembling that of
a monkey or a pig; it lived only a few hours. In this case, if the
widow were declared to have been childless, she could not claim
her husband's estate, which then would pass to the family of the
deceased, his brothers. The existence, however brief, of a child and
heir, however, entitled the mother to receive her husband's inheritance upon the child's death, "by substitution."

Maître Robert Robin and Maître Simon Houdry, who were entrusted with protecting the rights of the deceased child, and consequently those of his mother, defended the idea that, however deformed he may have been, the child was nevertheless human, and
was therefore his father's heir. Concerned with defending the human character of the progeny, which the Church had denied, and
anxious to reaffirm the virtue of the mother, Houdry argued: "I
said that even if he had the face of a monkey, given that all the rest
of his members were proportionate to those of the human body, he
could not have been, in any way, different in species from the rest
of mankind, especially since, having been begotten of man and
woman, he had to take on, consequently, the specific form that
characterizes all men, for like causes produce and engender effects
similar to their nature" (p. 34). On this now familiar point, Maître
Robin liberally quoted Aristotle, who remained the ultimate authority. But even though he emphasized that the monster was entirely human—a key point for the defense—Robin reminded the
court that, despite the tendency for things to reproduce and resemble each other, "God, the author of the universe, likes to make
us admire his ineffable power in the diversity of his effects" (p. 37).
The cloven foot was too strongly reminiscent of the devil not to call
to mind the Creator of all things. Anxious as well to reaffirm the
virtue of the mother and to dismiss all suspicion of marital infidel-
ity, the lawyer persisted:

> Aristotle and Hippocrates attributed [monstrosity] to the ardent
> and obstinate imagination that the woman may have while she

conceives, through some object or fantastic dream of a nocturnal vision. That is how Hippocrates saved a Princess accused of adultery for having begotten a Moorish child, unlike his father, who was white like her, because there was, at the foot of her bed, a portrait of a Moor . . . And the reason is that imagination has so much power over the seed and progeny that its imprint and character remain on what is born. Similarly, I can say that the deformity of the child's face, which has been the subject of debates between the parties, may have been caused by the mother's imagination during the child's conception. This imagination, though it may imprint a mark or character upon the child that is conceived that makes it somehow externally dissimilar to the rest of men, nevertheless cannot prevent the participation of natural causes, nor can it obviate the necessity that the body, having been formed and organized in conformity with the human body, a reasonable soul should have been infused at a time predetermined by God, the author of Nature. (pp. 43–44)

Here the law took a stricter position than the Church and determined that the child should have been baptized: "monstruosus homo est tamen homo" (a monstrous man is nonetheless a man) (p. 44).

In this summary of traditional opinions, the mother's imagination is again precisely defined as plastic art. It is because the mother's imagination has been led astray that it gives shape to a monstrous child; and it is because imagination shapes only the exterior part of a child's body that the monster is human. This plea is not without importance insofar as it directly addresses the question of legitimacy and representation. Everyone knows that like begets like, and that this is Nature's law, noted Claude de Tesserant in his *Histoires prodigieuses* of 1567.[39] But in the case of a monstrous birth, like produces unlike, and the mother's imagination, moved by an illegitimate desire—that is, a desire not directed toward her husband—allows a false resemblance to be born. Thus, tales of monstrous progeny faithfully illustrate Aristotle's definition that: "anyone who does not take after his parents is really in a way a monstrosity." Since the monstrous mother erases the image of the real father, the monster can be seen as the most illegitimate of offspring. This radical erasure of the father's image is not the least scandal of monstrosity. Or rather, what made monstrosity monstrous was that it served as a public reminder that, short of relying on visible resemblance, paternity could never be proven: that if nothing were more undeniable than maternity, paternity could never be verifiable or physically ascertained. Resemblance played such a major role in theories of generation because it alone, along rather tenuous lines, could offer what appeared to be a natural link between the father and his child. Conversely, the considerable importance granted since Aristotle to effects of resemblance in nature stems from the fact that what is always at stake in resemblance and likeness is the fate of paternity itself. "Aristotle says," Montaigne writes, "that in a certain nation where the women were in common they assigned children to their fathers by resemblance" (II: 37, p. 578). But if resemblance creates a visible connection between father and child, it also conceals the questionable character of all paternities. At the same time that it suggests filiation by instituting a "natural," visible, link between the progenitor and his child, resemblance, used as a criterion for establishing paternity, ignores the fact that filiation can never be certain. Thus resemblance imposes a temporary, if superficial order, while masking a fundamental, primordial disorder. And what resemblance conceals, the monster unmasks.

In a political culture where the notions of inheritance, name, title, and lineage were reinforced by multiple rights (birthrights, rights to inheritance, entails, and so forth), the question of paternity had considerable urgency. The uncertainty of legitimacy also explains the success of a theory that attributed a lack of resemblance to the power of the mother's imagination. The importance given to the *vis imaginativa* of the monstrous mother thus also conceals the question that weighs heavily on paternity itself. From a legal viewpoint, Robin and Houdry's successful defense reinforces the necessity of avoiding the question of paternity or filiation. And inasmuch as resemblance alone answers for paternity, it attempts to close an unbridgeable gap: the distance between fathering and childbirth.

While the erasure of the father is punished by the unseemly appearance of the child, the mother's imagination also dooms her offspring by usurping the vital principle of procreation—the father. This is why, we are told, monsters often die so young. The child is condemned to an early death, not so much by the extent of the deformities that define it as a "monster" in the first place as by the erasure of the father's principle. Treatises give numerous examples of monstrous offspring, marked only by a superficial likeness to an image or an object that did not participate in their creation, but who were not able to survive. A superficial desire, an *envie*, may leave only a birthmark, but a deeper fascination capable of erasing the father's image dooms the progeny.

In an epistemology strictly defined by the laws of resemblance, it could be said that the monster is truly that which resembles *what is not* its father. The monster is thus the very definition of imposture: while dissimulating its legitimate filiation to its rightful father, the monster assumes the appearance of that which it is not. One might add, in the case of the accounts considered, that the monster assumes the appearance of that which *is not*, that is, the appearance of something that does not exist, something that is already itself a mere appearance, a reflection, a portrait.

Enriched by the classical culture of Plato and Aristotle and fueled by the Reformation's contention over images, the thesis of the monster-engendering imagination was to take its place within philosophical and anatomical treatises of the European Classical Age, and give rise to numerous debates among scholars. As it was about to begin its scientific career, the idea of the power of the pregnant woman's imagination would find its greatest audience at the height of the Age of Reason.

2

Parental Singularity

During the Renaissance, the monster had been considered, in the words of Jean Céard, a "véritable hiéroglyphe divin."[1] In the seventeenth century it became the object of methodical investigations more concerned with its natural causes than with its possible prophetic message or cosmic significance. Katharine Park and Lorraine Daston suggest that this evolution in attitudes concerning monsters might have been caused by progress in medical knowledge and by the widening gap between "high" and "low" culture. "Francis Bacon's reflections on the study of monsters," they add, "represent an intermediate stage in the gradual process of naturalization begun in the wonder books. Where Paré and other wonder authors countenanced a mixture of supernatural and natural causes in the generation of monsters, Bacon insisted on a strict division between marvels of natural and supernatural origin; henceforth compilations of each sort of event were to be kept separate."[2] Although it is difficult to identify one specific turning point, treatises describing monsters as prodigies, marvels, signs, and prophecies had been largely replaced by scientific discourses by the time Descartes entered the debate on generation and William Harvey published his *De Generatione Animalium* in 1651.[3]

But even though the study of monstrosities was now integrated with more rigorous scientific investigations, the fact remains that one of the most intriguing paradoxes of the so-called Age of Reason was the enduring fascination of doctors and philosophers with the power of the maternal imagination over the fetus. The incorporation into medical literature of the widespread belief that the maternal imagination played a major role in the formation of the fetus, whether normal or monstrous, was one of the most significant features of the transition from the Renaissance to the European Classical Age. The popularity of the imaginationist theses impassioned philosophers and physicians; it also provided numerous opportunities for jurists and theologians to redefine the legal and divine nature of body and soul and to pass statutes on the all-important question of Baptism. By now the theory assigning to the pregnant mother's imagination the responsibility for the outcome of her pregnancy was completely detached from the corpus of anachronistic and outmoded works of the *merveilleux*. But it continued to fascinate researchers by insistently posing a problem as pertinent to the seventeenth and eighteenth centuries as it had been to the Renaissance, namely, the question of resemblances. This question was made more troubling by the important discoveries being published at the time about the generation of life. The imaginationist theses—now falling into the domain of medical research and expertise—found solid supporters and sparked intense debates in Europe. Within the medical community, the debate would not end until the close of the eighteenth century, for reasons that had little to do, as we shall see, with scientific data. In its description of monsters resulting from the mother's desiring imagination, the Renaissance had implied that a moderate and sensible imagination would produce a child who *did* resemble the father; still, the Renaissance had been more concerned with exploring the dangers, the extremes, than the norm. The growing emphasis on the role of the maternal imagination in the seventeenth and eighteenth centuries must be understood in the context of the intense, as well as contentious, development of ideas and speculations on the generation of life.

The Medical Field

"Embryology from the third century B.C. to the seventeenth century A.D.," remarks Joseph Needham, "is meaningless unless it is studied in the light of Aristotle" (p. 54). The seventeenth century provided the first serious challenge to the belief (attributed by tradition to Aristotle) that the mother's role in reproduction was an essentially passive one, that "the semen gave the 'form' to the inchoate 'matter' of the menstrual blood" (p. 55).[4]

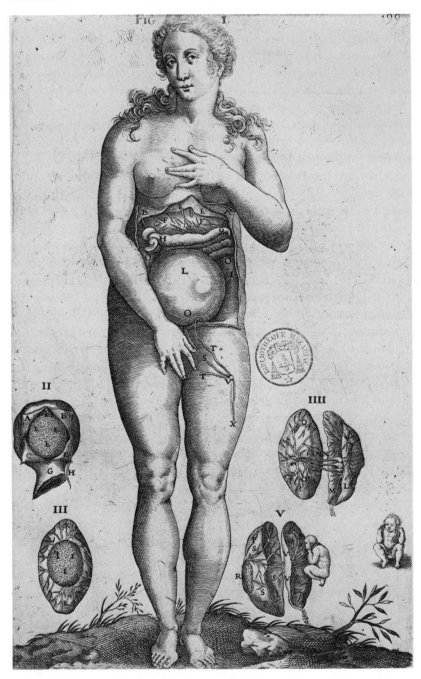

Anatomical engraving, seventeenth century.

In his notes on the generation of animals, Descartes (1596–
1650) speculated on an ancient question that held renewed interest
for the European Classical Age: what determines the sex of a
child? Descartes's answer, that sex depends on the position of the
fetus in the womb, constituted the leading theory on the subject
until the end of the eighteenth century.[5] Within that tradition,
males were thought to be positioned higher in the womb and were
thus brighter, because the purer part of the semen is carried
higher; females were thought to be lodged in the softer part of the
womb, thus accounting for their broader pelvises. At the same
time, the old concept of preformation, anticipated by Averroes and
Albertus Magnus, gained a new and growing audience. It was summarized by Joseph de Gli Aromatari (1586–1660) in his small pamphlet *Epistola de Generatione Plantarum ex Seminibus* in these words:
"As for the eggs of fowls, I think the embryo is already roughly
sketched out in the egg before being formed at all by the hen."[6]
The first important debate of the time over procreation would be
between preformationists—who believed that the human being exists as a whole in the sperm or the egg—and the partisans of *epigenesis,* or the gradual development of the fetus. This debate would
later be complicated by the discovery of ovaries and animalcules.

William Harvey, who discovered the principle of blood circulation and made a major contribution to the history of generation
with his *De Generatione Animalium* (1651), fought vehemently
against the idea of preformation. His theory was based on observations of chickens' eggs and of the does King Charles I had gen-
erously allowed him to kill in the royal forests. What Buffon later
termed "a massacre for the sake of knowledge" led to Harvey's firm
stand in favor of the slow development of the fetus, or epigenesis:

> There is no part of the future foetus actually in the egg, but yet
> all the parts of it are in it potentially . . . I have declared that one
> thing is made out of another two several wayes and that as well in
> artificial as natural productions . . . So likewise in the Generation
> of Animals, some are formed and transfigured out of matter al-
> ready concocted and grown and all the parts are made and dis-
> tinguished together *per metamorphosin,* by a metamorphosis, so
> that a complete animal is the result of that generation; but some
> again, having one part made before another, are afterwards
> nourished, augmented, and formed out of the same matter, that

is, they have parts, whereof some are before, and some after, other, and at the same time, are both formed, and grow . . . These we say are made *per epigenesin,* by a post-generation, or after-production, that is to say, by degrees, part after part, and this is more properly called a Generation than the former . . . The perfect animals, which have blood, are made by Epigenesis.[7]

Furthermore, for Harvey, the entire female body is "irradiated" during conception; a "kinde of contagious property" brings about fertilization and also serves to explain resemblances.[8] In Jean Rostand's words: "While the entire female body is inseminated, there is, however, only one place in this body that has the capacity to conceive the fetus, in the same way that the brain alone can conceive ideas. Both these concepts—the physiological and the psychological—are analogous: the ideas conceived by the brain resemble the images the brain receives from the senses; similarly, the fetus, which is the idea produced by the womb, resembles what originated it, and this is why the child resembles his father."[9]

Nicolas Steensen (1631–1687) is said to have been the first successfully to explain the role of the ovaries in the production of eggs, an idea further strengthened by the discoveries of Regnerus de Graaf (1641–1673), published in 1672 in Leyden under the title *De Mulierum Organis Generationi Inservientibus Tractatus Novus, Demonstrans tam Homines et Animalia, Caetera Omnia Quae Vivipara Dicuntur, Haud Minus Quam Ovipara, ab Ovo Originem Ducere.* In 1672, Marcello Malpighi contributed important observations on embryos to the development of ovism, and drew what then seemed to be the logical conclusion that live organisms were preformed in the egg. It is worth noting that this theory, which should have excluded the role of the mother's imagination in the formation of monstrosities, not only managed to accommodate the idea of the monstrous maternal imagination, but eventually was itself described as a monstrosity by modern history of science. Thus, Joseph Needham describes this credo as "the cloven hoof of preformationism" (p. 167).

For Regnerus de Graaf, both an ovist and a preformationist, the function of the father's semen is simply to carry the egg down from the ovary into the womb. As Rostand puts it, "The mother is the only true author of the child. She alone lives on in the child. There is no collaboration between the father and herself . . . that contributes to the creation of this new being. Of course, according to this hypothesis, heredity must be strictly maternal. Antiquity's idea of male and female collaboration is abandoned; one sex alone—the female—generates life. The father is deposed, devalued, assigned the role of stimulant" (pp. 66–67). Thus, clearly stated, is the principle I would call *parental singularity*, that is, the idea that only one parent is essentially responsible for procreation. This concept would enjoy unprecedented popularity throughout the seventeenth and the eighteenth centuries, assigning sometimes to the father, sometimes to the mother, sole responsibility for progeny. Later it would provide fertile ground for the Romantic imagination.

The concept of parental singularity was echoed, as well, when several scientists argued over who had been first to discover the egg: notably van Horne, de Graaf, and Swammerdam, the last of these publicly accusing de Graaf, in front of the Royal Academy of London in 1672, of plagiarizing his ideas. A similar controversy over the discovery of spermatozoa later involved Ham, Leeuwenhoek, and Hartsoeker. Even if Swammerdam did not discover the egg first, his work contributed to the arguments already published by de Graaf an important element that directly concerned the production of monstrosities: the theory of *emboîtement,* or encasement, which gave new support to theories of preformation.

"Swammerdam's support for preformation," writes Needham, "came from a different angle. He had been investigating insect metamorphosis, and, having hardened the chrysalis with alcohol, had seen the butterfly folded up and perfectly formed within the cocoon. He concluded that the butterfly had been hidden or masked *(larvatus)* in the caterpillar, and thence it was no great step to regard the egg in a similar light. Each butterfly in each cocoon must contain eggs within it which in their turn must contain butterflies which in their turn must contain eggs, and so on. Before long, Swammerdam extended his theory to man. 'In nature,' he said, 'there is no generation but only propagation, the growth of parts. Thus original sin is explained, for all men were contained in the organs of Adam and Eve. When their stock of eggs is finished, the human race will cease to be.'" (p. 170)[10]

The concept of a living being's preformation within the seed, or the egg, and the idea of the almost infinite encasement of eggs, seemed to exclude the possibility of monstrous anomalies, or at least it should have excluded the possibility that the maternal imagination could modify the shape of a progeny that had already been formed since the beginning of time. It is an added paradox that one of the encasement theory's most prolix advocates, Nicolas Malebranche, would also be one of the most energetic defenders of the idea of the maternal imagination's power over the fetus. Nevertheless, theories of preformation, and more specifically theories of encasement, made it difficult to explain anomalies; Brunner emphasized this problem as early as 1683, though a complete case would not be made until Isidore Geoffroy Saint-Hilaire published his classic work on monstrosities in 1836.

The principle of parental singularity took on another meaning when Antoni van Leeuwenhoek announced the discovery of animalcules in 1677. It is neither in the ovaries nor in the female's eggs that one should look for preexisting beings and the principle of generation, he argued, but solely in the male sperm. The discovery of animalcules unleashed as many passions and controversies as had the discovery of the egg. John Farley notes: "Discovering the animalcules independently in March 1678, [Nicolas Hartsoeker] argued that they were joined to the egg by an umbilical vessel in the tail and contained an infinite number of other animalcules, so that the first male of each species 'had been created with all those of the same species that have been engendered and will be engendered until the end of time.'"[11] Both enthusiasm and derision greeted the discovery, which was the talk of Europe. Although the theory of animalcules gave rise to discussions as lively as those surrounding the egg, John Farley notes that it "never enjoyed the popularity that ovism did. In an age dominated by theories of preexistence and the outlook that nature appeared to do nothing without a purpose, this was not surprising. Spermism implied an enormous wastage, for only a minute fraction of the little homunculi found an egg in which to develop" (pp. 20–21).[12] This "enormous wastage" was illustrated not only by the rarity with which an animalcule encountered an egg, but also by the fact that the encounter might result in a monstrosity. Once again, Aristotle's view that the female is a necessary deviation justified by her ultimate function, whereas the monster is an absolute and useless deviation, was echoed in the desire that nothing be lost—even morally, because of deformity—in the living being. The idea of a preformed monstrosity was utterly abhorrent to many scientists of the time. But while the discovery of animalcules did not modify the belief in preexistence, parental singularity once again changed sides. Now, the father was solely responsible for reproduction. As Jean Rostand remarked: "A great number of physicians and philosophers abandoned ovism for the thesis supporting animalcules. In their view, it was no longer the female sex that procreated, but the male. The woman was relieved of her procreative function, which was now restored to the male" (p. 83).

The two opposing factions in the question of parental singularity—ovists and animalculists—were further divided according to whether they supported the theory of encasement or simple preformation, or whether they supported epigenesis or the idea of differentiation and growth in the womb. Fontenelle was an animalculist, Leibnitz a defender of animalculism and preformation; Malebranche was an ovist and a partisan of preformation; Harvey defended epigenesis; Linnaeus was a supporter of ovism; and Voltaire unleashed his irony against animalculism—in his view, the most ridiculous thing in all Europe. The unresolved question remained the one posed by Aristotle in *Generation of Animals:* how to explain resemblance? It is over this point that issues became clouded and that thinkers from both sides, whether preformationists or not, turned toward the maternal imagination as the cause of abnormal births as well as legitimate resemblances.

The argument continued unabated until the end of the eighteenth century. Efforts by Maupertuis and Buffon to advance the hypothesis of a real collaboration by both parents would meet with little success. Epigenesis was losing supporters as well. Haller, who had started his career as a partisan of epigenesis, changed sides: "In the body of the animal therefore, no part is made before any other part, but all are formed at the same time . . . If I said that in the animal at the moment of conception one does not find the same parts as in the perfect animal, I have realised abundantly since then that all I said against preformation really went to support it." [13] Charles Bonnet (1720–1793), an ovist and preformationist, purportedly was beside himself with joy on hearing the news of Haller's discoveries and conversion: "For him," writes Jean Rostand, "the monster of 'epigenesis' had been brought down forever" (p. 133).

Despite the importance of the work, Caspar Friedrich Wolff's (1722–1794) defense of epigenesis in *Theoria Generationis* (1759) was attacked from all sides. "Epigenesis," notes John Farley, "teaches that development is not the mere mechanical unfolding of preformed parts, but is a process of simultaneous growth and differentiation from a completely homogeneous beginning. As Caspar Wolff, the foremost epigenesist of the eighteenth century, remarked in 1759, 'Those who teach the system of predelineation do not explain generation but deny that it occurs'" (p. 30). Wolff was forced to leave Germany, and only received true recognition in the nineteenth century, more specifically from the French terato-genist Camille Dareste.[14] Finally, mention should also be made of the fruitful research conducted by the Italian priest Lazzaro Spal-lanzani, who is credited with the first artificial insemination. His discoveries were published in 1780 under the title *Dissertazione di fisica animale e vegetabile*. With his work, the theories of ovism and preformation seemed to triumph again.

The idea that, through the role of eggs, women might be solely responsible for generation may have triggered Poulain de la Barre's fervent defense of the strength of men entitled *De l'excell-ence de l'homme* (1675). "Men are stronger than women. This differ-ence is founded on reason and meant by nature. In order to per-petuate the species, nature has given to males, who contribute as active and effective cause, the qualities most favorable to this duty, which are heat, dryness, and strength. Nature has given to females, who are only a passive cause and who need more humors for the reproduction and nourishment of their fruits, weaker qualities, so to speak, and less active ones."[15] This text is particularly significant in that it *precedes* the discovery of animalcules by two years and therefore could be read only as a strong Aristotelian reaction to recent ovist discoveries. It also suggests how important, perhaps indispensable, was the subsequent discovery of animalcules, which managed to reinstate the father in his active role, and compensated for the extraordinary success of ovism.

It was within this context of impassioned debates, in a climate of obstinate and irreconcilable opinions that have little in common other than assigning the essential role in procreation alternately to one parent alone, that the imaginationist quarrel would develop. Although the debate between ovists and animalculists at times be-

came, so to speak, a battle of the sexes, the question of the m<
imagination seems to have transcended the dispute rather th<
have been invoked to support both ovism and epigenesis, whe<
would have fit more logically into the scientific background. T<
belief in the power of the mother's imagination survived not because of the scientific discoveries of the seventeenth and eighteenth centuries, but in spite of them. Similarly, the eventual demise of this theory toward the end of the eighteenth century had
little to do with the current state of knowledge regarding reproduction, but was related, rather, to the still enigmatic question of
the role of resemblances in Nature's scheme.

Malebranche: Imagination and Philosophy

Malebranche was a priest of the Oratory who became fascinated by
studies on generation and conducted his own experiments on the
development of eggs. Strongly influenced by René Descartes's
posthumous work *Traité de l'homme, et un traité de la formation du foetus* (1664), which attempted to apply mechanical principles to embryonic development, Malebranche was equally well acquainted
with the more general debate on epigenesis versus preformation.
His deep belief in the power of the mother's imagination over the
fetus is all the more remarkable in that he sided with the ovists and
the partisans of preformation.[16] The entire second book of *De la
recherche de la vérité*, first published in 1674, is devoted to imagination. Malebranche's intentions speak for themselves: "This is the
order we observe in this treatise: it is divided into three parts. In
the first the physical causes of disorders and errors of the imagination are explained. In the second some of the most general errors of the imagination are explained in terms of these causes, and
we shall also speak of what might be called moral causes of these
errors. In the third part we speak about the contagious communication of strong imaginations."[17] The rationalist prejudice against
imagination is made explicit in these lines. Malebranche associates
imagination with errors and disorders; further, he views the effects
of imagination as "contagious" (already a favorite idea of Paracelsus, who had conceived that imagination played a role in the propagation of the plague). For Malebranche, imagination disseminated ideas and images just as, in former times, it had supposedly

spread diseases. The intensity of the rationalist prejudice against imagination was in proportion to the considerable role imagination played in the moral and philosophical concerns of the time.

Malebranche defined the act of imagining as follows: "If the agitation originates through the impressions made by objects on the exterior surface of our nerve fibers and is communicated to the brain, then the soul senses, and it judges that what it senses is outside, i.e., it perceives an object as present. But if the internal fibers alone are lightly disturbed by the flow of animal spirits, or in some other way, then the soul imagines, and judges that what it imagines is not outside, but inside the brain, i.e., it perceives an object as absent. This is the difference between sensing and imagining" (p. 88). This important distinction, whereby sensation refers to, and identifies, present objects, and imagination refers to objects that are absent, establishes a definite hierarchy without revealing the full danger—great indeed—that is posed by imagination.

Malebranche specified: "However, it sometimes happens that persons whose animal spirits are highly agitated by fasting, vigils, a high fever, or some violent passion have the internal fibers of their brains set in motion as forcefully as by external objects. Because of this such people sense what they should only imagine, and they think they see objects before their eyes, which are only in their imaginations" (p. 88). But to Malebranche, the real threat posed by imagination lay not only in imagination's ability to mislead our judgment, but in the scope of its influence. The two distinctions he added between the *active imagination,* that of the soul, and the *passive imagination,* that of the body, reinforced the idea of the imagination's considerable powers. As we know, imagination's greatest power was described as the ability to *imprint* images on the brain: "So the faculty of imagining, or the imagination, consists only in the soul's power of forming images of objects producing changes in the fibers of that part of the brain which can be called the *principal* part" (p. 88). This "impression," that is, literally, the imprint made by the imagination on the brain, is also a form of writing: the indelible image of an absent object that is perceived as, or made to be present through, these representations. Such impressions can be compared not only to writing, but, because of its figurative character, to the work of art. "Now, just as the breadth, depth, and clarity of the strokes of an engraving depend upon the pressure applied to the burin, and the pliancy of the copper, so the depth and clarity of the traces in the imagination depend upon the pressure of the animal spirits, and upon the constitution of the brain fibers" (p. 89).

Malebranche in turn posited the theory of the maternal imagination as formative of the fetus within the context of ovist and preformationist thought. He began by explaining, from a mechanistic point of view, why the fetus' fragility renders it vulnerable to the mother's impressions:

> Infants in their mothers' womb, whose bodies are not yet fully formed and who are, by themselves, in the most extreme state of weakness and need that can be conceived, must also be united with their mother in the closest imaginable way . . . Thus, the passions and the sensations, and in general all the thoughts of which the body is the occasion, are common to mother and child. These things seem incontestable to me for many reasons. Consider only that a mother who is very frightened at the sight of a cat begets a child with a horror that surprises him every time this animal is presented to him. It is easy to conclude from this that the child must have seen with the same horror and emotions of spirit what its mother saw when she carried it in her womb. (pp. 112–113)

In Malebranche's view, the child is more apt to receive his mother's image because his fibers are delicate, in the same way that sensitive and delicate individuals feel pity and empathy when they see violence inflicted on others and experience others' pain in the very same parts of their bodies.[18] The monster, then, is nothing more than the sign of *disorder* in a system whose objective is to reproduce beings similar to their progenitors, a disorder brought about through the plastic role of imagination. Malebranche tells us that after seeing the execution of a criminal on the wheel, a mother gave birth to a child whose body was broken in the same places as the condemned man's:

> About seven or eight years ago, I saw at the *Incurables* a young man who was born mad, and whose body was broken in the same places in which those of criminals are broken . . . According to the principles just established, the cause of this disastrous accident was that his mother, having known that a criminal was to be broken, went to see the execution. All the blows given to this mis-

erable creature forcefully struck the imagination of this mother
and, by a sort of counterblow, the tender and delicate brain of
her child . . . At the sight of this execution, so capable of frightening a woman, the violent flow of the mother's animal spirits
passed very forcefully from her brain to all the parts of her body
corresponding to those of the criminal, and the same thing happened in the child. (p. 115)

The monstrous birth thus can result from an expectant mother's
witnessing a harrowing event, as a manifestation of the effects of
terror. "The explanations of this accident are broad enough to explain how pregnant women who see people marked on certain
parts of the face imprint these same marks on their unborn children" (p. 116). And if terror can disturb the imagination, sometimes to the point of causing the death of the infants in the womb,
so can—and even more so—"some ardent desire, or some other
violent passion of their mothers" (p. 116).

Malebranche also expands on the theories of birthmarks, already popular during the Middle Ages and the Renaissance, by
examining how a fetus bears the image of the mother's unfulfilled
desires. These desires, all the more violent since they have been
frustrated, leave their imprint, or their "writing," on the child, and
can even deform the entire body. As Malebranche writes:

There are many other examples of the power of a mother's imagination in the literature, and there is nothing so bizarre that it
has not been aborted at some time. For not only do they give
birth to deformed infants but also to fruits they have wanted to
eat, such as apples, pears, grapes, and other similar things. If the
mother imagines and strongly desires to eat pears, for example,
the unborn, if the fetus is alive, imagines them and desires them
just as ardently; and, whether the fetus be alive or not, the flow
of spirits excited by the image of the desired fruit, expanding
rapidly in a tiny body, is capable of changing its shape because of
its softness. These unfortunate infants thus become like the
things they desire too ardently. (p. 117)

For Alain Grosrichard, this text makes explicit the hidden sin of all
births. "It is probably no coincidence that all the examples of monsters cited by Malebranche in [this] case are examples of fruit/chil-
dren. Each and every monster, for Malebranche, tends perhaps to
take the form of an apple . . . the monsters spell out to the mother

what progeny say without showing it: that they are, literally, the fruit of a sin." [19] By echoing other unexpected connections between generation and theology, the birthmark becomes literally the mark of the forbidden fruit.

The most striking example of a wandering maternal imagination is related by Malebranche as follows:

> It has not been more than a year since a woman, having attended too carefully to the portrait of Saint Pius on the feast of his canonization, gave birth to a child who looked exactly like the representation of the saint. He had the face of an old man, as far as is possible for a beardless child; his arms were crossed upon his chest, with his eyes turned toward the heavens; and he had very little forehead, because the image of the saint being raised toward the vault of the church, gazing toward heaven, had almost no forehead. He had a kind of inverted miter on his shoulders, with many round marks in the places where miters are covered with gems. In short, this child strongly resembled the tableau after which its mother had formed it by the power of her imagination. This is something that all Paris has been able to see as well as me, because the body was preserved for a considerable time in alcohol. [20]

The monstrous child, fashioned after a painting of St. Pius, looks not like St. Pius, but only like the representation of him. The original artist had reduced the saint's forehead, because Pius was looking toward the heavens. The mother-beholder, viewing the painting from below, reproduced indiscriminately what was only an artistic effect. We recognize in this story all the elements of an almost perfect monstrosity: the erasure of the legitimate father, the visible similarity to a false model, and the grotesque result of a poor artistic imitation of an image already once removed from its original model.

For Malebranche, however, imagination was not only the predictable agent of monstrous births, but was also endowed with the power to shape all progeny, whether normal or abnormal. This marked an important change in the medical history of the maternal imagination. Malebranche added:

> It is true that this communication between the brain of the mother and that of her child sometimes has bad results when the mother allows herself to be overwhelmed by some violent pas-

sion. Nevertheless, it seems to me that without this communication, women and animals could not easily bring forth young of
the same species. For although one can give some explanation of
the formation of the fetus in general, as Descartes has tried successfully enough, nevertheless it is very difficult, without this
communication of the mother's brain with the child's, to explain
why a mare does not give birth to a calf, or a chicken lay an egg
containing a partridge or some bird of a new species; and I believe that those who have meditated on the formation of the fetus
will be of this opinion. (p. 117)

Imagination shaped the progeny in a quasi-mechanical way. Although the general shape of the child to come was already determined, the mother's imagination, moved by immediate impressions (not just the particular father's face, but that of the human
species in general), communicated those imprints to her child's
body. In this passage, Malebranche gave imaginationism its most
general and poetic formulation. Its formative power makes imagination the fundamental principle in the organization of living
beings. Moreover, this function is central to Malebranche's beliefs
on generation, as illustrated by his careful examination of the respective importance of preformation and communication between
the child's brain and the mother's.

This belief in the formative power of imagination appears incompatible with the preformationist theses Malebranche openly
embraced. How indeed is it conceivable that preformed beings
could be so modified by the mother's imagination during pregnancy that they might be born marked or deformed each time the
mother's imagination failed to convey the proper impression? Ultimately, Malebranche evaded the problem:

It is true that the most reasonable thinking, that which conforms
most closely to experience in this very difficult question of the
formation of the fetus, is that infants are already almost completely formed even before the action by which they are conceived, and during the gestation period their mothers do nothing but provide them their normal growth. However, this
communication of the mother's animal spirits and brain with
those of the infant seems to serve to regulate this growth, determining the particles used to nourish it to be arranged gradually
in the same way as in the mother's body; which is to say, this communication of the spirits renders the child like its mother, or of
the same species. (pp. 117–118)

Although the child is already in its near-final form, the maternal imagination, driven by immediate impressions, its perception of the human species, and the father's image, communicates these imprints to the infant, who, in turn, shapes and adopts them as his own. Without contesting Aristotle's principle of resemblance, this theory brings into play two new ideas: First, that the maternal imagination is generally responsible for the *form* of the child whether it be normal or monstrous, and through imagination's influence, the species reproduces itself as form and resemblance; in other words, the imagination does not just receive images resembling beings, it is itself the agent for the resemblance between beings of the same species. Second, while it was long thought that daughters should resemble their mothers and sons their fathers, here resemblance to either parent is the work of the mother alone.[21] In the seventeenth century, then, the persistent belief in parental singularity would attribute to one parent alone the full responsibility for the birth's merits or deficiencies.

Yet precisely because imagination plays such a considerable role in procreation, its eventual breakdown could have dramatic consequences. The imagination of women may be all powerful in shaping their progeny, but it is also severely flawed in many ways. Malebranche remarks: "This delicacy of the brain fibers [responsible for accidents and misleading perceptions] is usually found in women, and this is what gives them great understanding of everything that strikes the senses" (p. 130). This idea places an important restriction on the power of the mother's imagination. In one of the most Platonic passages of *Search after Truth,* Malebranche gives the following example of the relationship between image and idea: "A mother, for example, who is moved to the love of God by the movements of the spirits that accompany the trace of the image of a venerable old man, because she has attached the idea of God to this old man's image . . . this mother, I say, can only produce in her child's brain the trace of an old man, and a strong liking for old men, which is not at all the love of God that had moved her. For in the end there are no traces in the brain that can, of themselves, arouse any other ideas than those of sensible things" (p. 123, translation modified). This passage illustrates an important point: that imagination is fallible precisely in its incapacity to establish a link between image and idea. This account also recalls the story of the child whose monstrous shape had been caused by the contemplation of a painting of St. Pius. In both cases, the mother had given in to idolatry. Not only do ideas yield to images, but images created through the power of imagination give but a pale reflection of the ideas that motivated them in the first place. In this way, Malebranche remains faithful to the commonplace view that women's beliefs in religion, and in religious subjects, are tainted with sensation since women are both less abstract and less spiritual than men. If Malebranche grants women, through imagination, the considerable responsibility of ensuring the proper continuation of the species, he also holds them fully responsible for the births of male children who, even if not physically monstrous, are suddenly "womanlike" in their terrors, their prejudices, and their sensitivity. The incapacity of the female brain to produce something intelligible rather than sensible, or to imprint ideas rather than forms on the child that will be born, also emphasizes the fact that, however vast it may be, the role of imagination is entirely devoid of intention—it has no teleology. Imagination translates the mother's desires in a way that escapes her will, her wishes, or her own understanding; it cannot even produce an aesthetic effect. Imagination deals only with resemblances, and resemblances without interpretation. By generalizing the part played by the imagination in reproduction, Malebranche also conceived of a greater number of secret aversions, irrational terrors, and unspeakable desires that can be transmitted to the child in the womb. In fact, he attributed all childhood fears to the traces left by the mother on her child's brain during pregnancy.

Although the imagination had been an object of speculation since Antiquity, and its influence on women had often been measured in terms of excess, Malebranche emphasized that imagination functions differently according to sex: "It is for women to set fashions, judge language, discern elegance and good manners," added Malebranche. "They have more knowledge, skill, and finesse than men in these matters. Everything that depends upon taste is within their area of competence, but normally they are incapable of penetrating to truths that are slightly difficult to discover. Everything abstract is incomprehensible to them. They cannot use their imagination for working out complex and tangled questions. *They consider only the surface of things,* and their imagination has insufficient strength and insight to pierce it to the heart, comparing all the parts, without being distracted" (p. 130, emphasis added). For Grosrichard, imagination in Malebranche illustrates the classical understanding of language elaborated by Port-Royal: "The relationship between ideas and traces, vertical and reciprocal, necessary yet arbitrary . . . belongs to the theory of signs posited by the Logic of Port-Royal. But here the sign is viewed not as the instrument of thought but rather as its *very* element; to imagine is to think not *by* signs, but first *in* signs . . . Structured like a language—as it is understood at the time—imagination has all of language's powers and surprising effects" (p. 24). Malebranche, however, was on the opposite side of Port-Royal, both on the question of generation and that of grammar, as was illustrated by his virulent dispute with Arnauld.[22] Certainly it is true that, for Malebranche, imagination functions *like* writing, particularly in its capacity to imprint the image of absent objects on the fibers of the brain, but this writing is neither necessary nor arbitrary. Grosrichard's generalization can be sustained only if one views the monster not as an accident of nature but as the very manifestation of nature as it should work. Yet for Malebranche, though the monster is the privileged accident that can illustrate the hidden workings of nature, the main reason for this accident is the monster's failure to accomplish nature's purpose: monstrosity is nature's ultimate disorder.

The writing of monstrosity has neither grammar nor rhetoric; it illustrates a purely Cratylist notion of language that relies on the figurative link between the absent object and the trace it leaves on the fetus. Women make judgments on language, Malebranche remarks, yet at the same time "everything abstract is incomprehensible to them." Their own specific writing is marred by their incapacity to consider the abstract, that is, the meaning of signs. This writing depends entirely on a resemblance between the absent object and the mark the object leaves on the progeny. Moreover, in a complementary fashion, the imaginative power that makes women so good at judging taste and manners is a matter of pure *form*. In fact, it is not the substance of language that is feminine, but merely its figures and contingent choice of words. In this sense, the monstrous progeny is the very emblem of the *mother tongue*, the reverse of the logic of Port-Royal. The monster is thus a maternal language, or linguistic function, centered entirely on the signifier, in the exercise of an imagination that communicates a figurative desire to the unborn child.

In French Classicism, the theory of women's imagination sought to contain the danger of a language whose form would be entirely unrelated to its substance, of a writing in which the signifier, like the monster, would prevail over the signified (that is, the father, the origin, the root of words) or worse yet, would be capable of doing without it entirely. The monster was neologism, an object of exclusion. Often it was not baptized; it did not receive a Christian name; and it was not formally recognized by its genitor. The monster thus represented the terror of a signifier detached from its legitimate origin, just as it bore no visible resemblance or relationship to the father who conceived it. The monster also conveyed the possibility that words might carry meaning as if by contagion, as if they could freely communicate notions over which neither logic nor reason could exercise the slightest control. In this golden age of eloquence, and in the supposedly feminine sphere of preciosity, the mother's imagination spoke a purely formal, unpredictable language, and a dangerous one at that, for it always referred to absent objects that were erroneously perceived as present, while erasing the very present, but superficially absent, genitor. Indeed, the greatest absence the monster signaled and proclaimed was that of the father, the ultimate referent whose signature it did not bear.

More generally, in Malebranche's view of women's imagination, the concrete prevails over the abstract, and the image triumphs over the idea that it is supposed to represent, as in the case of the old man who replaces the abstract idea of God. (Here, the Reformation's influence is still being felt.) Furthermore, the maternal imagination is unable to "compare all the parts." Malebranche is describing here precisely what the relationship between the monster and the imagination had demonstrated for centuries: the inability of the maternal imagination to interpret. For it is interpretation, the ability to go beyond the surface of things and establish comparisons in order to analyze, that interests the Platonic artist; he is concerned with proper proportion, in relation not to the model of his inspiration, but to the viewer who will behold his work. All this, as well as the ability to envision the finished work, is foreign to the maternal imagination, which is entirely absorbed by the present.

Malebranche assures us that there are probably exceptions to his views; however, he concludes: "Suffice it to say of women and children that since they are not involved in seeking truth and teaching others, their errors do not sustain much prejudice, for one hardly takes their proposals seriously" (p. 131). Thus, the discredit that befalls women also affects their children. A few pages earlier, Malebranche had written: "It is enough that I can conclude here, from what I have just explained in this chapter, that all these false impressions that mothers imprint in the brain of their children falsify their minds and corrupt their imagination, and thus most men are subject to imagining things other than as they are, attributing some wrong color to them, or bestowing some irregular trait on the ideas of the things they perceive" (p. 124).

Such was the paradox of the role of imagination in the French Classical Age. The maternal imagination is thought faithfully to reproduce what it sees and feels. *It is truthful and literal,* almost impersonal to the extent that the images' impressions left on the monstrous brain of the fetus show no sign of critical intervention, that is, of interpretation or judgment. Yet, for the same reason, the maternal imagination is a source of errors, because appearances are deceiving, and the imagination of women is concerned only with "the surface of things"; images are dangerous and the maternal imagination cannot differentiate between the model and its representation. Due to the incapacity of her imagination to distance itself from the model that so fascinates it, the mother "corrupts" not only the monster, but to a lesser degree, any being she engenders. Her imagination is responsible, in turn, for men's irrational fears; it is the source of their misjudgments and terrors, a weakness directly inherited from their mothers.

The child who was born insane and "broken" because his mother had witnessed an execution demonstrates this paradox. The monster is the living image of the tortured criminal, mangled in the very places where the wheel had marked the felon. He is also the criminal's untruth, because he is *other,* living, innocent of the crime whose punishment he bears. He is insane from being at once error and truth, insane because of the limited, superficial, and irrational image of justice his mother's terror has left on his brain. Whereas phantasia was associated with light *(phaos)* in Antiquity, this particular view of imagination is linked to darkness, to the blindness of a justice that so inequitably punishes the guilty and the innocent.

3

The Age of Imagination

"Nature always strives to her ends; sometimes she does not succeed. This is when she bears monsters, who are her sins and bastards," wrote the duke of Orleans' chaplain, René de Ceriziers, in 1643 in *Le philosophe français*. "But," he added, "if [monsters] run counter to Nature's ways, they do not shock in any way those of God, who suffers their presence in the world in order to give luster to its beauties."[1] Thus, while the monster in no way offends God, it is nevertheless the constant reminder of nature's, and specifically woman's, weakness in her contribution to generation. The persistence of this belief may help to explain why, in the seventeenth and eighteenth centuries, certain texts revived a theme that had been extremely popular during the Middle Ages, but had lost some of its virulence in subsequent years: the inner monstrosity of women.[2]

Monstrosity and Sexuality

Two particularly explicit treatises reminded the reader that, especially in women, procreation is both glorious and shameful. At the beginning of the eighteenth century there appeared a French translation of Liceti's *De Monstrorum Caussis*, prefaced by *Description anatomique des parties de la femme qui servent à la génération*, written by Jean Palfyn.[3] Liceti's text had been loosely translated and "enriched" (by a certain Gérard Blasius), as had been common practice in the previous century. What was new was the association of a treatise that simultaneously discussed prodigies, miracles, and monstrous births in the Renaissance manner with an essay on anatomy that opened with a violent diatribe on the female's "shameful parts." This is all the more surprising as Jean Palfyn (1650–1730) was a physician and scientist of some renown who had been interested in all the new theories on generation and had sided with the ovists and preformationists. Although ovism did not necessarily entail a new respect for the mother's body, it certainly suggested that as the mother came to be credited with a greater role in generation, her reproductive physiology at least deserved further medical scrutiny.

Description anatomique is prefaced by a series of considerations, which were commonplaces in the Middle Ages and would become clichés of the Victorian era, but remain surprising in the century of the Enlightenment. Palfyn warns:

> Now, so that the reader may have a clear and distinct idea of the Womb, as well as the other bodily parts of the Woman which are used in generation, we will preface this book (which concerns Monsters) with a Description of the Female Organs used for this purpose; that is, those parts of the body which cause women a thousand miseries, that irritate men in a thousand ways, that have allowed women—themselves weak and defenseless—to triumph over the strongest of men, overthrow several very powerful Kings, undo august Emperors, make fools out of wisemen, trick the learned, seduce the prudent, drive the healthy to loathsome ailments, strip the rich of their wealth, and strike down the most celebrated heroes. These organs are the cause of most of our ills, as well as our pleasures, and I dare say that almost all of the world's disorders, past and present, can be traced to them . . . Like some secret enchantment, these parts of the body can reduce the most prudent of men to a sort of folly. (p. 2)

The female organs are thus, above all, the source of errors: individual errors, political and historical errors, errors that allow a tragic reversal of the natural law that the strongest triumph over the weakest. Palfyn then evokes the fall of Nero, David, and Troy, of course, as examples of the fateful influence of the female organs. These organs, the site of lies, illusions, and unnatural power, must be unveiled to show their true nature. Palfyn continues:

> [Men] believe these organs in women to be full of sweetness, charm, and beauty, when in reality there are none in the body that are uglier and more subject to several very loathsome ailments, often infected with contaminated blood and much filth.

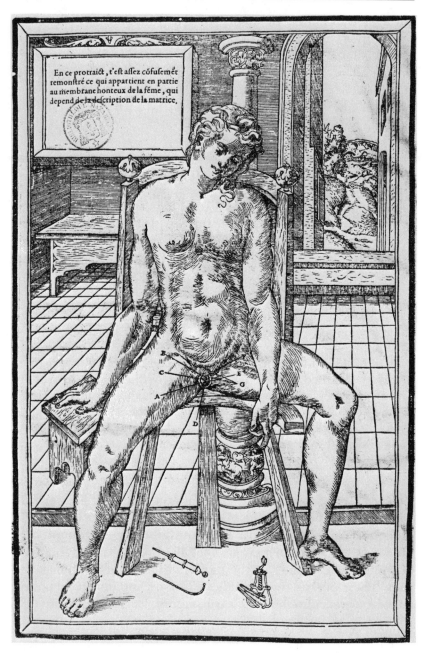

En ce protraict, c'est assez côfuseme͠t remonstré ce qui appartient en partie au membrane honteux de la féme, qui depend de la description de la matrice.

A woman's shameful parts, seventeenth century. The legend reads: "In this portrait is shown somewhat modestly that which belongs to the shameful membrane of woman, which depends on the description of the womb."

They are soiled and soaked each day by urine and emit a stinking and sulfurous odor, and they are relegated by the Author of Nature to the most contemptible place on the body, as if not fit to be seen, right near the Anus and its Excrements; they are themselves the main sewer for all elements. It is here, I say, in these bodily parts, into which all the body's filth flows and accumulates like a pit, that the Author of Nature nevertheless wanted Man—this superb Animal, whose final destiny is the Heavens—to be conceived, shaped, and formed, so that remembering afterward the time and baseness of his origins, he be not proud. (p. 2)[4]

In 1708, the meaning of these reflections takes on a special dimension. The very instrument of generation in women is monstrous in that it inverts all natural hierarchy, from the simplest to the most complex. The female organ appears to be an enchantment when it is only a sulfurous pit, it tricks the senses and reason, it defies science and scientists. If the monster is nature's disorder, the female instrument for procreation is the cause of all the disorders in nature. It is no wonder women passionately desire that which both seduces them and horrifies them, since it is in the very nature of women to join within themselves seduction and repulsion, life and disease, contamination and abjection.[5] What women hide, what women are, is monstrosity itself. With a perverse turn, this argument furthers the Aristotelian belief that like engenders like. Is it not logical indeed that women—so monstrous in their private parts—sometimes bring into the world the perfect resemblance of their inner monstrosity? It is only in relation to the father who sired his progeny that the monstrous child *dissembles*. The monster faithfully reveals his resemblance to the innermost being of the woman who conceived him in the madness of her imagination, the rapture of her desire, and the horror of her very being.

Ten years after Palfyn, Lorenz Heister published in Altdorf his *Compendium Anatomicum.* Heister himself was on the side of ovism and believed with the majority that birthmarks were the result of the mother's unfulfilled desires. But his contributions also include a somewhat grandiose rehabilitation of the "shameful parts" involved in procreation. Regarding the human reproductive organs, Heister wrote:

It is not without reason that they are called the noble parts, for they assist in the most admirable of nature's work. In the past

they have received the same homages as the Gods: the Sun and
the other Stars had less reason to be honored as Divinities, because their influence offers nothing as marvelous as the fertile
dew that emanates from these natural parts . . . True scientists
would never imagine the sight of these parts to be an insult to
their modesty. They believe rightfully that one's curiosity can be
directed toward any of the objects of Physics—toward those very
parts that are called, through a bizarre contradiction, both noble
and shameful . . . However, not all minds are so elevated and
just. They are weak minds dominated by the senses and the
imagination . . . they would have the name of these bodily parts
cut from Books on the Art, perhaps they would even have them
cut from the human body; at the very least their hollow scruples
seem to accuse nature of having chosen a shameful channel for
the propagation of human life.[6]

Although Heister is vigorously opposed to Jean Palfyn's anachronistic view of the "shameful parts," and defends both the nobility
of the organs used in human reproduction and the right to describe them explicitly in books lest medicine be metaphorically cas-
trated, the two positions have several points in common. In both
cases, the genitalia, whether considered noble or shameful, attain
religious proportions. More worthy of adoration than the gods of
Antiquity for Heister, these same parts for Palfyn are as hideous
and sulfurous as Hell itself. Both Palfyn and Heister believe that
these parts are the source of human errors of sense and judgment.
For both, they cause aberrations that, in Palfyn's view, ruin the
strongest of men, and according to Heister, mislead the most
learned. Moreover, "the weak minds that are dominated by the
senses and the imagination" behave like the women described by
Malebranche. Once again, the imagination acts contagiously: not
only can it make the fetus normal or monstrous, but it can impas-
sion the very scientist who studies the question of generation or the
man who reads the scientist's work. As a privileged example of this
form of aberration, the theory of animalcules would later be called
by Heister, like monstrosity, the product of a deranged, "heated
imagination" (p. 235).

The science of monsters and generation was itself troubled by
obscure yearnings: it was either hideous or deified, prone to error,
bearing the marks of an imagination moved by desire, horror, and

passion. Heister's remark—that those seeking to remove the names of the body's reproductive parts from books might wish, perhaps, that the same parts could actually be removed from the body—ascribes to the scientist an attitude similar to the power of the maternal imagination that produces the monster (a "mutilated animal," in the words of Aristotle). For Heister, these scientists also confuse objects and their representations: and just as the monster reveals woman's hidden desire, so these scientists' treatises on monsters and generation themselves imitate monsters by their form, their excesses, and their omissions. Texts such as Palfyn's, Heister suggests, are similar to the very mistake of nature—the monster— that their authors attempt to describe and explain. If the monster is the sin of Nature, these works on generation are the sins of Art.

Indeed, not only can the maternal imagination corrupt nature to the point of producing monsters, but the mother's body can so trouble the imagination that it produces monstrous disorders within society, politics, and finally science. The use of Latin rather than vulgar ("mother") tongues was predicated both on the tradition that Latin was the privileged scientific language and on the belief that anatomical descriptions would be less shocking if expressed in words removed from everyday exchange and communication. Ambroise Paré had upset Renaissance readers by choosing to write in French. The choice of a vulgar tongue became more frequent in medical treatises of the eighteenth century. Similarly, scientists opted to use descriptions referring to animals rather than directly to humans: "So as not to expose such minds to indecent subjects," writes Heister, "we will say about the chicken's reproduction what we fear to say about man's" (p. 223). It was, of course, obvious to Palfyn and his contemporaries that exposure to "indecent subjects" had the power to affect the public just as much as contemplation of a holy image could affect a pregnant woman's imagination. While the monster was losing its singularity through the generalization of the process that produced it, the science of generation was, in turn, beginning to become monstrous.

Two Quarrels

Two specific quarrels linked to the question of monstrosity further complicated the already intense debates on ovism, animalculism, preformation, and epigenesis. If the ovists, who were often in favor of preexistence, were right, how could monstrosity be explained?[7] How could one imagine that God would have allowed for preexisting monstrous germs? In his *Système de philosophie, contenant la logique, la métaphysique, la physique et la morale* (1690), Pierre-Sylvain Régis made explicit the Jansenist view:

> Nothing prevents us from believing that, in the beginning, the germs of monsters were produced in the same way as those of perfect Animals . . . It is of no use to say that God cannot be the author of Monstrosities and that He would [have to] be, however, if monstrous germs [were proven to exist] since the beginning; for it is easy to answer that there is nothing in the world, except moral evil, that God has not created and produced Himself very positively and freely. Conversely, it would be useless to argue that God in truth produces Monsters, although He would rather there were none, but that He is obliged to do so in order to satisfy the Laws of Nature: for we shall answer that the Laws of Nature are not different from God's will.[8]

Jacques Roger comments on this passage by pointing out: "The fact is Régis does not absolutely reject the accidental origin of monsters: he admits easily that too narrow a womb can produce hunchbacks and limping children; he also admits that the maternal imagination may engender monkeylike children or that double monsters are the result of two germs accidentally stuck together. But those 'accidents' cannot be attributed to chance happenings independent of God's will, that reigns alone . . . At any rate, directly or indirectly, monsters emanate from God and from his one and simple will. From this perspective, are they still monsters except to our limited understanding?" (p. 402).

Régis' book provoked a fierce exchange between Malebranche and the Jansenist Antoine Arnauld in the *Journal des Savants* of 1694. Malebranche defended the opinion that the birth of monsters could only be the result of accidents such as those caused by the maternal imagination, while Arnauld and Régis argued that God's perfection and sacred will did not exclude preformed monstrosities. Scientists were divided between these two beliefs, and many debates in the Academy of Sciences in Paris were devoted to the subject. In 1716, Jean Méry presented a monster he thought could only have been preformed, but in 1724, Louis Lémery wrote an adamant refutation of the doctrine of monstrous germs. Winslow and Haller replied in favor of the theory of preformed monstrosities. In 1738, Lémery launched a more articulated attack against the idea that God could have allowed what he describes as "disorganization, disorder, disturbance, confusion, and faulty executions." He asks, "Can such contradictions be imputed to the Author of nature? Yet, if one adopts the theory of eggs that are monstrous from the origin, one imputes monstrous births to God."[9] In a second memoir, Lémery added, "The system of Eggs that are monstrous from their inception always revolted me."[10] Twenty years later, after the deaths of the two principal adversaries, Lémery and Winslow, the debate had progressed no further. Roger comments: "The idea that God was directly responsible for monstrosities was revolting to reason. In order to solve this dilemma, the idea of preexisting germs, that is, the idea that nature was passive, had to be abandoned" (p. 418). In that perspective, the role of the maternal imagination in the formation of monstrosity also appeared as an exoneration of God. Disorders, confusions, and contradictions could be made to fit within an orderly and reasonable system that perfectly explained the occurrence of the monstrous accidents that troubled the otherwise perfect organization of God's Nature. Although most of the treatises that fed the quarrel of imaginationism were written not by leading scientists but rather by physicians addressing themselves to other practitioners and to women (the latter is a new factor as well), they were also written as an extension of the debate that involved or exonerated God in the birth of monstrous progeny.

The Imaginationist Quarrel itself may be said to have started in 1687 when Nicolas Venette, a physician with a taste for travel and writing, published an extraordinarily successful work entitled *Tableau de l'amour considéré dans l'état de mariage*. This book was translated into German, English, and Dutch, and was regularly reissued during the eighteenth and nineteenth centuries. Venette had previously written on scurvy, mineral waters, and the art of tree trimming. He was to find lasting fame with his modest essay on generation.[11] Although the scientific aspect of his work is of little interest, Venette addressed the important question of resemblance and filiation in a startling new way, and his conclusion would become the recurrent message of anti-imaginationists: the true monster is none other than the theory attributing monstrosity to the mother's imagination. "In truth," he wrote, "it is men's imaginations that are stronger than women's, and it is only the former's imagination that invented these sorts of reasoning: they were unable to find natural causes for what happens; they thus alleged apparent ones." [12]

The quarrel intensified in England when Daniel Turner published a medical essay entitled *De Morbis Cutaneis: A Treatise of Diseases Incident to the Skin* (1714) in which he reaffirmed the now-familiar view that birthmarks were caused by the mother's imagination and could not be cured or erased. He gave the example of a young girl born with burn marks on the back of her head, caused by the terror her mother had experienced when her hand was burned during pregnancy. Attacked for his views, Turner then published a *Defence of the Twelfth Chapter of the First Part of a Treatise De Morbis Cutaneis*, a letter addressed to Dr. James Blondel, the author of a book entitled *The Strength of Imagination in Pregnant Women Consider'd* (1726). Despite the book's title, Blondel was in no way a supporter of the imaginationist thesis. Quite the contrary: he unleashed his fury against Turner with a new edition of his book, augmented by a virulent preface and now entitled: "*The Power of the Mother's Imagination over the Foetus, examined in answer to Daniel Turner's book* . . . [13] Blondel meant to clarify his position: Turner had misquoted him. His own views on the question were unequivocal: "The great Misfortune is, that by repeating so often that the Effects of *Imagination* are incomprehensible, Persons are apt to make a Merit of Ignorance and for Truth worship Falsehood, because 'tis intricate and contrary to Reason. My Design is to attack vulgar Error, which has been prevailing for many years, in opposition to Experience, sound Reason and Anatomy: I mean the common opinion that Marks and Deformities, which children are born with, are the sad effect of the Mother's irregular Fancy and Imagination" (preface).

Blondel based his argument first on experience: "a great many of these stories are silly and ridiculous," and second on the imaginationists' failure to give a convincing explanation of their system: "The Imaginationists are so ingenuous as to confess, that they have nothing else to say for their opinion, but 'tis so because 'tis so" (p. x). And Blondel added his personal version of the metaphor of generation as art: "'Tis silly and absurd, for what can be more ridiculous than to make of Imagination a Knife, a Hammer, a Pastry Cook, a Thief, a Painter, a Jack of all Trades, a Juggler, a Doctor Faustus, the Devil and all? 'Tis mischievous and cruel: it disturbs whole Families, distracts the Brains of credulous People, and puts them in continuous Fear, and in Danger of their Lives: In short, 'tis such a public Nuisance, that 'tis the Interest of every Body to join together against such a MONSTER, and to root it entirely out of the World" (p. xi). As we see, Blondel was suggesting a new medical conception, a new metaphoric propagation, capable of destroying the only monster that really mattered: superstition.

But Blondel also confronted the leading theories thoughtfully, reviewing many stories handed down through the ages and taking particular care to undermine Malebranche's theories. While admitting that imagination can affect pregnancy, he claimed that this happens in ways that have nothing to do with the capacity to imprint an image on the body of a child: "Frightful and Ugly Objects, which are shocking even to *Men* of courage, are to be carefully removed from the Sight of pregnant Women, as being apt to disturb their Minds, and to fill them with Horror, Fear, and Apprehension. Anger is a Passion that puts the whole Fabrick of the Body out of Frame. Cholerick Persons in their *Furor* have been seised with Fits of Apoplexy . . . In that Case, 'tis much to be feared, that the Blood, flowing with great Vehemence towards the *Uterus,* may separate the *Placenta,* and cause an Abortion" (p. 3). The superstition Blondel was most anxious to dispel is the following one: "Most people . . . believe, that the *Imagination* of a pregnant Woman is able to imprint upon the Child the Representation of the Object, which the Mother has in View; as for Instance, that the strong Desire for *Peaches,* or *Cherries* not being satisfied does cause the Colour and Shape of a *Peach,* or of a *Cherry* upon the *Fetus;* that the mere Longing for *Muscles* is sufficient to *transubstantiate* the true and original Head of the Child into a *Shell-Fish* . . . They quarrel about the Extent of its Power. In short, their Opinion seems to be a *Hydra* with one single Tail and several Heads" (pp. 4, 8).

Part of Blondel's refutation of imaginationism also stems from the view that imagination should not be the power or burden of women alone: "Yet several good Authors have formerly pretended, that the *Imagination* of the *Male,* as well as of the *Female,* in any Kind of living Creatures, does contribute to the Colouring of the *Foetus*, as appears by *Pliny 7.12 Cogitatio* utriusque, *Animum subito transvolans, effingere similitudinem aut miscere existimatur.* 'The Thought or Imagination of [Male and Female] passing suddenly through the Mind, is reputed to imprint, or confound the Similitude'" (p. 8). Blondel then gives a lively account of some well-known historical cases where the mother's imagination was thought to have affected her progeny. He evokes the time when some assassins

> entered [Mary Queen of Scots'] Apartment Sword in Hand, and in a very rude and disrespectful Manner, stabbed *David Rixio* her Secretary, who, thinking to save his Life, did immediately seize the Queen about the Waste, crying for Mercy, at the same Time that the Executioners were repeating the Blows. It is impossible to express the Height of Fright and Consternation that Princess was put to . . . and yet, when the *Royal Prince,* King JAMES *the First* was born, not one single Scratch was found about his Body, nor any Similitude of Wounds; tho' I am apt to believe, that *Imagination* is no Respecter of Persons, and was not afraid, if she meddled with that Royal Babe, to be indicted for High Treason (p. 15).

As for the tradition that King James could not bear the sight of a naked sword, Blondel replies that the king was "as much disordered at the Report of a Gun" (p. 15), and blames the king's lack of courage on the misfortune of a disastrous education.

Blondel's answer to Malebranche, whose story of the monstrous child resembling St. Pius ("a *Popish* Saint") is quoted in its entirety, is lapidary: "Ther's nothing in all this, but meer Enthusiasm and Bigotry" (p. 27). The mother lied, presumes Blondel (an argument that had never been made by those disagreeing with Malebranche), and Malebranche was too naive to recognize this. Of course, it helps Blondel's cause that he is a firm believer in animalcules and thus tends to diminish the overall role of the mother to that of nourishing the fetus. But Blondel echoes Venette when he finally suggests that resemblances, rather than dissemblances, ought to surprise us: "Deformities ought not to be so amazing as the wonderful *Uniformity,* that does commonly reign among the living Creatures of all Kinds" (p. 130). His concluding paragraph stands out as one of the rare appeals for the dismissal of imaginationism along with the burden of guilt it had placed on women for so long:

"Thus you see, the Mother, under the specious Pretence of *Imagination*, is wrongfully brought in Guilty, when she is entirely innocent; and that the Deformities complained of are very often owing to remote Causes, which have taken Effect, even a long Time before she came into the World" (p. 142).

Turner retaliated with *The force of the mother's imagination further reconsider'd,* published in 1730, immediately followed by *The force of the mother's imagination upon her foetus in utero still further reconsider'd* (1730). Neither side was giving up. Turner's initial treatise was published in French in 1743 under the title *Traité des maladies de la peau;* Blondel's first book was also translated and published in Leyden in 1737 under the title *Dissertation physique sur la force de l'imagination des femmes enceintes sur le foetus.* Both texts were quoted often by the French authors who continued to argue the question vigorously for another half century.[14]

Imaginationism came under renewed attack with the publication in 1745 of Isaac Bellet's *Lettres sur le pouvoir de l'imagination des femmes enceintes,* "which combats the prejudice whereby the Mothers' imagination has the power to imprint the aspect of objects that have caught their eye on the body of the child they bear."[15] Bellet's approach was original in several ways. He chose to address not the medical profession, but women, who were, after all, more directly concerned. Critics have thus far not mentioned that Bellet's work directly prefigures Diderot's *Rêve de d'Alembert* and his *Entretien entre d'Alembert et Diderot,* both probably written in 1769. Bellet had developed the long metaphor of the body as harpsichord before Diderot made it famous for posterity. Examining the nature of sensation, Bellet remarked:

An exterior object, a flower presents itself to your eyes, your soul is informed, it acquires the idea of this object. What mechanism allows this sensation to operate? Here it is. Between the flower and your eye is a fluid body that you cannot perceive . . . It so happens that the spirits that flow back to the brain through various nerve fibers and that escape through various points meet in passing different fibers that they agitate, just as the plectra of a harpsichord pluck different strings in response to the key on which the hand has been placed. Such is the way our soul distinguishes one object from another, according to the brain's fiber that was set ringing, just as you distinguish a sound from another according to the harpsichord string that was plucked. (pp. 13–17)[16]

Bellet extends the metaphor to the idea of an "ocular keyboard" where a chord would pluck several strings and produce complex ideas. Moreover, though Fontenelle had preceded him in writing a scientific discourse for women, Bellet innovated by creating the "dialogue/letter" genre which was addressed to well-read women, spoke of female physiology, and prefigured the well-known conversation among Bordeu, d'Alembert, and Mademoiselle de Lespinasse.

Bellet stated from the beginning that most essays, whether imaginationist or not, do not have women readers in mind: "One ascribes to the imagination of pregnant women the power to imprint the aspect of objects that have caught their eye on the children they bear. This prejudice is very widespread and detrimental to the tranquillity and health of pregnant women. Several scientists have already been working to eliminate it. We already have a Dissertation by a Dr. Blondel, translated from the English into our language. I do not wish to judge the validity of the arguments advanced there against the power of the imagination, but I will say that this Dissertation is not appropriate for instructing and convincing Ladies" (pp. iii–iv). It is not the least of the paradoxes of this work that what is distinctive to "ladies," in Bellet's view, is precisely an intelligence modified by the very specific character of the female imagination—the difficulty of thinking abstractly—rather than by knowledge and reason. Another "genus" was "born": a medical text on questions specifically related to women's physiology and directly addressed to them. As Bellet describes it: "A work on this matter of specific interest to women was all the more difficult to accomplish in that it implied combining a knowledge of physics and anatomy, establishing principles with clarity, linking together their consequences with scrupulous exactness, and focusing the mind on abstract objects by treating them in such a way as to make them understandable" (p. vi). Further on, addressing himself directly to his imaginary female reader, Bellet writes: "Permit me, Madam, to protest the injustice of your suspicions. I am far from thinking that a Lady is incapable of understanding philosophical reasoning . . . Such is the effect of a prejudice that forbids them the study of the sciences . . . Ladies possess a delicacy of mind superior to men, a lively imagination able to grasp a principle in its entirety, and rarely are they mistaken on its consequence . . . No, Madam, I only fear that a matter, abstract in itself, may become, through my treatment of it, wearisome" (pp. 10–12). Had Malebranche decided to address himself to women (which in his time would have been inconceivable), he might perhaps have used similar words.

For Bellet, it was not imagination that caused abnormal births, but rather the imaginationist prejudice: "A prejudice all the more harmful in that women are intimidated by it during pregnancy. Worried and alarmed by the least incident, they lose their gaiety, their tranquillity, and their sleep. Their blood is altered; their fear of imaginary illness causes them real pains and becomes harmful to the health of their children" (p. 3). So, in fact, very little separated Bellet from the imaginationists. For though he later refuted all their theories patiently and confidently, the very notion that the mother's fear could alter her child was precisely the credo of imaginationism. Bellet supplied another example of this persistent belief when he attacked Malebranche's story of the child born insane and broken in the very places where a criminal had been tortured in front of the mother's eyes during her pregnancy. Bellet writes, "The example of the broken child does not intimidate me, Madam; it cannot possibly prove that ideas, passions, fear, terror, are communicated from the mother to her child" (p. 213). Bellet's refutation was a purely mechanistic one: In his view, the child had been marked by involuntary muscular contractions. What remained to be explained, of course, was the cause of these particular contractions. Bellet was an ovist and a preformationist. Given his belief that the human being was preformed, the remainder of his argument hinged on the inference that alterations could take place only at the moment of fertilization. "These external marks that are mistakenly attributed to the power of the imagination are the effects of the mechanism that fertilizes the egg containing the child" (p. 5).

Moreover, in Bellet's view, imaginationists suffered from the same conceptual error as did the monstrous mother—that of taking appearances for reality: "Although all men love truth, most go no further than the appearance of truth" (p. 45). Finally—and

Bellet developed this theme extensively in his *Lettres*—there can be no communication between the mother's brain and the child's, contrary to what Malebranche had stated. The difficulty is as much mechanical as it is philosophical: "I believe that I have proven that there can be no communication of ideas between mother and child. Hardly any of the fixed quantity of spirits that provoked the idea of grapes in the mother are passed to the child's body; the spirits found in the bloodstream dissipate with such ease during its lengthy circulation, they are divided into so many arteries, that not even a thousandth of these spirits reaches the child. Judge, then, whether there remains some trace of the original disposition received by the mother's organs" (p. 53).

Objections to the imaginationist view were equally strong on philosophical grounds. The mother, Bellet argues, receives only ideas, not images, from her imagination: this claim is a radical departure from traditional theories of imagination. How could she therefore imprint any images on her child's body? The mother's ideas are shaped by her memory, which the child lacks: "In any case, if it were necessary for the images of objects to be outlined on the brain tissue when the mind perceives them, the memory could never represent them, since nothing, in the absence of these objects, could render for the spirits spread throughout the brain the combined colors and movements necessary to outline the objects' surfaces" (p. 75). He continues: "The mother's imagination, therefore, can imprint nothing on her child's body. May I be so bold, Madam, to flatter myself that I have convinced you?" (p. 79).

The last point Bellet emphasized, a familiar one by now, is that if one were to assume that imagination played a role in the formation of the fetus, why would the mother be such a poor artist?

> Those who defend the imagination's power must recognize not only the uncertainty of this claim, but also an incomprehensible oddity: it seems that imagination must never be affected by the beautiful; its power is limited to depicting deformed objects. A woman contemplates the beauty of a portrait; however, it is neither the drawing's proportions or forms, nor the subject's noble and even features that will affect her imagination and reproduce themselves later on the child's body. No, Madam, her child will be born with a hideous drapery or have the pallor of a dying virgin. (pp. 191–192)

But it seemed that the imaginationists would have the last printed word in the eighteenth century and in the beginning of the nineteenth. In an extraordinary work, *Dissertation sur le pouvoir de l'imagination des femmes enceintes,* published in 1788, Benjamin Bablot, king's physician and advisor at Châlons-sur-Marne, established a masterly and remarkably well-informed compendium of references to the subject, from Antiquity to the eighteenth century. This was, in fact, the first scholarly work on the power of the mother's imagination.[17] Bablot's own views on imaginationism were faithful to the tradition that imagination had a plastic function in the formation of the fetus. In one of his commentaries on Heister's *Anatomie,* Bablot described his own beliefs when he wrote: "In this author's view, resemblance between the child and his father could result from the actions of these plastic Natures that model the face in function of the mother's ideas. Thus, as a child presents sometimes more his mother's features than those of his father, those attributing the cause to imagination say that the mother's thoughts were completely absorbed by her loving passion during conception and were unable to focus on her husband's features" (p. 81). Though Bablot himself contributed no new supporting elements to the imaginationist cause, he provided several examples with which he was personally familiar, since all had taken place at Châlons-sur-Marne, where he was practicing medicine. "Five or six years ago," he writes, "a woman of this town, who had been pregnant for a short while, took a walk on the public square where a painting of a Giant, whose figure, height, and beauty echoed the majesty of his size, had been exposed. This Lady considered the Painting with complacency, and thought of it from time to time during the remainder of her pregnancy. She gave birth to a child who had a face modeled after that of this Giant" (pp. 93–94). The child did not live.

Another story relates the drama of a pregnant woman so frightened by the spectacle of a public hanging that she gave birth to a dead child with contusions around his neck. These two examples are, of course, reminiscent of Malebranche's much-discussed cases of a child fashioned after a painting of St. Pius, and another born with the marks of the torture afflicted on a condemned man whose execution his mother had witnessed while she was pregnant. The enduring fame of Malebranche's examples, and the striking similarity of the examples given by Bablot, suggest that there may be more than a passing relation between the contemplation of a painting and that of an execution. Such contemplations could be said to represent a turning away from life. The artist "executes" a portrait and will later substitute the painting for the real-life model. The executioner's work is to put an end to life. In both cases the mother chooses art and death over life itself, and in both cases her imagination is moved to imprint the image of what she has seen on the body of the child she is carrying. By letting her imagination take over the normal process of nature, the mother produces an image, a representation, the painting of a painting, but above all *a dead body.* Inasmuch as the work of imagination may be comparable to that of an artist, these haunting stories of monstrous births suggest that death always presides over the work of art.

Bablot assembled an impressive list of examples that give a clearer idea of the extent of these beliefs at the end of the European Classical Age. To the authors previously discussed, he added Dr. Courtin (*Oeuvres anatomiques et chirurgicales,* Rouen, 1665), Lazare Rivière (*Pratique de médecine,* Lugduni, 1672), Jean Riolan (*Opera Anatomica,* Lutetiae, 1649), the Chevalier Digby (Sir Kenelm Digby) (*Dissertation touchant la guérison des plaies, par la poudre de sympathie,* Brussels, 1678), and Dr. Verduc (*Opérations de chirurgie, avec une pathologie,* Paris, 1694). He cites two contemporary examples from Digby's work, one of them particularly interesting for our purpose:

> Lady Fortescu, niece of this English Knight, and Count Arondel's daughter, had such a marked passion for black velvet patches [*mouches*], that she put them all over her face, so to speak, believing that by doing so she was adding still to her natural charms. As she was pregnant, d'Igby [*sic*] warned her that because of the pleasure she took in watching so many velvet patches in her mirror, she should fear that the infant to whom she was going to give birth be born with a face speckled with black patches. She listened to her Uncle and threw away her velvet patches: but the fear that his unfortunate prediction could come true so occupied her Imagination during her pregnancy that her Child was born with a black spot of the size she had imagined, right in the middle of the forehead. This amazing accident was known throughout England, so the author tells us. (pp. 67–68)

This example suggests two different ways in which the maternal imagination might make an imprint on the progeny; in the first one—the most traditional—imagination imprints an image too often or too intensely contemplated; in this case, the mother's own reflection in the mirror, her face marked with the black velvet patches that were fashionable at the time. But imagination can also imprint an image created by fear alone. Although the doctor is mainly preoccupied by the mother's contemplation of her face in the mirror, the fear created in the mother by the doctor's warning is the ultimate cause for the birth of a marked child. As was the case in the past, the idea of monstrosity remains associated with a suggestion of adultery. Instead of thinking about her husband, the mother has given in to two dominant preoccupations: a narcissistic delight in her own image, followed by an overwhelming anxiety associated with her doctor's remarks. One could say that in this case again, the father's role is erased by both the doctor's intervention and the mother's frightened imagination.

Bablot added more scientific support to the imaginationist thesis: the decision by the Faculté de médecine de Louvain (Belgium) to acknowledge that "when the matter is still soft and malleable, the Mother's violent Imagination, or a fear, can so transform and disfigure the form of the child she is carrying that it is born inhuman with all the appearances of a beast" (pp. 72–73). He also hoped to demonstrate one of the major weaknesses of the anti-imaginationists' position by focusing on Maupertuis' treatment of the question in *La vénus physique:*

> He denies the [imagination's] power to imprint on the *Fetus* the form of the object that has terrified the Mother or that of the fruit that she desired to eat because he argues that *fear and desire do not resemble the object that provoked them, and that the mother's feeling, motivated either by desire or the sight of a fruit, does not resemble in any way the object that caused it to be in the first place.* So that, according to him, Imagination cannot influence facial features nor modify them, nor influence the phenomenon of resemblances or dissemblances. However, if we believe this witty Author, a few lines above, he had written: "There certainly is an intimate communication between the *Fetus* and the mother, so much so that a violent agitation in the spirits or in the Mother's blood is transmitted to the *Fetus,* and causes disorders to which the Mother's

parts can resist, but to which the delicate parts of the *Fetus* succumb. Consequently, a woman troubled by some violent passion,
who has been terrified by some hideous animal, gives birth to a
deformed Child" . . . Maupertuis is obviously contradicting himself. (pp. 85–86)

The difference between Maupertuis' and Bablot's positions is not
immaterial. For Maupertuis, the maternal imagination may provoke a deformity, but its function as plastic art cannot be sustained
since fear and passion are emotions, not images; still, for Maupertuis, fear and passions remain the primary causes of deformities.
But for the imaginationists, since the result of fear and passion is
always recognizable as the very image of that which occasioned the
fear or passion, the mother's extreme feelings have to be mediated
by the mental function that retains and reproduces imprints, that
is, by imagination as plastic art. Bablot added numerous and varied
examples of extravagant marks: a young woman of "rare beauty"
born with the mark of a perfectly formed caterpillar on her neck,
the result of her pregnant mother's difficulty in removing a live
caterpillar that had fallen on her own neck, is one example (p. 87).
He concluded the first part of the book with the more ironic tale of
a woman so in love with a bishop that she gave birth to a child who
strikingly resembled the "respectable" prelate. "The Bishop decided to see for himself the reality of this phenomenon; and from
then on he became so interested in the young person that, thanks
to her benefactor's generous gifts, she enjoys today the sweet happiness of being able to assist at will her parents' needy old age"
(pp. 95–96).

In the second part of his *Dissertation,* Bablot considered in detail
all the objections raised against the imaginationists' views, and he
concluded with an impressive list of philosophers, scientists, and
theologians whom he considered supporters of this theory. The list
is worth quoting, as it provides an extraordinarily vivid example
both of the genealogy of thinkers who transmitted the concept of
imaginationism, directly or indirectly, willingly or unknowingly,
and of the historical tradition that supported the concept in the
eyes of eighteenth-century physicians:

Let us conclude. When one finds among the Supporters of the
power of imagination in pregnant women the most famous

names of Antiquity—without mentioning the SACRED HISTORIAN
of God's People—names such as Empedocles, Hippocrates, Soranus, Galen, Plato, Aristotle, Cicero, Pliny, Plutarch, Avicennus,
Marcile Ficinus, Albertus Magnus, Majoli, and Valedio; when
one finds among the Reverend Fathers who adopted the same
opinion the names of Saint Jerome, Saint Augustine, Saint
Thomas, and so many others; when, in Centuries closer to ours,
one finds the same Opinion defended by Rhodinus, Fernel,
Lemnius, Delrio, Aldrovandus, Christophorus of Vega, Schen-
kius, Thomas More, Montaigne, Paré, Pigrai, Mercado, Fienus,
du Laurens, and Courtin; when one finds, at the beginning of
the seventeenth century, three bodies of one of the most famous
Universities in the world, adopting unanimously the same Opinion; when at last, today, in spite of Medical Physics' progress, one
finds the very same Opinion defended by superior Geniuses such
as Descartes, Rivière, Riolan, Digby, Hecquet, Lemeri, Dodart,
Malebranche, Verduc, Andry, Maupertuis; finally, to abbreviate
citations, by Boerrhave and Van-Swieten; it seems to me that one
should not dare challenge the power of the women's Imagination
on the *Fetus* too quickly. (pp. 194–95)

Bablot also offered a striking example of the general credit given
to the power of imagination by Jean-Sylvain Bailly in a report on
Mesmer that he presented to the Académie des sciences in 1784.
Bailly, a member of the Académie, had been asked to investigate
Mesmer's theses on magnetism, which while they were novel and
gaining in popularity, had not yet been subjected to scientific scrutiny. Bailly wrote a harsh report in which he argued that the so-
called effects of animal magnetism were in fact caused by the considerable power of the imagination. Bailly wrote:

The observed phenomena yield further results which we will
now put forward. These results concern Imitation and Imagination, *two of our most outstanding Faculties:* they are facts in this still
young Science that studies the influence of Moral elements on
the Physical. To this aim, we ask leave to enter into a few preliminary and purely philosophical details. Moral man, like physical
man, is and only becomes what he is through these two faculties:
He shapes and perfects himself by imitation; he acts and becomes powerful by imagination. Imitation is therefore the primary means toward perfectibility; it modifies man from birth to
death. Imagination is a progressive faculty. It is a highly active

faculty, the author of good and evil: all lies before it, the Future like the Present, the Worlds of the Universe like the point of space where we are now. Imagination magnifies everything it touches; it never stops exaggerating, and its exaggeration is its power. It is through this power that it puts into action moral resources and increases physical strength . . . Imagination renews or suspends animal functions; it revives through hope, or it freezes with terror.[18]

Whereas in the past imagination had been perceived, above all, negatively, as the source of error (this was illustrated by Malebranche) and more peculiar to women than to men, by the end of the eighteenth century, it was universalized as one of the basic forces of Nature. Now seen as the mainspring for resemblance through imitation, imagination was common to all human beings, and its effects on procreation were only one of the widespread examples of the extent of its power. The imaginationist thesis was illustrated again in several works. In 1769, Lieutaud made public his imaginationist convictions in *Précis de médecine pratique;* he was followed in 1771 by Baron Gerardi van Swieten with *Medici Doctoris Commentaria in Hermanni Boerrhave Aphorismos de Cognoscentis et Curandis Morbis.*

Jean-Baptiste Demangeon's *Considérations physiologiques sur le pouvoir de l'imagination maternelle durant la grossesse* . . . (1807) was the last major text dedicated to the question of imaginationism.[19] Demangeon presented the imaginationist theory in a rather straightforward way. His most interesting comment concerns a statement attributed to Zacchias: "Zacchias, after having opposed with solid reasons the effects attributed to imagination, later admits, p. 329, title V of his book entitled *Quaestiones Medico-Legales*, that imagination nevertheless can influence ordinary forms, as a painter would, who, by accident, would borrow something from another, though normally used to working after his own ideas."[20] This reappraisal of the aesthetic role of imagination underlines the idea that imagination always brings to bear a foreign element, "borrows" from an agent not directly involved in generation a shape or a coloring, thus introducing a lie into reproduction. By the time Demangeon was writing, however, looking at paintings was no longer necessarily thought to have a bad influence on pregnant women.

Like earlier critics of imaginationism, Demangeon believes that though imagination has the power to give shape to the fetus, it does not have the capacity to imprint images on it. The mother may be compared to a painter because art is a form of procreation, but she is no longer the artist reproducing on the body of her child the images of the object she has contemplated with passion. Not only does Demangeon seriously question Malebranche's argument on the transmission of images, but he considers the question of transmission itself the greatest obstacle to the traditional imaginationist theory. "I do not know if the idea of nerves linking the mother to the fetus as a way of explaining the effects of imagination should have led to the supposition of already formed images, transmissible from the brain to the other parts where the brain sends nerve ramifications. If such was the case, one should have asked the proponents of this ridiculous theory to show us transmissions of similar images to the various parts of a single body where the brain sends nerve [messages]" (p. 20). His next objections are not original, but they do situate the debate in the context of the new scientific concerns being defined at the time:

> Undoubtedly, the mother's imagination has the power to disrupt the shape or the primitive configuration through the trouble it may cause in blood circulation and in nutrition, but I see nothing that would allow us to presume that it can imprint a particular object: if it were true, the variety and the changes of form would be as diverse and multiple as the objects that strike the imagination, so much so that the newly born infant would necessarily belie his race by offering an amalgam of all his mother's peculiar imaginations; if this were the case, we would have no reason for the continuation and variety of species through generation; imagination alone, more powerful than the very organism of which it is only an imperceptible part, would dominate all living beings and could as well plunge them into the horrors of chaos, by destroying all the frameworks of natural history with an infinite variety of forms and organizations. (pp. 21–22)

Explanation and justification play a considerable role in Demangeon's book. They, in turn, transform the nature of a theory that had hitherto relied on the strength of its examples.

For Malebranche, the monster was the final proof of the way imagination influenced the fetus: for Demangeon, the lack of a satisfactory explanation disqualified any given "proof," that is, any specific deformity attributed to the mother's passion, no matter how superficially convincing it might appear. Demangeon's disbelief ultimately rests on the fact that nature does not admit chaos, and that imaginationism brings chaos into the orderly system of nature. At a time when monsters are slowly being integrated into the larger study of embryology as extreme variations of a recognizable order, Demangeon rejects all theories that would take disorder as a point of departure. Moreover, he believes that imagination cannot reproduce images, it does not have any plastic function. Resemblance, then, could not possibly be mediated through the power of imagination. Heredity has not yet provided the clues to scientific understanding of resemblance, and Demangeon admits that "the difficulty is to find the processes used by nature to produce resemblances, racial varieties, and monstrosities" (p. 24). "As for dissemblances," Demangeon adds, "it is not unreasonable to believe that, when they are not prompted by adultery, they result from some disorder in the functioning of the organs of nutrition" (p. 29).

We are witness here to the end of a tradition. Not only did the imaginationist thesis cease to convince physicians and medical commentators, but the very enigma that imaginationism had tried to solve—the question of natural resemblance between parents and offspring—was itself the object of a radical epistemological reexamination.

4

Unfaithful Resemblances

The belief, inherited from Aristotle, that resemblances testified to the organized character of life, was not seriously challenged even by those who opposed the theory that imagination in pregnant women was the unreliable agent of resemblances between parents and offspring. Still, at the same time that the Quarrel of Imaginationism was dividing the medical world, several thinkers radically contested not only the link between imagination and resemblances, but also the idea that resemblances emanate from the natural order of things.

An unexpected challenge to the source and meaning of resemblances between parents and children was published in 1687 by Nicolas Venette, though the importance of his view would not be recognized for many years. Venette's book, *La génération de l'homme ou tableau de l'amour conjugal considéré dans l'état de mariage,* was a publishing success,[1] yet only Benjamin Bablot realized the significance of Venette's argument.[2] As Venette shifted the debate to new lines of inquiry, he foreshadowed the demise of the imaginationist theory, recognizing simultaneously the power of women's imagination and *the dangerous power of women over their own imagination.* In a chapter entitled "Whether Children Are Bastards or Legitimate When They Resemble Their Fathers or Their Mothers," he wrote, "Because most jurisconsults, along with a few knowledgeable doctors, claim that a woman who thinks strongly about her husband in the midst of illicit pleasures can produce, through the force of her imagination, a child that *perfectly resembles him who is not the father,* we will examine whether a child's resemblance depends upon imagination or some other cause."[3] Venette added:

79

Sharing the views of some Physicians, Jurisconsults say that a woman's imagination is so quick and her mind is so sharp that no one should wonder that she imprints upon what she conceives from her womb a resemblance to what she passionately desires or strongly imagines . . . Thus, *Resemblance is not proof of filiation*, according to the belief of these same Jurisconsults. The child who resembles his father is not for that reason legitimate. This conjecture in no way justifies declaring him his father's heir. His mother, in her illegitimate embraces, could well have produced him to resemble her husband by the force of her imagination; for, by constantly thinking about her husband while she was in her lover's arms, she imprinted on the soft body of the child she was then conceiving the features of the body and all the mental characteristics of the man to whom her imagination had attached itself. (pp. 274–277, emphasis added)

These reflections do not represent a radical change in the legal discourse on imagination, except for one important point. For the jurisconsults, the *vis imaginativa* in women is such that an unfaithful wife can produce a non-monstrous child, perfectly resembling the husband who did not engender it, solely through the power of her imagination. For this reason, the nature of the relationship among resemblances, imagination, and the monstrous is fundamentally altered. The mother is no longer seen as a victim, prey to a passion or a desire that she cannot overcome. Quite the contrary, she is mistress of her own senses and imagination to such a degree that she can use them to conceal and further an illegitimate affair. In this case, the lively force of a devious imagination produces not a monster but its exact opposite: a child who actually resembles the legitimate spouse who did not father it, a child in perfect harmony with nature's plan. Yet here normality is nothing more than the fruit of imagination. The mother, in turn, is no longer the blind artist who reproduces images without art—what Plato termed likenesses. She has become, rather, the *fantastic* artist, one who masters proportions, captures perspective, and produces the deceptive appearances that Plato attributed only to the best sculptors and painters.

At the very moment when imagination is entrusted with the power to create and master all resemblance, and precisely because of this very power, resemblance ceases to be reliable; it ceases to be proof of any identity, filiation, genesis, or truth. No longer does the resemblance produced by imagination reveal the generation of beings; instead, it masks their identity, making the bastard seem so much like the legitimate heir that he might even take his place. Resemblance misleads justice; it produces the ultimate disorder. Whereas resemblance had always signified identity first and filiation second, it now testifies to nothing more than a perfectly mastered imagination, at once powerful and treacherous.

The imaginationist theory of monsters, carried to its ultimate logical consequence, also suggests that it is he who in every way appears to be his father's son—the child formed perfectly after the features of the man who *should have* engendered him—who is perhaps the real monster. The genetic mechanism that accounts for the rules of resemblance has not yet been modified theoretically, but the moral and legal consequences of resemblance undergo a radical transformation. Whereas Malebranche (and several authors before him) had suggested that no two faces in all the world are absolutely identical, and that nature tolerates great diversity, Venette's evaluation of resemblance can be said to be counter-natural. The guilty mother had previously been punished for her illegitimate desires and hidden passions by the visible monstrosity of her progeny; for Venette, the guilty mother remains not only unpunished, but so fully capable of dissimulating her sin that it is up to the law to contest and expose the triumphant power of her imagination.

For centuries, it was thought that the mother's frustrated desires resulted in monstrous births and that her imagination erased the features of the child's true, legitimate father. Here, however, the imagination is not subject to some frustrated or unconsumed passion, it is at the service of cold calculation. The monstrosity revealed by the child's resemblance to the legitimate husband who is not his father exposes the inner monstrosity of the unfaithful wife. The adulterous woman need not fear punishment (unless justice intervenes), for monstrosity, which had chastised moral adultery, now inhabits, unknown to all, the illegitimate progeny of actual adultery. The legal decisions discussed by Nicolas Venette invalidate what had been an important distinction between the monster and the norm, since any child, appearing normal in every way, might in fact be the fruit of a monstrous genesis. Whereas in the past a woman had to ward off suspicions of adultery when her child did not resemble his father—and in this, the imaginationist theory saved her from severe reprisals—she now has to face a more general suspicion, one impossible to avoid, that falls on all offspring, even those who do resemble their legitimate fathers.

Diderot's "Felicitous Audacity"

"Conception takes place without pleasure for women, they even experience aversion," wrote Diderot in his *Eléments de physiologie*.[4] Should both sexes experience pleasure simultaneously, he added, they will produce no offspring: "Point de conception, quoique avec le plus grand plaisir simultané des deux sexes." Diderot's idea that procreation excludes female sexual pleasure and even generates a feeling of aversion in women is reinforced by his belief that the womb is cumbersome throughout a woman's life. Far from being a harmonious part of female physiology, the womb wields a frightening power over women: "During [a woman's] middle years, [the womb] exerts a sovereign authority: it gives law, rebels, gets into a rage, constricts and strangles other organs as would an angry animal. The womb is active and has its own way of feeling" (*Eléments*, pp. 391–392). This angry animal, a beast that wreaks havoc on the political economy of the female body, challenging all laws in order to impose its own rebellious rule, in fact behaves very much like the fetus it is meant to carry and nurture. How could pregnancy derive from pleasure, or produce any form of pleasure, when its principal agent, the womb, "not an essential organ in female life" (p. 391), is itself so troublesome? Not surprisingly, "the child is *at all times* an inconvenient guest for the womb" (p. 406, emphasis added). Females are subject to a double jeopardy: not only must they suffer throughout their lives the imperious tyranny of the womb, but should the womb serve its final purpose, that of carrying a child, they must also endure its immediate desire to relieve itself instantly of this unwelcome burden. The womb acts like an independent agent, one that the mother must suffer and indulge as she does pregnancy itself, without pleasure and sometimes with repugnance. The reason the child is not systematically aborted is that "the womb would wound itself if it tried to expel the fetus at a time when, because of the strong adhesion of the placenta . . . they can-

Imagination, *Encyclopedia* frontispiece, engraving by Charles-Nicolas Cochin fils, 1764, first published in 1772. The legend reads: One can see Imagination about to embellish and crown Truth. Below Imagination, the Artist has placed the various genres of Poetry.

not be separated" (p. 406). "Organs have their own fears," Diderot continues, "their aversions, their appetites, their desires, their rejections" (p. 406). The womb's aversion duplicates that of the mother at conception. From the beginning, the child is marked for rejection by the womb, and, as soon as the placenta allows it, the child is expelled: "Delivery is a sort of vomiting," notes Diderot (p. 406). Not that women are incapable of maternal tenderness. The contrast is great between Diderot's description of nature's violence during delivery and his narrative of the mutual discovery of mother and child after birth: "Separated from his mother, the child is put into her arms, which hold him. She is held by the child's arms; he is under her eyes, she holds him, kisses him, embraces him, she holds him to her breast, he holds himself to her breast, she continues to feed him, these two beings are trying to reidentify themselves" (p. 407).[5]

But the female fate of carrying a womb, this independent agent of domestic quarrels, and carrying a child, an inconvenient guest conceived in aversion, radically undermines any attempt, by Buffon, Bordeu, Diderot himself, or others, to draw similarities between the male and the female bodies—unless the female body be reconsidered, reconceptualized, perhaps even saved by a new proposition. Is it surprising that Diderot emphasizes how unnecessary the womb is for the health of women? He thus describes Soranus' recommendation to remove all inconvenient wombs as a "felicitous audacity" ("heureuse témérité"; p. 394).[6] These thoughts on the relationship between the female body and procreation must be kept in mind when one reevaluates Diderot's well-known quips about the symmetry of male and female anatomies. Or rather, they should serve to illuminate the fact that when Diderot sets out to discuss similarities between men and women in *D'Alembert's Dream,* he is also, and in fact primarily, writing a treatise on monstrosities.

Elizabeth de Fontenay has written a spirited account of Diderot's deceptive symmetry, his initial refutation of physiological differences, perhaps inspired by Buffon, who had noted in his *Histoire naturelle, générale et particulière* (1749–1767): "When one reflects upon the structures of the parts that serve for generation of either sex of the human species, one finds so many resemblances and such a singular conformity between them that one is tempted to believe that these parts, which appear so different externally, are really the same organs."[7] Similarly, Fontenay remarks: "Diderot emphasizes . . . the strict similarity between the male and female parts: the ovaries are called a woman's testicles, and the clitoris is said to be similar to the penis."[8] All this culminates in Mademoiselle de Lespinasse's well-known "crazy idea" (idée bien folle) as she confides to Bordeu in *D'Alembert's Dream* that "l'homme n'est peut-être que le monstre de la femme, ou la femme le monstre de l'homme" (men are perhaps nothing but a monstrous variety of women, or women only a monstrous variety of men).[9] In *Making Sex,* Thomas Laqueur reads this reply as a direct echo of Galen's ancient theories on the symmetry between male and female anatomy.[10] But Fontenay perceives in *La Grande Mademoiselle*'s immodest proposition a challenge to all forms of symmetry: she sees a magisterial dismissal of the male as ultimate referent (first part of the proposition) followed by the reciprocal undoing of a female norm (second part of the proposition). The *Dream* expresses the discovery of a new state of nature. "In the ceaseless metamorphosis of the new system of nature," Fontenay writes, "in this indefinite and mutual monstrosity, one can no longer think an alternative, beast or man, male or female, life or death, but only the continuous vicissitude of more and less, right and left, inside and outside" (p. 40). However, as Fontenay argues, the terrifying existence of the womb undermines the idea that whatever monstrosity may be, it is mutual: "The womb inscribes in the female body an unfathomable difference, the irrevocable *cleavage* of her sex" (p. 45).

Diderot's thoughts on the womb shatter Bordeu's condescending response to Mademoiselle de Lespinasse's silly idea: "That notion would probably have occurred to you a good deal sooner," he replies, "if you had known that a woman possesses all the anatomical parts that a man has. The only discoverable difference is this—one has a pouch that hangs outside and the other has a pouch that is reversed so as to go inside the body" (*Dream,* p. 135). Bordeu is speaking here in terms of variations rather than fixed categories. Apart from the fact that women such as Mademoiselle de Lespinasse *have not* known it, whereas men such as Bordeu *have,* women are a variety of men just as men are a variety of women. They are simply instances of the variations produced by nature, two among the infinite number of recognizable divergences: "The original and primary differences between animal species must be sought in the bundle of threads. And variations within the bundles of a single species account for all the individual monstrosities produced by that species" (*Dream*, p. 135, translation modified). In this "materialist-vitalist perspective," notes Elizabeth de Fontenay, "the point of view of individuation is no less illusory than that of sexation."[11] While underlining the irreducible difference created by the existence of the womb—a difference acknowledged in many of Diderot's other texts—Fontenay stops short of reinterpreting the *Dream* accordingly. I propose an interpretation of the *Dream* that takes into account precisely what is so carefully negated by Bordeu, yet generates its own discursive and philosophical practice: the terrifying monstrosity of a difference that systematically exceeds Diderot's concept of natural variations.

Certainly *D'Alembert's Dream* suggests a reconsideration of the physiological difference between male and female, as well as that between monsters and normally organized beings; at least Diderot's description of women and monsters so emphatically stresses their basic similarity to their superficial opposites—males, or "normally" constituted beings—that his analysis reduces their specific physiological organization to just one of nature's infinite but recognizable variations. However, both women and monstrosities resist being fully integrated into the flux of nature's moving scheme. The character of this resistance illustrates as well the changing views of the time on the relationship between resemblance and generation. As Diderot's text invites the reader to speculate on the infinite variety of nature, so as to blur the traditional separation between species, between the sexes, or between norms and exceptions, it quietly provides a strikingly modern explanation for monstrous births reconsidered simply as a "variation within the bundle": "Man," notes the dreaming d'Alembert, "is merely a common phenomenon,—the monster a rare one; both are equally natural, equally necessary, equally subject to the general order of nature" (*Dream*, p. 124, translation modified). This description tends to erase the very notion of monstrosity. In Diderot's constantly moving universal order, in which not a single atom duplicates another, the Aristotelian concept of monstrosity—defined as a lack of resemblance to one's parents—no longer makes any sense. Consequently, it has been tempting to understand monstrosity in Diderot as a simple form of difference, no more and no less remarkable than sexual difference.

Indeed, Bordeu superficially agrees with the view of the sexes as variations of a single principle, a case of reversed symmetry perhaps comparable to Buffon's general observation on monstrosities. But the pivotal element of Diderot's argument is that monstrosity itself serves to illustrate the superficial character of the difference between the sexes. Open the *Eléments* and witness the case of a hermaphrodite: Diderot is fascinated by monstrosities that would diminish one way or the other the distinction between male and female identities. He quotes a letter from a physician of Strasbourg, published in the *Gazette des Deux-Ponts* in 1775, that describes the case of a twenty-two-year-old soldier whose autopsy revealed he was carrying a fetus:

> In the early days of August 1773, a soldier, aged twenty-two years and a few months, suffered recurrent nausea, tiredness, aversion, etc. Soon, his abdomen started swelling. This man . . . felt acute abdominal pains on February 3, 1774 . . . all efforts [to save him] proved useless; the pain became more and more acute, convulsions started, and the patient died after ninety hours of suffering . . . The case was too extraordinary not to open the body; imagine the surprise of the assistants when, upon opening the abdomen, they saw a cyst or pouch which when cut open revealed a male fetus, dead and well formed . . . This cyst was a complete womb. [The young man] had only this organ in common with the female sex; otherwise he was perfectly male, inside and outside. (*Eléments*, pp. 408–409)

Recurring notes about various forms of hermaphrodism have been read to suggest that in Diderot's mind sexuality, like monstrosity, could be measured only in terms of degree of variation.[12]

Yet, this case of hermaphrodism is hardly presented as a mingling of the sexes, the way Fontenay suggests that, for Diderot, men and women are all more or less hermaphrodites. The Moravian soldier does not represent a hypothetical middle ground between the sexes, or a somewhat unusual combination of sexual characteristics. Rather, his is a "perfectly male" body, that is, a complete and completely recognizable human body, that of a man fatally burdened with the double inconvenience of a womb and a child, doomed by the female supplement of that other foreign object: a perfectly well-formed male fetus. Hermaphrodism as encasement. "There was no doubt as to the way in which this man could have been capable of engendering," adds the physician. "His bed companion was seized, put into irons, and, after repeated threats, confessed to what had been strongly suspected" (*Eléments,* p. 409). This case of fertile homosexuality is doomed by the monstrous femininity that inserted itself in a perfectly male body, killed it, and revealed for all to see the deadly character of the procreative mechanism. Diderot does not comment but moves on to another case whose only similarity to the preceding one is that it reveals the devastating effect of a womb which lacks the means to expel the fetus it so painfully endures. One cannot entirely agree with Jean Mayer when he writes: "[Diderot] comes to consider monstrosities not as unfortunate exceptions or awkward designs in the spontaneous organization of matter, but rather as the norm (*la règle*) in the living order. A viable being is a monster slightly better organized than a contradictory being; women are a variety of men, or, reciprocally, [men are a variety of women]. The notion of normal being becomes ideal, or at least relative." [13]

But the nature of women cannot be subsumed by any variation. The nature of sexual difference is monstrous, as Mademoiselle de Lespinasse observed, or rather, either of the sexes is monstrous relative to the other, and this monstrous distinction can never be either erased or fully contained by the scheme of nature. In fact, both the nature of women and that of monsters haunt Diderot's thoughts as irreducible disparities that constantly *exceed* the simple variations observed elsewhere. Even Bordeu's description of the marked symmetry between men and women does not fully account for sexual difference. In *Eléments,* Diderot notes in his description of ovaries: "No organic molecules. There, nothing in common between the organization of testes in males and females" (p. 415). For all the seductiveness of an original model whose "variations within the bundle" would account for all forms of living beings, whether male or female, and beings from different species, there are "surpluses" in Diderot's thought, moments that undermine any conclusion too quickly drawn from a general scheme. Thus there are physiological elements in the organization of females that are not comparable to those found in males. These features do not produce a parallel, though reversed, figure of the male organs, and ultimately both male and female identities retain an irreducible quality that constantly disrupts Diderot's concept of natural variation. If not in their physiological organization, at least in their workings the female parts for generation produce a surplus—be it the "inconvenient host" in the womb or the womb's imperious behavior—that belies Mademoiselle de Lespinasse's playful comment. Sexual difference in Diderot takes the paradoxical form of a variation that constantly *exceeds* the very concept of variation.

"What is a monster? A being whose duration is incompatible with the existing order" (*Eléments*, p. 418). Certainly, these words illustrate an important change in the traditional definition of monstrosity. A monster is no longer defined as a deformed creature or one unlike its legitimate parent, but rather as a being incapable of living more than a few hours, possibly a few years, in the current order of things. "The general order changes constantly; how can the duration of a species remain identical among so many vicissitudes?" (p. 418). The temptation is great to imagine that in Diderot's view, monstrosity is but a temporary, unusual variation of nature, one that will not allow a being to survive at a given moment, but one that might possibly become the norm in a different time, regulated by different needs. In his *Système de la nature* (1770), d'Holbach had almost entirely dismissed the idea of monstrosity. As Emita B. Hill notes, "In the absence either of a god or of absolutes in nature, monsters would no longer pose a problem. Holbach, militantly materialistic, declared that the notion of monsters was meaningless, the very name a misnomer; in his materialism, monstrosity was an empty concept; all things in nature were on a plane, equally reasonable, equally natural."[14] The monster is thus tamed, naturalized, safely included in the great chain of beings. Its genesis is in no way mysterious and can be fully explained. Diderot's recurrent anxiety about monstrous beings seems always relieved by a mechanical explanation, as in the case of the Cyclops dissected by Dr. Dubourg, a friend of Diderot, and discussed in *D'Alembert's Dream:* "MLLE DE LESPINASSE.—Does anyone know the cause of this abnormality? BORDEU.—Yes, the man who has dissected the monstrosity and found in it only a single optic thread" (*Dream,* p. 133). Although certain sentences in the *Dream* have been read as an anticipation of modern theories of genetic coding, notes Jay Caplan,

> Dr. Bordeu does not construe the monster as the result of an *error* in genetic coding (as departure from the norm), but rather as *any* of the actual permutations of a combinatory set . . . In [Diderot's] view, certain permutations (Siamese twins, etc.) may indeed appear abnormal, but only from the standpoint of a "normal," self-important individual who lacks a sense of natural processes, which are in continuous transformation and flux, as a whole. The normal state of nature, so to speak, is not characterized by stable definitions and contours of species and individuals, but by volatile movement *away from* any such rigid patterning; nature is normally ab-normal ("away from the norm"), and all of life is "more or less monstrous."[15]

Monstrosity is not a challenge to the normal order. The challenge is rather to imagine the norm as monstrous without undoing monstrosity's own specificity, its own excessive supplementarity. The irreducible supplement of monstrosity betrays a form of anxiety that unexpectedly echoes Aristotle's. "Diderot has succeeded in justifying the existence of monsters, but they appear no less frightening and no less monstrous than before," notes Hill.[16] No doubt, the question of attribution is clearly resolved: the mechanical production of monstrosities is no longer the responsibility of the mother alone, but that of both parents. Mademoiselle de Lespinasse asks:

> "But aren't there some striking cases of original deformity, aside from hunchbacks and clubfeet—misshapen babies whose malformation might be attributed to some hereditary defect?" And Bordeu replies: "Innumerable cases. Just recently, at the Charity Hospital in Paris, there died at the age of twenty-five a carpenter, a native of Troyes, by the name of Jean-Baptiste Macé, who was a victim of complications resulting from a chest fluxion. His internal organs, both in the chest and in the abdomen, were transposed—the heart was on the right instead of in its normal position on the left; the liver too was on the right; the stomach, the appendix, and the pancreas were near the right hypochondrium; the major artery bore to the liver on the left side the same

relation as it would have if the liver had been on the right . . .
And, after all that, they still want us to believe in final causes!"
(*Dream*, p. 134)

For Aristotle, monsters did not invalidate the "purposive or final
cause," but were classified as unnecessary deviations.[17] Diderot offers monsters as proof that there is no purposive or final cause;
and in assigning to monstrosities the *burden of proof*, he also singles
them out and reasserts their singularity as capable of invalidating
an entire system of thought.

Thus monstrosities are both inside the system, as evidence of
variations, and outside, as proof that there is no other system to
look for, no cause, no final reassurance. Diderot's rhetoric of excess
has already asserted that there is indeed no final cause at any moment in the chronology of life: the womb is a female's unnecessary
burden, the child is the womb's inconvenient guest, the monster
proves that there is no purposive cause. What, indeed, is more gratuitous than a rebellious organ entirely superfluous to the health
of the body that carries it? What is more gratuitous than a child
only tolerated by the womb and "vomited" into the world as soon
as is feasible? Perhaps just one other thing: the tremendous
"waste" of the unfecundated male seed so vigorously deplored by
d'Alembert. The idea of such a waste, like the description of the
womb, offers another challenge to the "materialist-vitalist" conception of nature. The wasted fluid, like the womb for the female, the
child for the womb, is an unrequited supplement, a useless excess,
a "vomit" lost to both reciprocal pleasure and procreation.

Diderot's debt to Maupertuis' transformationist theories and to
Buffon's more moderate interpretation of epigenesis is well
known.[18] Remarkably enough, however, there still remain echoes
of imaginationist thought in Diderot. The source of Diderot's anxiety—inasmuch as his belief betrays both a fear of imagination in
pregnant women and his awe of pregnancy itself—may be detected in Bordeu's view of the womb as an organ "capable of terrible spasms, dominating women and creating in their imagination
all sorts of ghosts; while prey to hysterical delirium, women go
back to the past, rush toward the future, and all the times are present to them: all these extraordinary ideas emanate from this organ
proper to their sex."[19] Thus the womb speaks to the imagination of
women. To illustrate the article entitled "Matrice" (womb), the *En-*

cyclopédie had borrowed from Haller an engraving of a womb, the topic of Fontenay's article "Diderot gynéconome." [20] In *Eléments de physiologie,* Diderot referred again to Haller when conceding the power of imagination in pregnant women: "I do not believe in birthmarks. However, Haller admits, after having denied the influence of the mother's imagination, that though there is no nervous communication between the mother and her child, some children have been subject their whole life to convulsions brought on by terror and other violent emotions that the mother felt during her pregnancy. I would not wish for a mother to have to see a grimacing face throughout her pregnancy. Grimaces are contagious: we can catch them; if the mother catches them, why not the child?" (*Eléments,* p. 418). This text illustrates the enduring power of imaginationism in Diderot; it follows logically from his description of the violent and tyrannical womb. Diderot fears that visual impressions can have a contagious effect. "It is certain that strange sensations pass from the mother to the child, and from the child to its mother, explaining perhaps the latter's capricious desires" (p. 418).

This remark in turn underscores an idea Malebranche had evoked without developing: the communication between mother and fetus. Because the fetus can influence the mother, as the mother can the fetus, the mother behaves strangely. But this reciprocity (like Mademoiselle de Lespinasse's axiom) does not entail any form of equality. Although the mother can influence the unborn child, and the child the mother, the effects of this mutual communication are by no means comparable. The mother may become capricious because of the child she is bearing, her pregnancy moving her to violent desires that will cease after delivery. The child, however, will be marked for life. [21]

It has been pointed out that Diderot's originality, and his modernity in relation to other thinkers of his time, consist in his apparent "universalization" of the monstrous as part of all that is in nature. Diderot provides further evidence of the perceptible change in attitude toward difference and resemblance: "Why shouldn't man, why shouldn't all animals, be species of monsters that have greater longevity? The monster is born and disappears. Why shouldn't nature, which exterminates the individual in less than a hundred years, exterminate the species over a longer period of time? The Universe sometimes seems to me to be but a collection of mon-

strous beings" (*Eléments,* p. 418). If all beings are but a variety of
monstrous creatures, how else to explain the monster, if not as the
manifestation of a different temporal order? Monstrosity is relative
in character, that is, it cannot be understood in its essence, nor can
it be defined by the lack of resemblance to one's parents; it can only
be understood in relation to conventions that ultimately constitute
an arbitrary norm.

But once again Diderot's normalization of the monstrous creates
a paradox closely linked to his view of women as a monstrous variety of men. The article "Monsters" follows the article "Fetus" in
Eléments. At one point in the *Dream,* Bordeu tells Mademoiselle de
Lespinasse: "Perform in thought an operation that nature often
performs. Mutilate one of the threads . . . Now perform again in
your mind one of nature's occasional experiments. Eliminate a second thread from the bundle . . . Eliminate the thread for the ear
. . . Keep on eliminating threads, and the animal will be deprived
of its head, feet and hands; it won't live long but it will have lived
. . . And that's not all. If you double . . . If you jumble . . . If you
fuse . . . you will have every imaginable kind of monstrosity"
(p. 132–133). These lines fit naturally within Diderot's mechanical
explanation of monstrosity, but what remains striking is Bordeu's
injunction to Mademoiselle de Lespinasse to *imagine* performing
these operations that will produce monstrosities: "Perform in
thought . . . Now perform again in your mind." Mademoiselle de
Lespinasse, under Bordeu's orders, is thus requested to repeat the
imaginative process that, for centuries, was credited with the birth
of monstrosities. In doing so voluntarily, she also anticipates the
role of the teratogenist who, a century later, would similarly proceed to produce anomalies in the laboratory by conceptualizing the
category, or the "family," of monsters to be deliberately conceived.[22]

Here, however, the monstrous conception takes place in the
woman's mind. Thus one can read Mademoiselle de Lespinasse's
"idée bien folle" in a new light, one that, once more, unexpectedly
recalls Aristotle: "La femme [est] le monstre de l'homme," she suggests; Aristotle had noted: "The first beginning of this deviation
[from the generic type] is when a female is formed instead of a
male."[23] Of course, the monstrous relationship of females to males
has no reciprocity in Aristotle's thought, where the principle that

like produces like further requires that males take after their fathers, females after their mothers, and that males remain the fixed norm from which all deviations are measured.

When Diderot *imagines* that males are but a monstrous variety of females or, indeed, that all living creatures might be a collection of monstrous beings, he introduces a reciprocity that undermines the unique monstrosity of females in relationship to males. But in doing so, he also takes the voice and the place of the female, and, specifically, those of Mademoiselle de Lespinasse as she responds to Bordeu's fecundating injunction to create monstrosities through her imaginative powers. Although Diderot rejects the possibility of a fixed norm, he nevertheless retains the normative principle that alone allows him to measure monstrosity as supplement (and he speaks at length of monstrous births that show a surplus of organs, particularly Siamese twins), and to speak from the place of the surplus. It is no accident that the female herself carries within her the excessive, temperamental womb, a supplement unnecessary to her survival, a supplement so poorly suited to carrying a child that the fetus itself will always be felt as an additional burden, a *surplus* as well, that is, already a monstrosity.

The universalization of monstrosity in Diderot can be read only as a radical reevaluation of procreation itself: the supplement without pleasure that presides over all births, including those of the *Dream*'s protagonists. The monstrous norm is that of pleasureless conception, pregnancy, and expulsion into the world. Nature's flux is a dynamics of rejection, echoed by man's dynamics of castration, Soranus' felicitous audacity. Monstrosity is both general in that it presides over the process of life, and particular in that its exemplary excess, the womb, can never be reduced to the norm except by its removal, which would then prevent the process of life, and thus the normalization of monstrosity, from taking place. Diderot's monstrous audacity performs its own rhetoric in the *Dream*. Following Bordeu's injunction to Mademoiselle de Lespinasse, Diderot performs his own thought experiment, a case of philosophical surgery. It is only through the felicitous audacity of reducing monstrosity to a dispensable excess—while maintaining monstrosity's own excessive singularity and its power to give life—that he can propose a global economy of comprehensible variations. But there is a price to pay for all the pleasureless conceptions, the "vomits," the removed wombs, the monstrous births, and the loss of the purposive cause: *imagine,* if you will, the Waste.

La Donna è Mobile

In 1800 there appeared in Paris a work that testifies to the radical change that the ideology of resemblance underwent at the end of the eighteenth century. Expanding on a subject that was extremely popular at the time, Jacques-André Millot published an essay entitled *L'art de procréer les sexes à volonté ou système complet de la génération (The Art of Procreating the Sexes at Will or Complete System of Generation).* In the chapter entitled "On Resemblances, or More Precisely, on Dissemblances," Millot took a position diametrically opposed to the Aristotelian doctrine according to which like produces like and which grounds the identity of beings and things on this resemblance. On the contrary, wrote Millot: "Resemblances are so rare, and dissemblances so excessively frequent, that to me it seems more appropriate to seek the cause of dissemblances than those of resemblances."[24] Like Diderot, one of the rare supporters of Buffon, Millot believed in the still controversial thesis that two seeds, masculine and feminine, actively and equally collaborate in procreation. He developed his theory in the following way: "If a single being could produce another, there would necessarily be more resemblance; but since two beings collaborate in the formation of a third, there is necessarily dissemblance, because the affinity of the atoms cannot be perfect . . . It is obvious according to this definition, that what we call *chance* [*le hasard*] plays a greater role in resemblance than anything else; for a few atoms more or less between each feature, or between only a few of them, produce a marked dissemblance" (pp. 294–296). So the order of nature is to "dissemble" itself. It is resemblance that marks disorder, the abnormal, or the result of extraordinary chance. Resemblance is uncanny. Contrary to the Aristotelian definition, he who does not resemble his parents is not a monster but a normal child; the monster is a rarity, the result of pure chance, he who *does* perfectly resemble his parents. This new evaluation of the question of genesis and resemblance, the view that like produces unlike, would modify as well the definition of progeny and filiation. Moreover, insofar as the theory of generation has always been a theory of art, this change is also reflected in aesthetic debate at the end of the eighteenth century.

To illustrate the play of dissemblances between parents and children, and to demonstrate that the natural order of things is marked by dissimilarities, Millot evoked the painting of a portrait. This comparison fits within an ancient tradition according to which works of art are used as privileged metaphors for the process of generation. In 1731, Dr. François-Marie Pompée Colonna repeated what was already a commonplace when he wrote in *Les principes de la nature ou de la génération des choses (The Principles of Nature, or of Generation):* "There is nothing shameful in admitting that the first principle of all the marvels of the universe is unknown to us, and its workings are hidden; the universe is a Painter and a Sculptor who exhibits his paintings and his work for our admiration, but not in order to show us his craft."[25] Millot used the same metaphor to illustrate the principle and the importance of dissimilarity: "The most skillful sculptor or painter cannot make two statues, two paintings of the same object, without involuntarily introducing some slight dissemblance, for the reasons I have just given, that is, because of the interval that exists between the parts" (p. 301). The interval to which Millot refers is the time interval that the sculptor or the painter requires in order to execute two works of art that he would like to make identical. In Millot's perspective, art still imitates nature, in an ultimately Aristotelian manner, for nature itself produces only dissimilarities, unfaithful images, and marked differences.

Millot claimed to have witnessed a peculiar scene of portrait painting, and offered this experience as empirical evidence of his belief in the priority of dissimilarity in generation and art. At the beginning of each new sitting, he tells us, the portrait failed to bear any likeness to the model whom it had so faithfully resembled the previous day. It was as if the drawing, which had perfectly reproduced the model's features one day, differed from them so markedly the next day that it had become useless to the painter, who aimed to make a true-to-life image of the young woman who was sitting for him:

[The painter] realized at the second session that what he had drawn at the first no longer resembled his model; he erased his work and began again. At the end of this sitting, he found his work a very good likeness, and another session was scheduled for the next day. Upon the lady's arrival, the painter made a comparison with his work of the previous day; he was not pleased, and clearly acknowledged that there was no resemblance. Once more, he decided to erase his drawing and to start over again. He devoted a very long sitting to making the work more precisely resemble the model; at the end of the sitting, he congratulated himself, but admitted, "I thought I had done just as well yesterday." He scheduled another session for the following day. Fresh and vivacious, the young lady arrived at the painter's studio, and once again the comparison disheartened the painter. He despaired and said that he knew that beauty was changeable, but that he had never seen such a variety, and that there was something extraordinary about it. He sent her away and asked her to take me along. The young lady's complaints about the excessive cold in the spot where my friend made her pose had already given me the key to the enigma, for the season was harsh; but I wanted to have confirmation of my idea. I accompanied this lady to my friend's studio and allowed him again to begin his painting, which was this time on another canvas, so that he might have the other sketch as an object of comparison. I observed this lady with as much attention as if I had had the talent to paint her, and after about three quarters of an hour, I noticed the change that her pretty face had undergone. I drew my friend's attention to it and told him that soon his model would resemble yesterday's painting. I explained my opinion, and he agreed with me that there was no other reason for the dissemblance that appeared, since the cold tended to draw the features closer together . . . From this fact we concluded that resemblance consists not only in the exact proportion of features, *but especially in the interval that exists between them,* and that this is the point most difficult for the artist to catch, and the most rarely encountered in nature. Consequently, natural and perfect resemblance *is only an accident of nature.* (pp. 302–306)

The parallel between art and procreation apparently remains unchanged, but the painter, a modern father, finds himself powerless to make an exact reproduction of the model. Furthermore, his work remains sterile, insofar as dissimilarity prevents him from realizing the portrait in the conditions requested until a medical observer finally intervenes. One can observe the sterilizing effect of art on the living not only in the chill to which the artist subjects his model, but even more strikingly in the fact that by the end of each sitting, the model has grown so cold that she once again resembles the inert image in the painting of the previous day. This metaphor of reproduction—the artist, his model, and the portrait—was to become one of the recurrent icons of Romantic Art; it privileges the father both as artist and as the agent of artificially contrived resemblances. For Millot's narrative concludes with a point that is radically new: the superiority of art over nature. Nature is change-able and creates intervals that produce unfaithful appearances, unrecognizable images. As with Rameau's nephew, "Rien ne dis-semble plus de lui que lui-même."[26] Such is nature, and such is the father's role in reproduction. But when art is well thought out, when the painter successfully completes his painting, art triumphs over nature, even if we know that art can capture only *one* of the model's multiple and changeable moods. The mobility and the var-iability of the model's features escape the artist entirely; he cap-tures but a glimpse of a living being.

To better appreciate the aesthetic transformation suggested by Millot, we might briefly look back at a classic lecture by Charles Lebrun on "L'expression générale et particulière," originally read before the Académie royale de peinture et de sculpture in 1678, and first published in 1698. Lebrun wrote:

> As the exterior forms bear so near a relation to the nature of every animal, the Physiognomists tell us, that if it happens any Part of a Man's body is like That of a Beast we must thence draw our conclusions of his Inclinations. This is what they call *Physio-gnomy,* a word derived from the *Greek,* and signifies the Rule or Law of Nature, by which a coherence is kept up between the Af-fections of the soul and the Form of the body; and by this it ap-pears there must be certain and permanent Signs, which indicate the Passions of the Soul, that is, Those which reside in the sensi-tive part. Some Philosophers have asserted that this Seience might be exercised by *Dissimilitude* or Contraries; for instance, if the Hardness of the hair be a sign of Roughness and Brutality, its Softness will denote a Sweet and Tender nature; so if a breast full of thick hair, be the sign of a Hot and Cholerick disposition; a breast without hair, shews a Meek and Sweet temper.[27]

Although it was opposed to similarity, *dissimilitude* for Lebrun still worked within a system of positive interpretation entirely regulated by the idea that if a resemblance suggests a definite association between two objects, dissimilitude implies a corresponding antagonism between these two elements.

For Millot, dissimilarity no longer retains any possibility of positive interpretation. It has become, more radically, the impossibility of deriving meaning from any system of resemblance or dissimilitude, because the law of nature cannot be contained or explained by similitude or likenesses. They are the work of chance, uncanny occurrences, and if Lebrun could add to his lecture a complete series of forty-four drawings as predictable, recognizable images of all human passions, Millot's text is located within an aesthetic that no longer valorizes resemblances between models and images, or similarities between passions and forms.

This conceptual shift modified as well the definition of resemblance. Resemblance is no longer a representation of features, as it had been for the Platonic artist, but rather a matter of *intervals*. It is no longer measured by the similarity of features to each other, but rather by the reproduction of distance—in other words, the *difference*—between features. Resemblance is no longer a property of the thing itself (which "dissembles" itself through the effect of time and climate), nor is it anchored in any identity but rather in the changing distance between elements of the same thing. Resemblance comes into play not only between the portrait and its model, but also between the model and itself. At this point, the interplay of dissemblance and resemblance is displayed not in signs, but in their spacing. It then becomes inevitable that the notions of identity and legitimacy will be destabilized. For what kind of credibility can be granted to a resemblance that may depend on nothing more than the deceiving nature of imagination, and what stable identity can be derived from appearances that are so mobile that they have no duration whatsoever?[28]

The discredit which had fallen upon resemblance is illustrated as well in two articles devoted to the subject and published in the *Encyclopédie* in 1765. The first reads as follows: "Resemblance (logical, metaphysical): Relationship between two things, formed by the operation of the mind. When the idea that one has developed of an object is properly applied to another, these two objects are called similar [*semblables*]. This new name that they are given simply indicates that the idea that represents one also represents the other; *this in no way proves that resemblance is really in the objects,* but it means that the relationship of *resemblance* is in the mind" (emphasis added). How far this is from a system in which nature gave order to knowledge founded upon recognizable resemblances between beings and things; and in which the mother's imagination had the power to reproduce, and then to confound, nature, to institute false resemblances, and perversely to introduce an ideological and social disorder. The *Encyclopédie* article suggests that since resemblance exists only in the judgments that we make about things, judgment alone may finally answer for progeny. Ultimately, the fate of monstrosity—the visible monstrosity of the deformed child, and the hidden monstrosity of the resembling offspring—resides in the sentence cited above: "This in no way proves that the resemblance is really in the objects." Like resemblance, monstrosity is in the eye of the beholder.

A second, even shorter *Encyclopédie* article makes the following comment under the heading "Resemblance (Painting)": "Conformity between the imitation of the object and the object imitated. One speaks of catching a person's resemblance. It is a talent that seems to be independent of study; rather mediocre painters may possess it to a certain degree; and those who are much more skilled in all other respects may in this respect be their inferiors."[29] As we have seen, from the perspective of French Classicism the maternal imagination was like a bad painter in just this way, because *it could catch resemblances* without skill or any intent to interpret a model.

Thus as the monstrous mother was finally credited with the power to create beautiful, but false and misleading, resemblances, two new interpretations emerged: one, illustrated by Millot and the *Encyclopédie,* denigrated the value of all resemblances and posited that the order of nature was to produce dissemblances; the other generalized the power of imagination to mediate all forms of thought, knowledge, and artistic creation. Thus, in 1781, the celebrated Charles Bonnet, corresponding member of the Royal Academy of Science in Paris and London, would write in his *Oeuvres d'histoire naturelle et de philosophie:* "IMAGINATION, infinitely superior to the MICHELANGELOS and RAPHAELS, retraces in the soul the faithful image of objects, and from the various paintings it composes there takes shape in the brain *a painting gallery,* whose parts all move and are composed with an inexpressible promptness and variety."[30] This reappraisal of the power of imagination to recreate a faithful image of nature, to equal or transcend the artistic process by creating an exact "painting" of the objects observed, is entirely separated from the nature and the role of the mother's imagination. This universal quality belongs equally to men and women; far from being deceived by the changing, movable character of all things, imagination reflects the variety and variations of all things promptly and without fail. But its field of action is limited to the soul.

Thus the theory of imaginationism slowly disappeared as both the power of imagination and the nature of monstrosity came to be defined according to a new set of criteria. The debate was never, at any point, won or lost by either side, nor was it affected in any way by medical discoveries: in fact, nothing in the considerable scientific progress made during the period suggests definitively that the maternal imagination might not be at least partly responsible for the actual shaping of the child. However, although imaginationism had found defenders of its theories in almost all schools of medical thought, it would not survive the new perception—and "perception" rather than "discovery" is the appropriate term here—that resemblance is the work of art rather than of nature; that nature produces only diversity, variety, and dissimilarity. From this perspective, the natural diversity of things allows for every monstrous variation, without the least intervention of the maternal imagination.

Popular tradition was no doubt far from abandoning the theory of birthmarks and the belief in different forms of imaginationism,[31] and medicine continued to investigate the monstrous variations of nature. But within the framework of rational thought on natural deviations, the monster became nothing more than a variation, a definable category of living species. Nothing reflects this new understanding of the monster more clearly than the change in meaning that the terms "anomaly" and "abnormality" underwent in the nineteenth century. Georges Canguilhem explains it this way: "'Anomaly' comes from the Greek *anomalia* which means unevenness, asperity; *omalos* in Greek . . . means that which is level, even, smooth, hence 'anomaly' is, etymologically *an-omalos*—that which is uneven, rough, irregular, in the sense given these words when speaking of a terrain. But the etymology of the word 'anomaly' is often mistakenly derived, not from *omalos*, but from *nomos*, which means 'law,' hence the compound *a-nomos*. This etymological error is found even in Littré and Robin's *Dictionnaire de médecine*. Since the Greek *nomos* and the Latin *norma* have closely related meanings, 'law' and 'rule' tend to become indistinguishable. Hence, in a strictly semantic sense, 'anomaly' denotes a fact—it is a descriptive term—while 'abnormal' implies a reference to a standard of value; it is an evaluative, normative term."[32]

The category of the monstrous is reduced, like the etymology of the word "anomaly," to the category norm/normal. The monster is no longer perceived as a being that only a mother's fevered imagination could have produced and for which she could be held accountable. Rather, it has become a simple variant in the orderly interplay of familiar norms. Thus the mother becomes both innocent and *excluded from* the genetic process regulating resemblances and differences. Canguilhem notes: "When monstrosity has become a biological concept, when monstrosities are divided into classes according to constant criteria, when we presume to imagine that we can provoke them experimentally, then the monster is naturalized. The irregular submits to the rule, the prodigy to the predictable."[33]

5

Monstrous Father: The Birth of Teratogeny

In *Eléments de physiologie* Diderot had written, "No imagination without memory; no memory without imagination."[1] The eventual substitution of the concept of memory for that of imagination, as that which characterizes the maternal contribution to the unborn, was illustrated in this brief nineteenth-century account of a monstrous birth mentioned in one of Villiers de l'Isle-Adam's most horrifying tales, "Claire Lenoir": "Have you given any thought to these human monstrosities, such as beings speckled with bicolor marks or furry monsters—cephalopods, doubles, horrible errors of nature, all issued from a sensation, a whim, a *sight,* an IDEA that occurred during the mother's pregnancy? . . . A woman whose husband was stabbed to death delivered an infant girl five months later. At age *seven,* this child fell prey to fits of hallucination. She would then scream, 'Help! Here are men armed with knives about to kill me!' The little girl died during one of these fits, and blackish marks, similar to smeared blood, were found on her body. In spite of the sexual differences, the marks duplicated on the heart the wounds that the father had received seven years earlier, when the child was not yet among the mortals."[2] What impresses Villiers is not the power of imagination, but rather the persistence of the idea.[3] The monstrous mother has transmitted a memory rather than a simple image. Not only is the body of the child "imprinted," but the child remembers, as it were, the kind of violence that killed her father before she was born. Contrary to the earlier tales of monstrosity it seems to repeat, Villiers' narrative shows that monstrosity does not erase the father but *resurrects* him, bringing him back to life, so to speak, for seven more years. At the same time

103

that the power of the maternal imagination was more vividly described in terms of memory than images, the concept of resemblance was replaced by the notion of heredity—the heredity of in-
nate characteristics, whose mode of transmission was still hotly
debated in the nineteenth century, and the heredity of acquired
characteristics, itself the object of many experiments now long forgotten.

Heredity and Patrimony

The notion of heredity was just as mysterious, uncertain, and unpredictable for the nineteenth century as the maternal imagination
had been for earlier times. When William Brooks published *Law of
Heredity* in 1880, he defined heredity as "a power to produce a definite adult animal, with all its characteristics, even down to the
slightest accidental peculiarity of its parents."[4] Brooks's choice of
words is significant: the word "definite" has replaced "similar";
"characteristics" is used where "features" used to appear. Yet, one
overriding question remained constant: is monstrosity transmissible? The sciences of generation, noting the monster's profound
uselessness, which Aristotle himself had emphasized, had long believed that Nature compensated for its own accidents by making
the monster sterile. The monster's sterility echoed as well the sterile
woman's inner monstrosity. In a new scientific debate in which all
notions of resemblance, all visual and external assessments, had
been devalued in favor of a conception of identity based on internal, infinitesimal variation, the question of the "accidental peculiarity," a euphemism for monstrous characteristics, would also be
viewed in terms of accidental transmission.

The shift of emphasis from imagination and resemblance to the
role of heredity revealed important changes in the perception of
the science of generation. The word "heredity" first meant "inheritance" in a legal sense. In a tale of parricide entitled "L'elixir de
longue vie" (1830), Balzac used the term "heredity" to designate
the laws that still governed inheritance and favored the eldest son.
In 1834, *Vocabulaire de l'académie française* still defined "heredity" as
"the right to succeed," and the "estate left by a defunct man."[5] The
same word came to be applied to the more elusive physical inheritance transmitted from parents to all their children, whether male

or female. Yet, whereas the earlier sense of the word "heredity" had conferred legitimacy on the eldest son, the laws of heredity tended to legitimize the role of the father by showing how the male organism remained, as Brooks put it, "the originating element in the process of evolution."[6] The notion of heredity reinforced ties between parents and children, ties that were shown to be as intimate as those that once connected the maternal imagination to the brain fibers of the child. However, the underlying conceptual *economy* of heredity—in contrast to the economy governing the maternal imagination—marked a subtle change in meaning and worth. Maternal imagination had been entrusted with the twofold task of accounting for legitimate similarities and for unrecognizable resemblances, in which the father's features were erased. Heredity's immediate objective was to explain, and to prove through laboratory experimentation, the *mode* of transmission of characteristics from parents to their offspring.

In their enterprise, if not in their scientific reasoning, the technical debates surrounding the transmission of hereditary characteristics reiterated the question that had divided scholars since Aristotle: where does resemblance come from, and what are its causes? But the focus now was on cell identity rather than individual identity, and resemblances no longer designated the superficial likeness of beings, but rather their internal configuration and patterns of behavior. Investigation in this area raised troubling questions. Which of the cells determine characteristics, and how? Regarding the transmission of hereditary characteristics, John Farley summarizes Eduard Strasburger's argument of 1884 that "upon fecundation . . . the nonnuclear material of the egg and sperm fuses, but the chromatin material lies in contact without actually fusing. Then the chromatin networks of the male and female nuclei divide into segments in the normal manner, distributing an equal amount of nuclear material to the two daughter nuclei so that each daughter nucleus will contain an equal number of paternal and maternal segments" (p. 167). However, August Weismann vigorously contested the idea that parental cells are equally distributed in the process of generation. In his view, there survived only what Jean Rostand terms "a limited legacy," which keeps cells of a certain type from producing anything other than their exact duplicate. The idea of "somatic segregation," what A. H. Sturtevant calls "the sorting out of hereditary elements," was adopted by Weismann, "who elaborated them into an intricate theory of heredity and development. According to this scheme, the chromosomes are bearers of the hereditary material . . . The different chromosomes of an individual may have been derived from many different ancestral lines, and they therefore differ among themselves . . . There is, in a sense, a competition between the various chromosomes, and the nature of each characteristic depends on the outcome of this competition at each critical time and place in the developing embryo."[7]

Independent of all scientific content, the most intriguing aspect of these texts on heredity is the parallel drawn between cellular systems and political organization: research on heredity above all establishes a hierarchical relation between cells capable of transmitting what Rostand calls "le patrimoine héréditaire" (hereditary patrimony)[8] and those whose role is only reactive. The extraordinarily complex inquiry that led to modern views on heredity and the privileging of cells actively capable of reproducing hereditary characteristics echoes in its semantics the hierarchical society of the Old Regime, with its distinctions of birth and its law of inheritance. The status conferred upon the "germinal band" is like a distant reflection of the ancestral lineage, of the royal bloodline.

An economy of resemblance associated primarily with images and the maternal is thus being transformed into an economy of heredity linked mainly to cellular functions that transmit a *hereditary patrimony*. This transformation challenges in turn the traditional definition of monstrosity. The monster is now conceptualized as a form of cellular organization. From this perspective, monstrosity is merely a function within a larger system of signification, a function that constantly reminds the observer that signs are both necessary and arbitrary. This change is also illustrated in the terminology that was developed to account for the laws of heredity, a language free of all traces of Cratylism. This language gives the father a recognizable role in generation, not in terms of images, resemblances, or likenesses, but in terms of words that describe invisible links, internal organization, and moral inheritance. The science of embryology and the discovery of the laws of heredity inaugurate a new discourse which defines the child's biological identity in terms of opposition and difference rather than resemblance and dissimilarity. A child's identity is no longer assessed in terms of recognizable appearances that establish, for all to see, a link between parents and offspring. In theories of generation, the maternal role had been explained mostly in terms that privileged both the *vis imaginativa* and the power of images. The maternal role found its most powerful logic in an economy of resemblances. But the role and importance both of the mother and of imagination were simultaneously erased in the scope and complexity of research centered on a system of transmission and communication of characters, that is, a form of writing. Villiers de l'Isle-Adam illustrated this phenomenon in his tales with the creation of Dr. Tribulat Bonhomet, Spallanzani's sinister disciple, who declares: "An analytical mind, a mind given to magnification and minute examination is so much the essence of my nature, that all my joie de vivre is confined to precise classification of the puniest tenebrioid, to observation of the strange tangles, *similar to an ancient script,* that are revealed in an insect's nerves."[9]

The development of a science privileging words rather than images also repressed a certain idea of sexuality, successfully shelving the long debates on the shame and glory of the reproductive organs. John Farley has persuasively argued that the history of genetics itself in the nineteenth century corresponds to a repression of sexuality similar to the repression affecting mores during the Napoleonic and Victorian eras. The favored model remained that of plants' "asexual reproduction." "Duncan Crow, whose description of sexual intercourse significantly paralleled the biological outlook of the period, was I assume, unaware, of the validity of the parallel to which he alluded. 'Ideally,' he wrote, 'women would produce children by parthenogenesis; failing that, male impregnation should take place in a dark bedroom into which the husband would creep to create his offspring in silence, while the wife endured the connection in a sort of coma.'"[10] At the same time, Crow's recent description of Victorian sexuality masks another important aspect of sexuality in the nineteenth century: the veiled desire that *males* should produce children as if by parthenogenesis. This idea found its most striking expression in fantastic literature, though it could be said that science, as well, furthered the conceit of the scientist as the sole father of artificially developed progeny. Such was the role and function of the scientist experimenting in his laboratory, a sol-

itary father whose goal it was to generate life alone, and more specifically, to generate monstrosities. A new science was born.

The Father of Teratogeny

Nineteenth-century science adopted and expanded the idea of the
monster's "naturalness." Indeed, the nineteenth century is credited
with having finally created a science of monsters, or teratology.[11]
Teratology, which first attempted to classify all monstrosities, was
founded by Etienne Geoffroy Saint-Hilaire (1772–1844) and his
son Isidore Geoffroy Saint-Hilaire (who coined the word in 1830).
In his *Traité de tératologie* (1836), Isidore Geoffroy Saint-Hilaire described monstrosity as a group of very complex and serious anomalies making it impossible or difficult to accomplish certain functions, and producing in those suffering from it a malformation
strikingly different from that ordinarily seen in the species. He described the monster not in relation to what could have produced it,
but in relation to its internal teleology; not in relation to its *cause,*
but with a view to its *function.* The monster is that which is incapable of performing certain functions, one of the most important
of which is reproduction.

Camille Dareste (1822–1899), who founded "teratogeny," or the
science of monstrous embryology, commented on Geoffroy Saint-
Hilaire's *Traité de tératologie* as follows: "Anomalies, especially monstrosities, were long considered to be facts completely foreign to
natural order, and consequently to science."[12] For Dareste, the
monster's integration into scientific categories was another example of its normalization. Of course, Dareste's assumption that
monstrosity had been foreign to science before the nineteenth century was erroneous: monstrosity had long been the unresolved
enigma that defined the limits of all theories of generation. Questions relating to monstrosities figured almost every month in the
proceedings of the French Académie des sciences. But Dareste's
interest was primarily in experimental science. Although scientific
thought had for many years speculated on the cause and the nature of the monstrous, it was modern science and laboratory research that would elucidate, and thus "naturalize," monstrosity.

In *Histoire des anomalies de l'organisation,* Isidore Geoffroy Saint-
Hilaire noted, "Monstrousness is no longer a random disorder, but
another order, equally regular and equally subject to laws: it is the

mixture of an old and a new order, the simultaneous presence of two states that ordinarily succeed one another."[13] According to Dareste, it was because the monstrous had recovered its rights as a creation of nature, and no longer of counter-nature, that its scientific study was fully justified. Dareste defined the monstrous as "the extraordinary result of purely natural causes" (p. 2). Summarizing Isidore and Etienne Geoffroy Saint-Hilaire's studies on teratology, Dareste added: "The most extreme form of monstrosity and the slightest anomaly are essentially phenomena of the same order— deviations from the specific type produced by a change in evolution. With this exception, that monstrosities affect a great number of organs concurrently and profoundly, whereas slight anomalies superficially affect certain isolated organs. The difference between these two phenomena results essentially from different intensities in the modificatory causes, as well as, perhaps, from the time these causes take place" (pp. 39–40).

Nothing could illustrate more explicitly the normalization of the monster by the scientific gaze: its submission to rules, norms, and variations. The monster is now the object of classification according to "types," with each type corresponding to a probable cause, purely mechanical and similar in nature to factors regulating the development of normal embryos. Teratology, or the science of monsters, was expanding. In fact, the expression "science of monsters" would have been inconceivable before the nineteenth century, if by "science" we mean a discipline primarily concerned with finding and establishing laws. In 1880, Dr. Ernest Martin wrote the popular and detailed *Histoire des monstres depuis l'antiquité jusqu'à nos jours*,[14] praising the efforts by recent teratologists to explain the current scientific view of monstrosity and its now predictable genesis. After five chapters devoted to the history of monstrosity, Martin introduced "modern science" with a classified organization of monstrosities: "simple monsters" and "complex monsters." In a chapter on heredity he considered diverging opinions on the transmission of monstrous anomalies. The most interesting chapter for our purpose is entitled "Imagination and Monstrosity." In this text, Martin briefly summarized the most important theories on the question, and concluded with the following remarks:

1. The imagination plays an undeniable role in the procreation of monstrous beings.

2. Its role is mechanical and the uterus is its agent. When excited by some nervous agitation, the uterus' contractility exerts a pressure that the embryo cannot bear with impunity.

3. Outside these cases, the imagination can also affect the embryo after a period of prolonged agitation, without, however, producing an actual monstrosity. It affects the embryo's general state, sometimes its intelligence, but it possesses nothing teratogenic.

4. In that imagination's main function consists in calling up images of objects and beings, it in no way has the power to reproduce these images: facts to the contrary are meaningless, they are purely coincidental, when not dictated by passion or superstition.[15]

Although the focus here is still on the mother's imagination, the word "maternal" never actually appears. Further, teratology reduces the role of imagination to no more than a mechanical determinant capable of being examined in terms of laws and norms. The restriction posited by teratology—that imagination does not have the power to reproduce images—also describes the unbridgeable gap between art and medicine that has widened since the beginning of the nineteenth century. The medical history of monstrosities had been enriched by experiments, testimony, and legends; it had produced a diversified tradition mingling facts and fiction to create a complex network of understanding. Teratology made a point of excluding this tradition, and more specifically imagination's creative function in generation, which it considered past "passion and prejudice." Previously, treatises on generation had always referred to art as a metaphor for nature; henceforth, the first concern of the new science would be not only to exclude art from its discourse, but also to separate imagination, as a mental faculty, from all creative processes. This exclusion of the role of imagination from embryology and teratology also entailed the exclusion of the mother.

"It is difficult to go back further than the last century," wrote Martin. "It was only then that descriptions worthy of the name began to appear in scientific writings, and at first, they were intermixed with details *foreign* to the subject. They reflected the superstitious concerns of their authors' minds; then, slowly, *imagination yielded to reflection*" (p. 114, emphasis added). Once again, we encounter the concept of the contagious imagination: as if the maternal imagination had in turn contaminated that of doctors, making them *conceive* of works that were *deformed* by foreign, illegitimate influences. The triumph of reflection over imagination echoes the successful efforts by teratologists to exclude the maternal factor, except in its purely mechanical aspect. The reduction of the maternal role to the "uterus' contractility" also illustrates new medical terminology. But the conclusion of Martin's book recalls a theme evoked earlier by those who had opposed imaginationism: that what is really monstrous is the theory that places on the mother's imagination the burden of deformed children. "Science had now undertaken to defeat Satan and his infernal cohorts, lies and superstitions, haunting thoughts, more hideous monsters than those whose story we have tried to expose in these pages" (p. 381).[16]

Not content only to discover the elusive laws of nature, teratology also hoped to formulate new laws that would permit this recent science to compete with nature, perhaps to surpass it as well. Thus was born the adjunct science of teratogenesis, whose objective was the controlled production of monsters in the laboratory. For nineteenth-century scientists, noted Martin, "one point still remained unclear: how are they formed?" (p. 119). Here science itself becomes a generative process, but with the express desire to exclude the creative (disorderly) role of the mother. "For the physiologist," Martin reiterates, "life alone can produce life, and it can be perceived through characteristics which are the expression of forces brought into play by the use of physical agents whose impact we know through science. Take the example of an egg that hatches; a living being has been formed inside it: how did this life come to be? We are sure that the heat from physical causes plays a decisive role: we may not know the essence of these causes, but we are in control of their application, and each time we apply them, we will produce a hatching similar to the first; we therefore make life appear" (pp. 131–132). This plural *we*, though not royal, is nonetheless male. This master discourse is that of the scientist in his laboratory, the modern womb. The scientist now takes the place of the mother. When Martin writes "we therefore make life appear," he means that "we" are in a position to replace (or to do without) the maternal, and that "we" likewise have the capacity to produce either normal or abnormal beings. The point here is not that the mother finally finds herself free of guilt, free of the tremendous responsibility that she was forced to bear for so long; indeed, what changes is not the status of the mother but primarily that of the monster. Nowhere is this better and more chillingly illustrated than in E. Geoffroy Saint-Hilaire's lapidary remark in his *Dictionnaire classique d'histoire naturelle:* "Monsters have their usefulness: they are means of study for our intellects." [17]

Teratogenesis, or teratogeny, the systematic production of monsters in the laboratory, was first constituted by a series of exclusions and reductions. The reductions were: reduction of the unusual, of deviation and *dissimilarity,* to a series of variations of the recognizable laws of nature; and reduction of the extraordinary character of the monster, who at times had been considered prodigious, demonic, or simply useless. Aristotle's conception of monsters—that although (like women) they are deviations from the norm, monsters (unlike women) do not necessarily exist in view of the "purposive or final cause"—was essentially redefined by Geoffroy Saint-Hilaire, who considered monstrosity a key to scientific knowledge. Science then became both the monster's final cause and its ultimate justification. The monster is no longer the product of the maternal principle; it is, rather, a useful object of scientific inquiry. Teratogeny also excluded the imagination's role in forming *and* perceiving the monster. For the teratogenist, the imagination cannot imprint images, nor can it successfully provide scientific evidence: "Imagination yields to reflection." And finally, teratogeny excluded the maternal from the laboratory as the ultimate cause of contagious disorder that could contaminate the regulated production of distorted life. These reductions and exclusions work to the advantage of the scientist. Indeed, with teratogenesis a new form of parental singularity emerges, one that claims to reproduce life at will, in all its variations and forms.

Teratogenesis, the outgrowth of teratology, was an ambitious field. Its goal was to study the genesis of deformities by actually producing monstrosities in the laboratory. The idea of trying to modify an embryo to provoke a monstrosity was not a new one. In 1605, Jean Riolan wrote, "Anyone can easily produce a monstrous bird." He suggested that by taking an egg containing two yolks and removing the membrane that separates them, one can obtain "a small bird with a single head, four wings, and four legs." He added, "Will you say that what was artificially accomplished might predict something sinister?"[18] But it was not until the nineteenth century that science, having definitely abandoned the theory of the preexistence of germs (normal or abnormal), considered the possibility that monstrosities might be deformations capable of systematic experimental reproduction. Etienne Geoffroy Saint-Hilaire pioneered the idea of producing monsters in a laboratory.[19] But the development and expansion of this idea was the work of Camille Dareste[20], a French scientist who defined the premises of teratogeny as follows in 1877: "If organization does not preexist in the germ, there is not, nor can there be, preexisting monstrosity. Anomalies and monstrosities appear at certain stages in the development [of the embryo] . . . Teratogeny, or, in other terms, the study of abnormal embryogeny, must consist—like normal embryogeny—in the direct study of the successive modifications determined by the evolution of organization. These two sciences form but one . . . But teratogeny's means of study are quite different from those of normal embryogeny. One can more or less obtain normal embryos representing common species of each class. Such is not the case with monstrous embryos."[21] This particular problem led Dareste to a radical solution: "Where shall we find the elements necessary to the study of teratogeny? Since direct observation cannot provide them, we must necessarily induce [their formation], obtain them from experimentation. If monsters do not preexist, if they are the result of accidental causes which modify the germ when it is produced or developed, why not try to obtain artificially what sometimes happens naturally; why not induce the birth of monsters by modifying the physical or biological conditions that determine the production and the evolution of normal beings?" Dareste added: "This strange problem, which on first observation seems to defy treatment, would have been considered blasphemous at various times in the past. However, modern science cannot, and must not, recoil from it." "Teratogeny," Dareste concludes, "must create its own object of study."[22]

Dareste wrote several memoirs on questions related to embryology ("Note sur un nouveau genre de monstruosité double appartenant à la famille des polygnathions," 1859, and "Note sur l'existence de l'amidon dans le jaune d'oeuf," 1868) before publishing in 1877 the results of his reflections and laboratory experimentations on embryos, *Recherches sur la production artificielle des monstruosités, ou essais de tératogénie expérimentale* (Research on the Artificial Production of Monstrosities or Essays on Experimental Teratogeny). His work reflected a general interest in both the origin of monstrosities and the idea that they resulted from accidental or so-called exterior causes. In 1860, the French Académie des sciences had proposed the following question for its national prize essay competition: "Experimental study of the modifications whose influence can be determined in the development of the embryo of a vertebrate through the effect of exterior agents." The Académie specified further: "Twenty-five years ago, Geoffroy Saint-Hilaire's experiments tended to establish that one could provoke anomalies in the organization of the developing embryo by modifying the conditions of incubation of a bird's egg. The Académie wishes to see this topic studied anew, and more completely, either in birds, batrachians, or fish."[23] The prize was divided between two scientists: Lereboullet, who had presented a memoir on anomalies in the reproduction of pikes, and Dareste.

Lereboullet's memoir had concluded with considerable caution that a few anomalies might be attributed to external causes, that is, causes subsequent to fecundation. Camille Dareste's assessment was more radical. With few exceptions, most monstrosities could be produced artificially in a laboratory. Although Dareste later wrote that he had once hoped to work on embryos that develop in a placenta, he later limited his experiments—though not his ambitions—to chicken embryos. The desire to expand the scope of his teratogenic investigations led him to claim:

> If the artificial production of varieties, at least for certain species, does not seem to pose any greater difficulty than the artificial production of monstrosities, it is not the same for the production of races. In this new problem it is necessary to act not on individuals, but on successions of individuals over a smaller or greater number of generations. Thus naturalists must have research tools of a completely different, and much more costly, nature. The laboratory is no longer sufficient: menageries are needed, or at least places where animals used in experiments can be raised. (p. 42)

Complaints about the shortage of necessary space to conduct large-scale experiments were to be a recurrent theme in Dareste's work on teratogeny. Dareste's obsession with the insufficient amount of laboratory space at his disposal recalls the ancient (masculine) belief that too narrow a womb would produce unsatisfactory progeny. To support his demand for larger experimental space, Dareste cited the naturalist François Vogt, one of Darwin's translators: "Menageries and zoological gardens must necessarily be transformed into zoological laboratories in which definite observations and experiments may be continued without interruption over a number of years" (p. 43). The expression "must necessarily be transformed" (devront nécessairement se transformer) seems to suggest that the inexorable character of the laws that govern evolution also applies to science. It is as if science were itself destined to broaden the scope of its teratogenic experiments.

Vogt was a respected naturalist, and Camille Dareste's work on chicken embryos earned the praise of Charles Darwin. Moreover, Dareste's work on monstrosities proved useful for the understanding of normal organisms as well. Similar teratogenic experiments were conducted in Denmark by the physiologist Panum and in Italy by Lombardini. Gould and Pyle note in *Anomalies and Curiosities of Medicine* (1896):

> From the appearance of the treatise by Geoffroy-Saint-Hilaire, teratology has made enormous strides, and is to-day well on the road to becoming a science. Hand in hand with embryology it has been the subject of much investigation in this century, and to enumerate the workers of the present day who have helped to bring about scientific progress would be a task of many pages. Even in the *artificial production of monsters* much has been done, and a glance at the work of Dareste well repays the trouble. Essays on teratogenesis, with reference to batrachians, have been offered by Lombardini; and by Lereboullet and Knoch with reference to fishes. Foll and Warynski have reported their success in obtaining visceral inversion, and even this branch of the subject promises to become scientific.[24]

However, far from opening the door to a larger field of inquiry, teratogeny, at least in the way Camille Dareste conceived it in his *Production artificielle des monstruosités*, was the last avatar of the traditional medical scrutiny that for so many centuries had sought to unveil the mysteries of monstrosities. Unlike the product of maternal imagination that it replaced, the teratogenist's creation was neither caused nor controlled by any external model, any plastic or living object, that inspired desire or horror in its genitor. The scientist was guided by a determined will that inscribed the monster in a greater scheme of things. Once the mother's punishment, the monster had become the scientist's trophy; once the involuntary expression of illegitimate passion, it had become mere evidence of laws anticipated by teratogeny. Once prophetic, the monster had become predictable. The pictorial model after which the mother had been thought to produce a monstrous child was replaced by a recognizable rule. And when monstrosity was understood in terms of rules, science no longer had anything to fear from the disorders of a maternal imagination.

Camille Dareste's *Production artificielle des monstruosités* illustrates the scientific reappropriation of monstrosity at the expense of the maternal role, and the far-reaching attempt to reproduce life without the mother. Dareste first posited that the scientist working on the production of monstrosities had to free himself from the power of imagination: "Although imagination has been given free reign in explaining teratological phenomena through mechanical or pathological causes, it sooner or later encounters a dead end, and must ultimately admit its powerlessness" (p. 18). But as we have seen, the teratogenist creates his own field of experimentation, imagines a new experimental domain.

In his research, Camille Dareste adopted Isidore Geoffroy Saint-Hilaire's classification of monstrosities and sought to reproduce each case to demonstrate how anomalies came to be born. There were four main categories: "Slight anomalies, designated by the term *hemiterata,* and serious or complex anomalies, which form three separate groups, *heterotaxia, hermaphrodisms,* and *monstrosities.*"[25] The reduction of the category of the monstrous to a subcategory of the anomalous also served to regulate or at least minimize what could not yet be entirely explained or subjected to experimentation. Hemiterata, continued Dareste, "are subdivided into anomalies caused by *displacement, change in connections, continuity, partition,* and *disjunction*" (p. 137). Later: "Simple monstrosities (that is, those formed by a single embryo) are divided into three categories, which are called *autosites, omphalosites,* and *parasites.* I set aside simple parasitic monstrosities, on which I have no personal documentation. In the current state of science, their interpretation offers insurmountable difficulties, so that I do not know if their existence in a separate category is truly justified" (p. 140).[26] This statement—I personally know nothing about such monstrosities; further, they cannot be explained; thus I can't say that they exist as a separate category—was founded on a logic that tended to exclude the unknown as possibly nonexistent, inasmuch as existence implied a "category." A footnote added that the suppression of this category (simple parasitic monstrosities) had been suggested as early as 1867.

Further subcategories described teratologic "types," with emphasis on anomalies of the eye. These were of special interest to Camille Dareste; however, no statement is more curious than his comment on the subcategory of omphalositic monstrosities: "The discovery of two new examples in the category of omphalositic monstrosities (examples not described by Isidore Geoffroy Saint-Hilaire) . . . may one day lead teratologists to the creation of one or two new families. Such a creation would be currently premature, for it is not impossible that new examples, as yet unknown, might be added to those we already know, thus unveiling new relations among all these monstrosities" (p. 145). Dareste's goal of reproducing in his laboratory all recognized categories of monstrosities betrays another purpose: the creation of new families. Although the creation of such families would be premature, Dareste warns, chances are good that still undisclosed monstrosities might appear (in his laboratory) to establish the remaining family connections needed to form a complete picture. The "family" scene described in Dareste's project also offers an interesting view of his "paternity." For all practical purposes, he has taken the previously silent, obliterated, place of the monstrous father. Not only does he claim his paternity but he also takes it upon himself to reject those monstrosities he "does not know personally"—those he has not reproduced, or "fathered"—and to claim his capacity to produce new anomalies that will yield a coherent view of the "family." Regarding the consideration of "double monstrosities," that is, monstrosities involving two embryos, this all-powerful father added, "The category of double monstrosities presents no theoretical difficulties" (p. 146). He then proceeded to dismiss entirely certain categories as "artificial," illegitimate families, drawing attention instead to unrecognized but existing family connections.

Dareste admitted to few scientific failures, and those he did describe shed new light on the nature of his dubious paternity. In a long endnote on hermaphrodism, Dareste wrote:

> My observations have taught me nothing on the origin of various anomalies designated by the name *hermaphrodisms* . . . Moreover, the origin of these various monstrosities in mammals and men—where they have been primarily observed—can today be very easily explained by theoretical considerations deduced from recently acquired knowledge of the evolution of the reproductive organs. It was long believed that the male and female reproductive systems were essentially distinct, presenting only the measure of harmony indispensable to the performance of their functions. When Etienne Geoffroy Saint-Hilaire sought to demonstrate the unity of their composition, he was led to believe that the reproductive systems in males and females offered not relations of harmony but analogic relations as well. He thus sought to find in both sexes a system of common organs, modified only functionally. Isidore Geoffroy Saint-Hilaire sought to explain the various forms of hermaphrodism by positing the principle of a fundamental unity. (p. 351)

Dareste goes on to explain that this approach did not, however, lead to a satisfactory explanation until a "brilliant anatomic discovery by J. Muller" proved that both male and female reproductive parts coexist separately, that is, *distinctly* and autonomously in the early embryo. Thus: "It sometimes happens that the 'Muller's filaments' are not fully developed in the male sex . . . These filaments then form . . . what is now called the *masculine uterus*" (p. 352).[27] Dareste then concluded by quoting M. de Lacaze-Duthiers: "To my mind, it has been amply demonstrated that glands develop in variable proportions; that a given individual is more male than female; finally, in other cases the proportions are equal" (p. 353). Moreover, Dareste noted that hermaphrodism of the superior organs of reproduction (ovaries and testicles) is "excessively rare" and that these facts have not been "scientifically established." Nonetheless, he claimed that hermaphrodism of the "middle system," that which may develop into a *masculine uterus,* had been completely elucidated by science, that is, "naturalized." The "superior system" of reproduction is at the origin of embryonic life, the "middle system" is the locus of gestation. It thus comes as no surprise that Dareste, who presided over the gestation of thousands of monstrosities and dreamed of an immense laboratory where new monsters would be created every day, should be perfectly satisfied by a theory of hermaphrodism that posits the existence of a masculine uterus.[28] For not only does the scientist assume visible paternity of monstrosities, but he also assumes the maternal role in generation. The question of hermaphrodism is then strategically reappropriated. Since hermaphrodism has not been produced in laboratories, and since, according to Dareste, it is easily explained, it hardly belongs to the category of monstrosities relevant to teratogeny. But it survives as a supplement in this long endnote to Dareste's last chapter on his teratological experiments.

Like the maternal imagination, the teratogenist *modifies*, through intervention, a process that left undisturbed would have produced normal progeny. "The fundamental, *dominant* fact, so to speak, of teratogeny is that teratogenic events are always the consequence of a modification in the embryo's evolution" (p. 354). The laboratory has fully and successfully replaced the womb, and rational, male intervention has been substituted for the female imagination. Just as the role of the maternal imagination was responsible not for the conception, but only for the formation—or rather the deformation—of the fetus, the scientist works on fertilized embryos that he then proceeds to deform and cripple.

Dareste saw himself as the promoter of a new science and believed that teratogeny was destined to have a long and prolific life. Geoffroy Saint-Hilaire's greatest claim to glory, according to Dareste, was having preceded him in his experimentations: "His work on the artificial production of monsters is certainly one of Geoffroy Saint-Hilaire's greatest achievements. But this great scientist was satisfied only to clear the way. Carried away by the fervor of genius, he would visit at the same time the most varied questions; he did not have the time patiently to follow long-term experiments whose first condition for success absolutely demanded the most untiring perseverance. He had imagined the method that was necessary for the creation of a new branch of the biological sciences; he left the application up to others" (p. 37). Teratogeny was conceived by a man "carried away" by his "fervor," capable of "imagining" the principles that would lead to the creation of monstrosities: expressions that recall descriptions of the maternal imagination at work in the creation of monstrous progeny. The description of teratogenic labor itself is not devoid of passion or excess; its demands are seen as pressing, and its agent must be tireless. Indeed, the *genesis* of teratogeny is described as a long delivery. Dareste describes the twenty-five years of research that led to the results published in his book as follows: "Working *alone* and without help, in the most adverse conditions—first in Paris, dependent on my own resources, then in Lille, on the totally insufficient resources of a provincial university laboratory, lacking everything, even room for my work—I had to battle innumerable difficulties, and I made very slow progress. I nevertheless succeeded in producing artificially almost all types of elementary monstrosity . . . I produced several thousand monsters, and I was able to study most of the teratological types at different moments in their evolution" (pp. 37–38). These are extreme examples of the power of parental singularity, whose role is not to imitate nature but to imitate artificially what was once counter-nature. Dareste's "thousand monsters" trivialize the question of monstrosity without diminishing the fervor it provokes: what was once the passion of creation has now become the passion of experimentation. This was the research to which, as Dareste put it, "I have devoted my life." He added, "[Research] has already enabled me to establish laws on the formation of monsters, and I hope it will permit me to collect data regarding the solution to one of the greatest problems our minds can pose us: the origin of the species" (p. 44).

As illustrated by the works of Camille Dareste, teratogeny posited the exclusion of the maternal imagination from the formation of the monster, the more general exclusion of imagination from the conception of the monstrous (on the assumption that imagination's connection to prejudice could only impede science from achieving its inevitable progress), and finally, the exclusion of the female from gestation, which could now take place in the laboratory. (It is interesting to note that Dareste admits having tried to produce monstrosities in embryos that develop in a placenta, but he finally gave up because of obvious technical difficulties.) And just as the mother's narrow womb had been thought to be one of the mechanical causes of monstrosity, too small a laboratory was said to impede the full development of the teratogenic project. In fact, according to Dareste, teratogeny itself risked becoming an aborted form of embryology if it did not get more experimental space, such as menageries and zoological parks. Finally—if not in theory, then in practice—the notion of parental singularity was reinstated in the laboratory at a time when scientific doctrine had dismissed it entirely. But if one is tempted to regard Camille Dareste as the modern father of the modern monster, then it would be more accurate to say that the teratogenic scientist rather than *being* the father *supplants* him: it is to the scientist that the monster owes its form and appearance. Rather than originating life, the teratogenist modifies it. Henceforth, the scientist will simultaneously occupy *both* the position once held by the desiring maternal imagination and that held by the model (image, portrait, animal) which prompted the deviation from the norm. Perhaps it is because he now occupies the position of both the mother and the model that the teratogenic scientist himself becomes the image of the monster he has engendered. For all the valuable scientific data it discloses and classifies, Dareste's work reads as fantastic fiction, his role that of an uncanny creature: a hermaphrodite that would not be sterile. To the extent that the role the teratogenist assumed paralleled that of the imaginative mother during pregnancy, it could be said that he was also the mother of monsters. The scientist carried within himself the model for future monsters; he was himself their model. The concepts of parental singularity and generative responsibility have changed sexual sides one last time. The monster's new "mother" accomplishes a work that is a long labor of passion, that presents all the signs of great desire, yet refuses to yield to the *vis imaginativa* long associated with maternal deficiency.

To recall the model proposed by Claude Lévi-Strauss in his "Elementary Structures of Kinship," one could say that the elementary structure of monstrosity also has four components: the monster's legitimate father; its imaginative mother; the model for the monster, that is, the object of maternal desire; and the monstrous offspring. In the final metamorphosis of the medical idea of monstrosity, this structure was modified as follows: just as the legitimate father had been "erased" from his progeny by an inscription that superimposed onto his likeness that of a foreign image, the mother now was excluded from the development of the embryo to which she had given life. She was banished from Dareste's laboratory, her existence no longer necessary. The teratogenic scientist had usurped the mother's place, his laboratory had become an artificial womb, and the model—the images of earlier times hanging in the church or in the conjugal bedroom—now belonged to a linguistic category: the endless taxonomy of "families" of monstrosities that living embryos would be made to replicate. This model can be described in terms of laws of variation established by the scientist, or by the scientist's own *vis imaginativa*. In a sense, imagination continues to play a role, but its role is that of the *fantastic* artist[29] who masters forms and dissimilarities, willfully producing false resemblances. To the extent that the monster's model, its mother, and the teratogenic scientist have now become one, the concept of parental singularity grows more complex. Whereas maternal imagination was always thought to be directed toward an external object of desire, the scientist is carrying out an inner project. A process of doubling takes place whose consequences have been best illustrated in works of fiction that constitute the teratogenist's lasting glory and his most troubling accomplishment.

Finally, to give life to a monster is to give death as well by anticipating the creation of a being doomed to live for only a few hours, a progeny unfit to live in any sense of the term. *Traité du droit criminel français,* published in 1826, made this chilling statement: "Il ne peut être commis d'homicide ni sur un monstre ni sur un mort" (there can be no homicide committed against a monster or a dead man).[30] That teratogeny thus conceived systematically produces death was the topic of many tales of monstrous conceptions in the nineteenth century. As Romantic aesthetics explored the nature of artistic creation, monstrous beings—such as Frankenstein's demon or the popular version of the golem—came to symbolize the singular and tragic power of the work of art. As writers staged scenes of creation—portrait painting or the production of automata—the question of the artist as single father challenged and repudiated the metaphor of birth as natural conception. The work of creation became an agony of labor. Virginia Woolf once remarked: "Novels are such clumsy and half extinct monsters at the best."[31] As science slowly "naturalized" monstrosities as variations of nature while maintaining its uniqueness through the development of the separate field of teratogeny, literature offered its own metaphor of monstrous conception, its version of a teratological tradition that had intimately associated art and progeny, albeit monstrous, through centuries of ceaseless inquiry into the role of imagination in the creative process.

Part II

Metaphors of Procreation

A man with a head in his belly,
from Ambroise Paré, *Des monstres et prodiges*, 1573.

The changing world of science was much more familiar to the literary world than we often remember. To mention only the French, Balzac dedicated *Le père Goriot* to Geoffroy Saint-Hilaire; Villiers de l'Isle-Adam followed the scientific discoveries of his time; and echoes of the new science of heredity structure many of Zola's works. But although the values underlying the Romantic metaphor of procreation are at times strikingly similar to those explicitly discussed in the practice of teratogeny, most tales of singular procreation precede the work of Camille Dareste by many years. Rather than the model for Romantic art, Dareste was science's own Romantic failure.

The following chapters illustrate the ways in which Romanticism, duplicating in its own terms the field of teratogeny, turned to tales of monstrosity to emphasize the uniqueness of its art.[1] The belief that the mother could imprint on the child she was carrying the mark of her wildest desires continued to be documented, mostly in popular culture, where it still is found today. But Romanticism did more than depict the fate of the maternal *vis imaginativa;* it reflected on the dark desire to reproduce without the other and rehabilitated the resulting monstrosity as a troubling but unique work of art.[2]

Thus the chapters in Part II tell a double story: that of a genesis, the anguish of procreation, and that of a monstrous progeny. *Frankenstein* is the best-known and most familiar of all tales of monstrous births. A productive line of inquiry has shown how *Frankenstein* dismisses the maternal element in its display of a motherless creation. I argue that, although the demon's conception dispenses with the maternal body, the novel, Mary Shelley, and her readers all have worked to erase the *paternal* image, to dispel the disquieting presence of a silent father. In this sense, *Frankenstein* may be seen as the last and most forceful example of the tradition that associated monstrous births with the erasure of the legitimate father's image.

Hawthorne, Poe, and Balzac, among others, reflected explicitly on the strange and monstrous quality of perfect reproduction. Reconsidering the power and deceptive character of similarities, they wrote about contrived genesis and the ambiguous nature of artificial resemblances. I have explored how this notion of art frames and subverts an Oedipal crisis that restores the powers of monstrous procreation to a lone father. But this subversion does not involve a simple shifting from the maternal to the paternal. It also entails a crisis in filiation, one that echoes the authors' troubled relationship to writing itself.

If success can be measured by the endurance of a work of art, Marie Tussaud may be both the most successful and the most neglected of all Romantic artists. The Wax Museum's attempts to reproduce lifelike images have generated the recognizable feeling of Romantic horror associated with monstrous reproductions. A closer examination of what a critic has called the Museum's "embryo," the Chamber of Horrors, reveals that Marie Tussaud, its singular inventor, carried her art to some of the excesses already explored by Frankenstein, finding the material for her museum in the charnel houses of England or the cemeteries of the French Revolution. Her practice of wax modeling added a complex dimension to the relationship between the work of art and its dead model, giving monstrosity a powerful political meaning. As a female artist—and this is not the least of the paradoxes of her extraordinary life—she both erased and claimed the role of the father in art. Far from rehabilitating the maternal body, Tussaud's work displays a troubled glorification of patrimony: in its monstrous womb, it displays a criminal progeny absolved by an all-powerful king.

Villiers de l'Isle-Adam chose a modern scientist as the hero of *L'Eve future*. Edison's creation may be seen as yet another metaphor for the work of art: the scientist produces a perfect female as intelligent as she is beautiful, but also sterile and doomed to an early death. As he devises his new Eve piece by piece, Edison demonstrates an explicit understanding of the tradition that attributed monstrous birth to the maternal imagination. But in Edison's economy of uncanny resemblances perfection itself, the ultimate erasure of an imperfect genitor, testifies to the monstrous nature of ideal beauty.

Early in the twentieth century, an Austrian-German author, Gustav Meyrink, wrote his own version of the old Jewish legend of the golem, the most ancient story of male creation, in which a rabbi animates a statue of clay by the use of words or letters. Meyrink gave new life to tales of artificial birth by writing the story from the point of view of the created subject, the golem himself. In his novel, the golem, subjected to the anguish of being born and the cryptic blessing of a surrogate father, bears the scars of the mother's loss. A vertiginous sequence of violent acts sanctions the murderous desire to reproduce alone and art itself becomes the agent of judicial retribution.

In their assessment of procreation all these artists commented on the tradition that endowed the maternal imagination with the power to create unique, if doomed, progeny. By writing about monstrous births, they also staged their own desire to create alone what no one else would or could produce. Beyond the desire to do away with the other, the artists' works convey that in their attempt to procreate they strive to produce not life itself, but a lifelikeness that no one can imitate precisely because it is *not* life itself. This lifelike image is the unique, fragile, unviable creation of a lonely genitor: it is a work of art.

In this context, the word "monster" takes on yet another series of meanings. As it had in the past, it designates progeny born from an unusual conception. But the reappropriation specific to Romanticism, the father's assumption of the maternal role in procreation, is a crime worthy of a double punishment: the birth of a hideous or doomed creature, the fateful work of art, on the one hand; and the monster's repudiation of its genitor on the other. This ultimate repudiation, a challenge to the father himself, takes on various forms—from the monster's explicit accusation of Frankenstein's failed paternity to Madame Tussaud's symbolic effigies of regicides/parricides in the Chamber of Horrors. Monstrosity always reveals a truth. In earlier times it disclosed the secret longings of pregnant women; and in Romanticism it reveals the very desire Diderot dared not make explicit in his *Eléments de physiologie*—the desire to do away with the mother herself. This desire, however, never leads to a simple repudiation. Rather, it yields an incestuous anguish mingled with the suspicion that the artist himself was born from a woman who considered images with a fateful admiration. Thus is art conceived.

6

Unwonted Paternity: The Genesis
of *Frankenstein*

Mary Shelley's novel, *Frankenstein or the Modern Prometheus,* was published in 1818, almost fifty years after Lazzaro Spallanzani's first attempt to produce artificial fertilization.[1] By the time of the book's publication, medical investigation into generation had shifted its emphasis from the mother's influence and experience to the lone scientist experimenting in his laboratory. In a way, the story of *Frankenstein* forecast the new form of science that culminated in the strange figure of Camille Dareste, the teratogenist. More recent readings of the text have emphasized its autobiographical character: the dramatic story of a monstrous birth seems to echo Mary Shelley's own tragic experience of maternity. She had lost a first child; her second child, William, was with her in Switzerland when the novel was begun; and she was pregnant again by the time the novel was completed. Her complicated family life, the subject of scandal for her contemporaries, was one that readers found illustrated or thinly disguised under her pen. But more troubling and more scandalous still was the description in *Frankenstein* of the murder of a young boy named William, who is described in terms reminiscent of Mary Shelley's own son. Thus not only did the novel describe the genesis of a monster, but it was itself proclaimed a monstrosity. Mary Shelley wrote in her Preface of 1831 this emblematic sentence: "I bid my monstrous progeny go forth and prosper. I have an affection for it, for it was the offspring of happy days."[2] The monster and the novel duplicate each other, both designated by the pronoun "it." But while the monster's fictive genesis is painful and tormented by troubled desires, the writing of the novel was perceived as the child of happier times.

Rather than inaugurating a new literary trend or foretelling a new way of creating life, *Frankenstein* plays a pivotal role in a tradition that had long perceived procreation as a work of art. For centuries, monstrosities had tragically illustrated the limits of the mother's imaginative talents, talents that produced horrible likenesses—eikastiken art—without ever mastering the art of resemblances—phantastiken art. Rather than the prototype of a new genre, *Frankenstein* may be seen as the last and most powerful illustration of eikastiken art, art without art. The birth of Frankenstein's monster is the last instance of parental singularity and of wild likeness obscurely moved by hideous desires. The genesis of Victor's monster offers no radically new vision either of imagination or of progeny but the question of resemblance assumes new urgency as the novel demonstrates that similarities, rather than differences, disclose the greatest monstrosity.

The idea that a father by himself should have the power to give life, albeit monstrous life, is an ancient theme powerfully embodied in the Jewish legend of the golem.[3] It could be said that Victor Frankenstein's creation is both a distant echo of the possibility of creating a golem and a prophetic image of the teratogenist scientist. But above all, the novel reenacts on its own terms the all-important question of imagination and portraiture.

Motherhood

At the beginning of the novel, Victor Frankenstein describes his fiancée, his cousin Elizabeth, in a most curious manner: "The world . . . to her it was a vacancy, which she sought to people with imaginations of her own" (p. 30). Elizabeth, it could be said, is pregnant with imaginary visions that give life to the emptiness of her world. If her behavior betrays a desire for motherhood, this desire relies on the very function that tradition credited with monstrous births. While Victor reads, Elizabeth studies drawing and thus becomes closely tied to the fatal power of images. But Victor imitates her metaphorically: "In *drawing the picture* of my early days," he writes, "I must not omit to record those events which led, by insensible steps, to my after tale of misery" (p. 32, emphasis added). The monster's birth is anticipated by another one as frightening and horrible—the birth of a passion. "When I would account to myself for the birth of that passion, which afterwards ruled my destiny, I find it arise like a mountain river, from ignoble and almost forgotten sources; but, swelling as it proceeded, it became the torrent which, in its course, has swept away all my hopes and joys" (p. 32). The object of this passion born of ignominy, aroused from unfathomable depths, is science. Science, like images, proves that the representation of nature, whether pictorial or symbolic, should not be substituted for nature itself. The natural object of Victor's passion is meant to be Elizabeth; any form of substitution will lead to disaster.

Victor's new passion is born and grows when he refuses Elizabeth and travels far from home as if to protect himself better from her influence. Just as there were both good uses of images and idolatrous excess, there are good ways of reading books (illustrated by the fatherly professorial characters of Krempe and Woldman) as well as the perverse fascination for texts that is represented in Victor's education by the choice of "useless" works and by the terrible effects of these works on a passionate imagination. It is no surprise that all the authors Victor first selects—Agrippa, Paracelsus, Albertus Magnus—wrote on questions of generation and monstrosity. Further, Paracelsus' theory that the propagation of serious epidemics such as the plague is an effect of imagination, and more particularly of women's imagination, is also illustrated in *Frankenstein* as the monster, the product of Victor's imagination and itself a modern plague, carries death and destruction wherever he goes. But this first stage of Victor's monstrous creative process, fascination with books, produces no progeny; it only serves to fire his imagination. Before the monster is born another event takes place, also marked by contagion: Elizabeth contracts a mild case of scarlet fever and infects Victor's mother, who dies.

The mother, the model of natural procreation, is buried and her death quickly dismissed by the narrator; yet it remains an underlying factor in the sequence of disasters that will destroy Victor's family and seal his fate as well. Victor refuses, with a strange admission, to fulfill his mother's last desire—that he should marry Elizabeth: "The time at length arrives, when grief is rather an indulgence than a necessity; and the smile that plays upon the lips, although it may be deemed a sacrilege, is not banished" (p. 38). Victor's sacrilegious repression of his mother's death opens the way for his equally sacrilegious enterprise, his own "motherhood." The terms of this lengthy process of conception are by now strikingly familiar: "I determined thenceforth to apply myself more particularly to those branches of natural philosophy which relate to physiology. The event of these inquiries interested my understanding, I may say my *imagination,* until I was exalted to a kind of transport" (p. 46, emphasis added). Critics have examined Victor's metaphoric "pregnancy" down to the smallest detail: from "days and nights of incredible labour and fatigue" (p. 47) to the approximately nine months of gestation: "Winter, spring, and summer, passed away during my labour" (p. 51). From the moment of "conception" Victor is physically changed: "My cheek had grown pale with study, and my person had become emaciated" (p. 49). But above all, the conception of Victor's creation bears the mark of his fevered imagination: "My imagination was too much exalted by my first success to permit me to doubt of my ability to give life to an animal as complex and wonderful as man" (p. 48). Nor does imagination cease to haunt him in the long preparation for the birth of the monster: "My employment, loathsome in itself . . . had taken an irresistible hold of my imagination" (p. 50).

Not surprisingly, Victor's first reaction when initially faced with his monstrous offspring is one of aesthetic shock, the sense of having failed in an important artistic endeavor: "How can I describe my emotions at this catastrophe, or how delineate the wretch whom with such infinite pains and care I had endeavoured to form? His limbs were in proportion, and I had selected his features as beautiful. Beautiful!—Great God!" (p. 52). Frankenstein has thus reproduced the eikastiken art of the monstrous mother, that is, art without interpretation, without proportion or the necessary betrayal of the model that makes the phantastiken object unfaithful to nature but at the same time aesthetically beautiful. And just as the monster had been the visible image of its mother's obscure desires, so Victor's monster is the reproduction of his most profound aspirations: "I had desired it with an ardour that far exceeded moderation; but now that I had finished, the beauty of the dream vanished, and breathless horror and disgust filled my heart" (pp. 52–53). But what specific model could have made such an impression on Victor's imagination as to shape this hideous progeny? The answer is provided in the scene immediately following the monster's birth when Victor, overwhelmed by emotion, falls asleep and has the following dream: "I thought I saw Elizabeth, in the bloom of health, walking in the streets of Ingolstadt. Delighted and surprised, I embraced her; but as I imprinted the first kiss on her lips, they became livid with the hue of death; her features appeared to change, and I thought that I held the corpse of my dead mother in my arms; a shroud enveloped her form, and I saw the grave-worms crawling in the folds of the flannel" (p. 53). In its own way, this dream retells the genesis of Victor's creation. Victor sees himself holding his mother, first disguised as Elizabeth, and then holding the monstrous corpse that issued from their incestuous embrace.

The monster is nothing but "the demoniacal corpse to which I had so miserably given life" (p. 53), notes Victor. His passion for books and for words has been replaced by the haunting image of his dead mother. Or rather, his passion for books had masked another passion now fully disclosed by the birth of a monster. The ultimate model for Victor's monster has been his mother. The monster's "straight black lips" recall the lips that "became livid with the hue of death" as soon as Victor kissed them in his dream. By creating a monster from stolen corpses Victor is obscurely attempting to resuscitate the mother whose death he had sacrilegiously forgotten. And by "giving birth," as many critics have shown, Victor is also taking the place of his mother. The first image in the dream, however, is that of Elizabeth. Only when Victor kisses her is she transformed into his dead mother. The dream also recalls that Elizabeth ultimately caused his mother's death. That Elizabeth brings death rather than life may also explain Frankenstein's visible repulsion toward his cousin and his own desire to give life without a woman. The thinly disguised incestuous embrace revealed by the dream thus elucidates the genesis of the monster, inspired by Frankenstein's desire for his mother as well as his desire to be like his mother. Commenting on this passage, Mary Jacobus writes, "The composite image, mingling eroticism and the horror of corruption, transforms Frankenstein's latently incestuous brother-sister relationship with Elizabeth into the forbidden relationship with the mother . . . Elizabeth in turn comes to represent not the object of desire but its death."[4] Finally, both experiences—the demise of Victor's mother and his own "delivery"—are innocently linked in a letter from Elizabeth: "Surely, Victor, you must have been exceedingly ill; and this makes us all very wretched, as much so nearly as after the death of your dear mother" (p. 59).

Portraits

Portraits of the dead mother play a significant role in *Frankenstein*. The monster, possibly believing that Victor's young brother is his son, kills the boy and steals the precious miniature portrait he was carrying. "[Elizabeth] told me," writes Frankenstein's father, "that that same evening William had teazed her to let him wear a very valuable miniature that she possessed of your mother. This picture is gone, and was doubtless the temptation which urged the murderer to the deed" (pp. 67–68). Again, Elizabeth has been the unwitting agent of death and acknowledges her deed readily when she exclaims: "O God! I have murdered my darling infant!" (p. 67). Although the portrait did not cause William's death, it had fascinated the monster, who later confesses:

> As I fixed my eyes on the child, I saw something glittering on his breast. I took it; it was a portrait of a most lovely woman. In spite of my malignity, it softened and attracted me. For a few moments I gazed with delight on her dark eyes, fringed by deep lashes, and her lovely lips; but presently my rage returned: I remembered that I was for ever deprived of the delights that such beautiful creatures could bestow; and that she whose resemblance I contemplated would, in regarding me, have changed that air of divine benignity to one expressive of disgust and affright. (p. 139)

In this seminal scene, inasmuch as Victor's mother served as a model for this monstrous progeny, the monster is contemplating the uncorrupted image of his own misshapen form. But in the miniature the mother's image is preserved from the corruption of death and from Victor's desperate attempts to resurrect her. The monster's longing for the possession of the "lovely woman" repeats his maker's incestuous desire. Moreover, the power of images is made more frightening still when the miniature becomes the agent of a second, more horrifying death—that of Justine. Justine was the adopted child who so admired Victor's mother that she became strikingly like her: "[Justine] thought her the model of all excellence, and endeavoured to imitate her phraseology and manners, so that even now she often reminds me of her," notes Elizabeth (p. 61).[5] Justine is thus the living portrait of Victor's mother; she is the successful reincarnation of the maternal ideal. The encounter between the monster—the image of the dead mother—and Justine—the delightful reminder of a youthful mother—is sealed by the precious miniature the monster stole from William. The monster says of Justine: "She was young, not indeed so beautiful as her whose portrait I held, but of an agreeable aspect, and blooming in the loveliness of youth and health. Here, I thought, is one of those whose smiles are bestowed on all but me" (p. 140). The monster faithfully repeats the very words he uttered when looking at the miniature, and his reaction is predictable: "She shall not escape: thanks to the lessons of Felix, and the sanguinary laws of man, I have learned how to work mischief. I approached her unperceived, and placed the portrait securely in the folds of her dress" (p. 140). In Victor's dreams "crawling worms" had been hidden "in the folds of the flannel" that his dead mother wore. Similarly, the portrait signals death for the young woman who so admired Victor's mother that she endeavored to resemble her in every respect.

This purloined portrait serves as a focus for a multiplicity of sometimes contradictory desires. We do not know who made it, but we know that it represents Victor's mother as a young woman. It belongs to Elizabeth, the woman destined to be Victor's bride, and is lent to William, who dies carrying it. The miniature is snatched by the monster, who longs to possess the model who inspired such a beautiful image. It is then hidden by the monster in the folds of Justine's dress while she sleeps. It will ultimately cause her death when she is accused of having killed William in order to possess it. That so petty a motive could be thought to be at the origin of so great a crime (a child's murder) is yet another sign of the power of images in general, and the power of this specific portrait in particular. Significantly, only the monster seems to understand that possessing the miniature is of no value, that if possession of the model could have brought him happiness, the miniature itself serves him best as an agent of death. Just as Victor, moved by the remembrance of his mother, created a horrendous being, the portrait in turn seduces the monster and impels him to commit a hideous crime. But the portrait is only illusion, a memory of an inaccessible maternal figure, and the monster demonstrates the proper use of images when he effectively condemns Justine to die for having stolen the miniature. She is convicted and executed in the most iconoclastic of cities, Geneva. Victor, who had allowed himself a "sacrilegious" smile soon after his mother's death, writes after Justine's execution: "Justine died; she rested; and I was alive. The blood flowed freely in my veins" (p. 85).

The disclosure of the truth, that it was the monster who killed William, takes place during a series of spectacular storms that illuminate a dramatic landscape, defined on one side by the dark slopes of the Jura and dominated on the other by the bright summit of Mont Blanc. "The storm, as is often the case in Switzerland," Victor notes, "appeared at once in various parts of the heavens. The most violent storm hung exactly north of the town, over that part of the lake which lies between the promontory of Belrive and the village of Copêt. Another storm enlightened Jura with faint flashes; and another darkened and sometimes disclosed the Môle, a peaked mountain to the east of the lake" (p. 71). The Môle, alternately revealed and darkened by the storm, overshadows the scene when the monster appears as criminal and simultaneously assumes a masculine identity: the scene when he is born a second time, one could say, both as a man and as a murderer.

But "mole" also refers to a condition associated with pregnancy and is well documented since Antiquity as the cystic transformation of the fetus. In *De Generatione Animalium*, Aristotle notes, "[*Mola uteri*] occurs in women occasionally only, but it does occur in some during pregnancy. They bring forth a '*mola*' . . . In such instances, the objects which make their way out of the body are so hard that it is difficult to cut them into two even by means of an iron edge . . . it looks as though Nature in these cases suffers from some inability, and is unable to complete her work and to bring the process of formation to its consummation."[6] The word "mole" thus describes an inability to fully produce a child and characterizes the generation and delivery of a shapeless body, as if the mother had been incapable of giving birth to a fully formed human being. The mountain bearing this foreboding name overlooks a scene of violence and discovery as Victor, devastated by William's death but unaware of the identity of the murderer, seeks in the bleak and dramatic scenery the echo of his inner torment:

While I watched the storm, so beautiful yet terrific, I wandered on with a hasty step. This noble war in the sky elevated my spirits; I clasped my hands, and exclaimed aloud, "William, dear angel! this is thy funeral, this thy dirge!" As I said these words, I perceived in the gloom a figure which stole from behind a clump of trees near me . . . A flash of lightning illuminated the object, and discovered its shape plainly to me; its gigantic stature, and the deformity of its aspect, more hideous than belongs to humanity, instantly informed me that it was the wretch, the filthy daemon to whom I had given life. What did he there? Could he be (I shuddered at the conception) the murderer of my brother? No sooner did that idea cross my imagination, than I became convinced of its truth; my teeth chattered, and I was forced to lean against a tree for support. The figure passed me quickly, and I lost it in the gloom. Nothing in human shape could have destroyed that fair child. *He* was the murderer! (p. 71)

The phrase "I shuddered at the conception" describes both the genesis of monstrosity and the thought that the monster is a murderer. The scene also describes the monster's rebirth, his coming into the world as a human being rather than a mole; this is eloquently revealed by the change of the pronouns (from *it* to *he*) that describes his newfound virility.

The question is then put to Victor and quickly answered: Is it possible that he might strongly have desired to produce a criminal? Was the murder of William an event obscurely anticipated by his imaginative fever? Barbara Johnson interprets William's death as the expression of so scandalous a desire that it has eluded all examinations of the novel: "It is only recently that critics have begun to see Victor Frankenstein's disgust at the sight of his creation as a study of postpartum depression, as a representation of maternal rejection of a newborn infant, and to relate the entire novel to Mary Shelley's mixed feelings about motherhood . . . The idea that a mother can loathe, fear, and reject her baby has until recently been one of the most repressed of psychoanalytical insights, although it is of course already implicit in the story of Oedipus, whose parents cast him out as an infant to die."[7] While autobiographical readings of the novel raise specific problems, William's murder certainly casts light on both the nature of monstrosity and the nature of the monstrous parent. Victor exclaims, "I considered the being whom I had cast among mankind, and endowed with the will and power to effect purposes of horror, such as the deed which he had now done, nearly in the light of *my own vampire, my own spirit let loose from the grave,* and forced to destroy all that was dear to me" (p. 72, emphasis added). The monster, an explicit image of his genitor's hidden secrets, appears as Victor's alter ego, so similar to his creator that generations of readers have mistaken the name of the father for that of the "son."

The monster's second birth, his newfound identity as a man and as the agent of William's death, also discloses a certain idea of filiation. "My brothers," notes Victor, "were considerably younger than myself" (p. 30), and William being the youngest of the two could easily be mistaken for Victor's own son. William tells the monster: "My papa is a Syndic—he is M. Frankenstein—he would punish you . . . Frankenstein!" Replies the monster, "You belong then to my enemy—to him towards whom I have sworn eternal revenge; you shall be my first victim" (p. 139). There is a suggestion, then, that William could have been murdered for seeming to be Victor's son, just as Justine was finally executed because she was like William's mother. Elizabeth writes, "If she could have committed the crime for which she suffered, assuredly she would have been the most depraved of human creatures. For the sake of a few jewels, to have murdered the son of her benefactor and friend, a child whom she had nursed from its birth, and appeared to love *as if it had been her own!*" (p. 88, emphasis added). Justine's execution is justified on grounds of both idolatry and infanticide, the very crimes attributed to the monstrous mother of the Renaissance, who, through her love of a portrait, erased from her progeny the legitimate traits of her husband, destroying the life of the child she was carrying. Just as the legitimate child was sacrificed by the mother who produced instead a monstrous being, so was William, the "legitimate" resemblance of Victor, erased to make way for the monstrous progeny, the newfound son.

"My Father's Desire"

Another painting plays a peculiar role in the novel. Described by Victor when he returns home after William's death, this large canvas represents Victor's mother lamenting the death of her own father:

> Six years had elapsed, passed as a dream but for one indelible trace, and I stood in the same place where I had last embraced my father before my departure for Ingoldstadt. Beloved and respectable parent! He still remained to me. I gazed on the picture of my mother, which stood over the mantlepiece. It was an historical subject, *painted at my father's desire,* and represented Caroline Beaufort in an agony of despair, kneeling by the coffin of her dead father. Her garb was rustic, and her cheek pale; but there was an air of dignity and beauty, that hardly permitted the sentiment of pity. Below this picture was a miniature of William; and my tears flowed when I looked upon it. (p. 73, emphasis added)

The painting is remarkable on several accounts: it contrasts with William's miniature both in its size and in the feelings it evokes in the beholder. The canvas representing Victor's mother when she was still Caroline Beaufort had been painted at the request of Victor's father and expresses in many ways his troubled desires. We are told that he had decided on the subject to be represented: his future wife in despair, kneeling by a representation of her father as corpse. The choice of this morbid scene, the portrait of a spouse in such pain that her life is actually in danger—"in agony"—casts a curious light on the otherwise benevolent image of Victor's father. It suggests, among other things, that first and foremost Victor's father loved the young Caroline as a suffering daughter, perhaps even because of her suffering. The tale of their wedding is as curious as that of the painting itself and may be metaphorically represented in the painting as well. Victor's father and Beaufort were of the same age and had been close friends: "My father loved Beaufort with the truest friendship, and was deeply grieved by his retreat in these unfortunate circumstances. He grieved also for the loss of his society" (p. 28). Hoping to persuade Beaufort to accept his help, he arrives at his friend's home too late and discovers the scene he will wish to remember in the painting: "[Caroline] knelt by Beaufort's coffin, weeping bitterly, when my father entered the chamber" (p. 28). Although Victor's father is as old as Caroline's, he decides, following her loss, to marry her. "It was not until the decline of life that he thought of marrying," notes Victor (p. 27).

The painting commissioned by Victor's father perpetuates not only the scene when he saw her again, but also her own suffering and loss. According to Victor's narrative, however, one element has been modified: Caroline's bitter tears have been replaced by an "air of dignity and beauty, that hardly permitted the sentiment of pity" (p. 73). The expression of filial grief prevents the beholder from seeing Caroline as anything but a forlorn daughter. More specifically, the painting, although presumably commissioned at a later time, represses Caroline's identity as spouse or mother. She is entirely absorbed by her grief, yet the austere representation of her pain precludes any feeling of commiseration. The beholder is not invited to share her agony or to feel pity. This representation of self-contained sorrow thus depicts, or repeats, the scene early in the novel in which Victor's father decided to marry Caroline Beaufort. The canvas, painted as Victor's father desired, also embodies an image of Caroline Beaufort as forever mourning the loss of a father, grieving over the death of the man who would be replaced by Victor's father: "He came like a protecting spirit to the poor girl, who committed herself to his care, and after the interment of his friend he conducted her to Geneva, and placed her under the protection of a relation. Two years after this event Caroline became his wife" (p. 28). The presence of the painting not only makes it impossible for Caroline Beaufort to forget her father's death or the man who came to take his place—that is, her husband—but also makes it impossible to think of her as a mother. She is portrayed primarily as a daughter in a state of deep agony at her father's deathbed. Whereas the miniature William later wore around his neck evokes the beautiful young mother, this painting of self-absorption reminds the beholder that filial grief presided over Caroline's life as a determining element of her destiny.

The scene illustrated by the canvas is reproduced several other times in the course of the novel, replayed by different characters arrested in the same position of distress and mourning. The painting becomes emblematic of all present and future deaths. Forced to confront the death of his best friend, Clairval, Victor writes, "I entered the room where the corpse lay, and was led up to the coffin. How can I describe my sensations on beholding it? I feel yet parched with horror, nor can I reflect on that terrible moment without shuddering and agony, that faintly reminds me of the an-

guish of the recognition" (p. 173). This "anguish of recognition"
certainly alludes to the monster's role in Clairval's death—his signature—but throwing himself on the coffin Victor reenacts the
painting's subject "in an agony of despair": "I gasped for breath;
and, throwing myself on the body, I exclaimed, 'Have my murderous machinations deprived you also, my dearest Henry, of life?'"
(p. 174). Another scene of recognition takes place at the same
time: Henry, who had so resembled Victor in life, in death becomes
the very picture of the monster. Victor notes, "The cup of life was
poisoned for ever; and although the sun shone upon me, as upon
the happy and gay of heart, I saw around me nothing but a dense
and frightful darkness, penetrated by no light but the glimmer of
two eyes that glared upon me. Sometimes they were the expressive
eyes of Henry, languishing in death, the dark orbs nearly covered
by the lids, and the long black lashes that fringed them; sometimes
it was the watery clouded eyes of the monster, as I first saw them in
my chamber at Ingolstadt" (pp. 179–180).

Similarly, when Elizabeth dies Victor writes, "I still hung over
her in an agony of despair" (p. 193), just as Caroline Beaufort "in
an agony of despair" had knelt by her dead father. But as was the
case with Henry, the face of the monster is superimposed on the
face of the victim, already hidden by "a handkerchief thrown
across her face and neck" (p. 193; a probable allusion to Rousseau's
Julie). Victor immediately "saw at the open window a figure the
most hideous and abhorred" (p. 194). But these repetitions of the
deathbed scene constitute an important reversal. Each time, Victor
assumes the grieving position of her who was to become his
mother; and each time, the face of the victim is transformed into
the face of the monster, as if the monster were always necessarily in
the position of the dead father, being himself "a spirit let loose
from the grave." The patterns of repetition and duplication characteristic of the novel make these scenes more complex still. It is
fairly obvious since the "birth" of the monster that Victor has not
given life; rather he has given birth to death, by animating not just
a corpse but a corpse that would bring death wherever he went.

The painting showing Victor's mother grieving over her lost father is thus reenacted with the image of the monster systematically
taking the place of the dead father, both as a reminder of his origin
and as the agent of all possible losses. Victor's position is also

marked by a series of shifting reflections: he assumes the kneeling position of his grieving mother, that is, the position of one who has lost a father; at the same time, he appears to lament the loss of someone who suddenly assumes the physical appearance of his own creation, of his progeny. In a sense, the enduring cause of Victor's grief is his failed maternity/paternity. He is lamenting only his incapacity to give life, to be a father. This may be why the victims are so quickly forgotten: their loss is less painful than Victor's permanent mourning. A sacrilegious smile erases superficially the dead mother; the blood of life erases Justine's death. Victor says of his father, he "could not live under the horrors that were accumulated around him . . . he died in my arms" (p. 196).

The last scene of the novel gives the painting its full signification. In that scene, the monster bends over Victor's dead body and succeeds in fulfilling the destiny of progeny: to weep over the death of a parent. Just as Caroline Beaufort before him had grieved over her father's death in an "agony of despair," the "daemon" exclaims, "Do you think that I was then dead to agony and remorse?" (p. 217). The monster finally accomplishes what Victor had been unable to do: he cries over his genitor's demise, giving vent to filial despair rather than erasing the loss with a blasphemous smile. The monster's promise that he will kill himself also fulfills the painting's implicit question: how can one survive one's parents if not through a father's misguided desires? Victor's father had fixed Caroline Beaufort's grief forever on canvas and had at the same time precluded all feeling of compassion for her loss by having her painted with an air of dignity "that hardly permitted the sentiment of pity." Victor may be thought to have erased his mother's death by giving birth to a dead body, perpetuating both the fact of death and the troubling desire to create life after a parent's demise.

Frankenstein is a tale of disrupted filiation, a story grounded in the belief that it is sacrilegious to give birth when death surrounds us. Further, the story is framed by a series of narratives: Walton's letters, which contain Victor's own tale and within which the monster's confession is almost a complete novel in itself. This specific literary organization, characteristic of many early nineteenth-century stories,[8] is a literal reproduction of the theory of *emboîtement* or *encasement*, the theory that posited that all future generations were contained in the seed of our first parents and that there would come a time when the last man or woman would be born. Thus each new life is also one less life to be counted toward future generations, since the total number of beings is finite and has been predetermined since the beginning of time. In a sense, the monster represents the last of the "human" beings or perhaps prefigures how the human race will end. *Frankenstein* opens and closes in a landscape of frozen immensities, in an echo of the belief, common at the beginning of the nineteenth century, that the world would end in a sea of ice.

The frozen plains of the North Pole serve as a metaphor for the demise of life in general and more specifically of the human race on the planet. Yet the fascination with the North Pole that evokes both the desire to explore new territories and an obsession with entropy is also expressed in terms reminiscent of the art of painting. Before meeting Frankenstein, Walton, who is attempting to reach the North Pole, writes to his sister to describe the loneliness of the landscape, the daunting aspect of those "icy climes," and his ambition to accomplish the miraculous exploit of finding an open passage near the Pole. The "Northeast passage" was to be the goal of many nineteenth-century travelers. The hope of finding an open sea beyond the ice fields, close to the Pole, led to many doomed expeditions, shipwrecks, and extraordinary tales of hardship, ice storms, northern lights, mutiny, and death before the Northeast Passage was actually found by Nils Nordenskjöld in 1878. Walton writes to his sister:

> I try in vain to be persuaded that the pole is the seat of frost and desolation; it ever presents itself to my imagination as the region of beauty and delight. There, Margaret, the sun is for ever visible; its broad disk just skirting the horizon, and diffusing a perpetual splendour. There—for with your leave, my sister, I will put some trust in preceding navigators—there snow and frost are banished; and, sailing over a calm sea, we may be wafted to a land surpassing in wonders and in beauty every region hitherto discovered on the habitable globe. Its productions and features may be without example, as the phaenomena of the heavenly bodies undoubtedly are in those undiscovered solitudes. (pp. 9–10)

Walton's imagination, consistent with many beliefs of the time, persists in picturing the Pole as a sea of fertility, a sea free of ice and rich in undiscovered species. "The sea is the father of monstrosities," a Renaissance writer had noted in his commentary on Pliny.[9] The rich picture provided by Walton's vivid imagination sustains him through days of hardship, but he admits in his letter to his sister: "My day dreams are more extended and magnificent; but they want (as the painters call it) *keeping*" (p. 14). Walton dreams of success, yet acknowledges, "I cannot bear to look on the reverse of the picture" (p. 15). Walton's hopes of finding at the Pole a scene of unsurpassed splendor, rich in life and unknown forms of existence, echo Victor's dream of creating a new form of human being, stronger, taller, more beautiful. At the conclusion of the novel, however, both men suffer a staggering confrontation with "the reverse of the picture": "We are still surrounded by mountains of ice," writes Walton, "still in imminent danger of being crushed in their conflict. The cold is excessive, and many of my unfortunate comrades have already found a grave amidst this scene of desolation" (p. 211). And two days later: "The die is cast; I have consented to return, if we are not destroyed. Thus are my hopes blasted by cowardice and indecision" (p. 213). And on September 12: "I have lost my hopes of utility and glory" (p. 213). "I have lost a friend," he adds, the first intimation that Frankenstein has died. The idea of the Pole as a miracle of fertility rather than a barren expanse of ice and snow is reminiscent of Frankenstein's ambition to be a lone father, to produce life where none seems possible.

The knowledge that led to the monster's birth will remain Frankenstein's secret. Critics were quick to attribute the mystery shrouding the monster's conception to Mary Shelley's lack of interest in scientific matters. Given Mary Shelley's education, such an interpretation can be easily discarded. Frankenstein's deliberate reluctance to disclose the process of procreation reflects the fact that the generation of monsters remains Nature's ultimate secret, never to be shared and impossible to reproduce. Frankenstein, having started work on the production of a female companion to his creation, drowns her before she comes to life. Is he moved by fear or the recognition that a monster is always unique in its absolute difference and can never be duplicated? Walton insists on being told the answer, but Frankenstein refuses to have his secret violated. Walton concedes, "Sometimes I endeavoured to gain from Frankenstein the particulars of his creature's formation; but on this point, he was impenetrable" (p. 207).

Genesis

For many critics, Mary Shelley's celebrated claim in her 1831 Introduction to *Frankenstein,* that she "did not owe the suggestion of one incident, not scarcely of one train of feeling, to [her] husband" settled the much-debated question of the real authorship of *Frankenstein.* Yet, as has been shown, her claim was somewhat inaccurate.

At the time of its publication, *Frankenstein* was believed by many to have been the work of Percy Shelley. It was he who sent the manuscript to Charles Ollier on August 3, 1817 (a letter wrongly dated 1818), with these words: "I send you with this letter a manuscript which has been consigned to my care by a friend in whom I feel considerable interest." [10] On the same day, Percy Shelley wrote an ambiguous declaration to Leigh Hunt: "Bye-the-bye I have sent an MS. to Ollier concerning the true author of which I entreat you to be silent, if you should be asked any questions" (letter 331, p. 237). A few days later, in another letter to Charles Ollier, Percy Shelley asked, "I hope 'Frankenstein' did not give you too bad dreams" (letter 332, p. 238). After Charles Ollier turned down the novel, Shelley sent it to Lackington, Allen and Co. It was apparently accepted as Shelley's own novel and he wrote a letter of clarification on August 22, 1817: "Gentlemen, I ought to have mentioned that the novel which I sent you is not my own production, but that of a friend who not being at present in England cannot make the correction you suggest" (letter 334, p. 240). If by "the true author" Shelley meant Mary, this sentence was, of course, patently untrue, since Mary was staying at Marlow at the time. Shelley, however, became more and more involved in the publication of the novel and revised and corrected the proofs himself after Lackington, Allen and Co. agreed to publish the book. Shelley continued: "As to any mere inaccuracies of language I should feel myself authorized to amend them when revising proofs," which he did (p. 240).

By contrast, Mary Shelley's *Journal* makes few explicit references to the novel and the vagaries of its publication aside from this dry note entered on August 24, 1817: "A letter from Lackington" and a postscript to her September 28, 1817, letter to Shelley: "What of Frankenstein?"[11] Later, on December 3, 1817, Percy Shelley wrote to Lackington: "Gentlemen, Inclosed is a dedication which has been transmitted to me by the author of 'Frankenstein,' and which should be printed as is customary immediately subsequent to the Title" (letter 346, p. 256). The dedication to William Godwin need not be interpreted as evidence of Mary Shelley's absolute creative control over the novel, since it came after an uncharacteristic reconciliation between her husband and her father. Indeed, the dedication follows an unusually affectionate letter from Percy Shelley to William Godwin (letter 345, December 1, p. 255) and precedes another warm and considerate message, dated December 7 (letter 349, pp. 258–260).

The first direct allusion to Mary Shelley's participation in the novel that Percy Shelley had handed to the publishers is found in his letter of December 16, 1817, to Thomas Moore, in which he discusses the recent and anonymous publication of the *Journal of a Six Weeks' Tour,* adding: "[Mrs Shelley] has another literary secret which I will in a short time ask you to *keep* in return for having *discovered* this" (letter 354, p. 270).

Even though *Frankenstein* had been rejected by Charles Ollier, Percy Shelley addressed a copy of the novel to him on January 2, 1818: "I send a copy of Frankenstein to be bound for me in some neat and appropriate binding . . . I should like to hear your opinion of Frankenstein" (letter 360, p. 277). The same day Percy Shelley requested additional copies of *Frankenstein* from Lackington, Allen and Co. "which may be placed to mine or to the author's account, as you please" (letter 361, p. 278). This request is curious indeed in that Percy Shelley had no other account with Lackington than *Frankenstein.* Visibly eager to have reactions to the novel, Shelley wrote to Charles Ollier again on January 15, 1818: "Do you hear anything said of 'Frankenstein?'" (letter 364, p. 280).

Frankenstein was an instant popular success but received mixed critical reviews. Although Walter Scott wrote a favorable account of the novel (and thought Percy Shelley was the author), the *Quarterly Review* published a devastating review of the book in January 1818:

Our taste and judgment alike revolt at this kind of writing, and the greater ability with which it may be executed the worse it is

... The author has powers, both of conception and language, which employed in a happier direction might, perhaps, (we speak dubiously,) give him a name among those whose writings amuse or amend their fellow-creatures; but we take the liberty of assuring him, and hope that he may be in a temper to listen to us, that the style which he has adopted in the present publication merely tends to defeat his own purpose, if he really had any other object in view than that of leaving the wearied reader, after a struggle between laughter and loathing, in doubt whether the head or the heart of the author be the most diseased.[12]

The public thought at this point that Percy Shelley had written the novel and Shelley lost no time disengaging himself from any responsibility for the much-criticized book. Thus, in a letter of April 30, 1818, to Lord Byron, he wrote, "I am commissioned by an old friend of yours to convey 'Frankenstein' to you, and to request that if you conjecture the name of the author, that you will regard it as a secret. In fact, it is Mrs S's. It has met with considerable success in England; but she bids me say, 'That she would regard your approbation as a more flattering testimony of its merit'" (letter 378, p. 305). Shelley's deliberate revelation comes at a time when he was being personally attacked as the author of the novel. Another letter, dated July 25, 1818, and written from Bagni di Lucca to Thomas Love Peacock, notes in a more sober style: "'Frankenstein' seems to have been well received; for although the unfriendly criticism of the *Quarterly* is an evil for it, yet it proves that it is read in some considerable degree, and it would be difficult for them with any appearance of fairness, to deny it merit altogether. Their notice of me, and their exposure of the true motives for not noticing my book, shews how well understood an hostility must subsist between me and them" (letter 384, p. 315). What is remarkable in this letter is that Shelley does not disclaim authorship as he had in his letter to Byron. The same day, he sends a more direct appreciation of the critical attack to William Godwin: "I hear that poor Mary's book, 'Frankenstein,' is attacked most violently in the Quarterly review. We have heard some praise of it, and among others an article of Walter Scott's in Blackwood's Magazine" (letter 385, p. 318).

Thus began the publishing history of one of the most mysterious literary procreations of the nineteenth century. While Percy Shel-

ley was busily arranging the details of publication, correcting the
proofs and anxiously awaiting his friends' reactions, Mary Shelley
seems to have been eerily detached from the fate of her novel. Neither the *Journal* nor her correspondence enlighten us as to her
emotions while she wrote the novel and saw its immediate popular
success. It is remarkable that the novel in which she later claimed
to have invested so much of herself elicited so little comment in her
Journal. Most of the *Journal*'s entries shed no light on how *Frankenstein* came into being. What the *Journal* does reveal, however, is that
most of the readings done by Victor Frankenstein were in fact
books that Percy Shelley, rather than Mary, was reading at the time
the novel was conceived.[13] Although there is very little mention of
the novel in the *Journal,* an enigmatic entry for Saturday, January
25, 1817, reads: "An unhappy day—I receive bad news and determine to go up to London" (p. 156). This is possibly the first indica-
tion that she was pregnant again.

The most significant entry of the *Journal,* one often quoted but
rarely adequately discussed, was written on Wednesday, May 14,
1817: "S. reads Hist of Fr. Rev. and corrects F. write Preface—Fi-
nis" (p. 169). As the editors discreetly point out by quoting Mary
Shelley's 1831 Introduction to *Frankenstein,* this detail flagrantly
contradicts Mary's later claim: "I certainly did not owe the suggestion of one incident, nor scarcely of one train of feeling, to my
husband, and yet but for his incitement, it would never have taken
the form in which it was presented to the world. From this declaration I must except the preface. As far as I can recollect, it was
entirely written by him."[14] Not only did Percy Shelley have more to
do with the novel than Mary Shelley later claimed, but the words
"write Preface" cannot possibly refer to Percy Shelley as a single
subject. However poor Mary Shelley's spelling was—and it was no-
toriously poor—this is not one of her usual mistakes. What the
Journal states most clearly, then, is that *she* did write the Preface, or
perhaps that they *both* did.[15] This curious disclaimer should alert
us to the extraordinarily complex genesis of the novel, for this is
only the first in a series of repeated contradictions on the part of
both Percy and Mary Shelley in regard to their roles in the writing
of *Frankenstein.*

Critics have been quick to point out the influence of Rousseau
on *Frankenstein*[16] and more specifically on philosophical questions

raised by the story of Felix and the scene of Elizabeth's death, when Frankenstein rushes to find Elizabeth with "her head upon her arm, and a handkerchief across her face, her neck" (p. 193). This appears to be a direct reference to the scene of Julie's death in *La nouvelle Héloïse*, where Julie lies with a handkerchief covering her deformed face. One of the plates in *La nouvelle Héloïse* shows Saint-Preux rushing to Julie and attempting to lift the veil.[17] From this point of view, it is important to note that according to Mary Shelley's *Journal* she did not read Rousseau's novel until a month *after Frankenstein* was finished. "Read Tacitus and Julie," she writes on Friday, June 27, 1817 (p. 175). But during the crucial summer of 1816 Percy Shelley was reading *La nouvelle Héloise* and was immersed in Rousseau when the idea of *Frankenstein* was first discussed. He wrote to Thomas Love Peacock on July 12, 1816:

> It is nearly a fortnight since I have returned from Vevai. This journey has been on every account delightful, but most especially, because then I first knew the divine beauty of Rousseau's imagination, as it exhibits itself in "Julie" . . . I read "Julie" all day; an overflowing, as it now seems, surrounded by the scenes which it has so wonderfully peopled, of sublimest genius, and more than human sensibility . . . I never felt more strongly than on landing at Clarens, that the spirit of old times had deserted its once cherished habitation . . . I forgot to remark, what indeed my companion [Byron] remarked to me, that our danger from the storm took place precisely in the spot where Julie and her lover were nearly overset, and where St. Preux was tempted to plunge with her into the lake. (letter 295, pp. 167–175)

This testimony is useful because, although Percy Shelley's contributions to *Frankenstein* have been carefully documented from the two manuscripts now on deposit at the Bodleian Library, from changes of words to discussions of longer episodes, little attention has been paid to Percy Shelley's more general literary influence on the novel. Furthermore, while the influence of Rousseau on *Frankenstein* has been examined as well, it has generally been assumed that this influence was due to Mary Shelley's reading of Rousseau, in spite of her own acknowledgment that she had not even started reading the crucial *La nouvelle Héloïse* by the time she finished writing *Frankenstein*.[18]

In his edition of the 1818 *Frankenstein*, James Rieger notes:

What has not been generally known is that Shelley oversaw his wife's manuscript at every stage. Not only did he correct her frequent grammatical solecisms, her spelling, and her awkward phrasing; the surviving manuscript fragments show marginal suggestions (all adopted by Mary) for the improvement of the narrative, interpolations that run for several sentences, and final revisions of the last pages. For example, it was Shelley's idea that Frankenstein journey to England for the purpose of creating a female Monster. His words contrast Frankenstein's personality with Elizabeth's and the Swiss republic with less fortunate nations. Most important of all, Shelley revised the ending from the last paragraph of Frankenstein's dying speech . . . to the Monster's disappearance in darkness and distance. Finally, in 1817, he corrected the proofs, with his wife's "carte blanche to make what alterations you please." His assistance at every point in the book's manufacture was so extensive that one hardly knows whether to regard him as editor or minor collaborator. (p. xviii)

Rieger's remarks provoked a debate as to whether the extent of Shelley's contributions indeed qualified him as a minor collaborator. E. B. Murray replied, "Some working writers (one thinks of Thomas Wolfe) do accept enough from creative editors with whom they have a close rapport to justify these latter as 'minor collaborators,' though their names do not appear on the title page, much less their words in a prefatory note."[19] One wonders, of course, why Percy Shelley's collaboration on Mary Shelley's novel seems so difficult to accept in the face of unimpeachable evidence. One of the difficulties, no doubt, lies in what Rieger maintains is "the worst distortion in the 1831 Introduction": the claim that "although Shelley 'incited' Mary in the composition of *Frankenstein*," she did not "owe the suggestion of one incident, nor scarcely of one train of feeling to [her] husband" (p. xvii).

Mary Shelley's thorough denial of any substantial collaboration between Percy and herself may be one of the most provocative elements in the complicated history of *Frankenstein*. Certainly, at one very practical level, she had good reason to claim the third printing of the novel as hers alone. By 1831, she had experienced endless difficulties publishing Percy Shelley's works posthumously. Her recent biographer Emily Sunstein notes: "On July 23 [1824], she was shocked to learn that Sir Timothy was infuriated by *Posthumous Poems* and would terminate her allowance unless she withdrew it from circulation, stopped publication of the prose, and moreover promised not to publish anything by or about Shelley during his own lifetime."[20] Although he had failed to conceal his interest in the novel's fate, Percy Shelley himself had been quite careful not to disclose his own participation in the writing of a text he had judged inferior to his own poetic works. Thus Mary Shelley certainly felt that it was not only prudent but legitimate to present the novel as her own creation. Furthermore, she desperately needed the money that the new edition of the novel, the most successful of her publications, would bring.

What is more interesting, however, is the nature of Percy and Mary Shelley's collaboration. We now know the details of Percy Shelley's annotations, marginal corrections, syntactic changes, semantic choices, and so on. But his participation hardly stopped there. It is curious to find in his earlier correspondence some of the keywords of the novel—words that fail to appear in Mary Shelley's *Journal* or letters of the same period. He wrote on March 16, 1814, to Thomas Jefferson Hogg: "Eliza is still with us—not here!—but will be with me when the *infinite malice* of destiny forces me to depart . . . It is a sight which awakens an inexpressible sensation of *disgust and horror,* to see her caress my poor little Ianthe, in whom I may thereafter find the consolation of sympathy. I sometimes feel faint with the fatigue of checking the overflowings of my *unbounded abhorrence* for this *miserable wretch*" (letter 233, pp. 86–87, emphasis added). This description of Percy Shelley's feelings toward his sister-in-law, Elizabeth Westbrook, is frequently echoed in the novel: "*Abhorred* monster! . . . *Wretched* devil!" (p. 94), full of "malignity" are common expressions describing the monster, who is also frequently called a "wretch" and "a figure the most hideous and abhorred" (p. 194). The monster itself exclaims: "No malignity, no misery, can be found comparable to mine" (p. 219; written in Percy Shelley's own hand on the manuscript).[21] More striking still are some lines from a letter written by Percy Shelley to William Godwin on March 6, 1816, in which Shelley writes from the same perspective the monster was later to adopt toward his creator:

> I lamented also over my ruined hopes, hopes of all that your genius once taught me to expect from your virtue, when I found

that for yourself, your family, and your creditors, you would sub-
mit to that communication with me which you once *rejected and
abhorred,* and which no pity for my poverty or sufferings, assumed willingly for you, could avail to extort. Do not talk of *for-
giveness* [author's emphasis] again to me, for my blood boils in my
veins, and *my gall rises against all that bears the human form,* when I
think of what I, their benefactor and ardent lover, have endured
of enmity and contempt from you and from all mankind. I cannot mix the feelings to which you *have given birth* with details in
answer to your views of my affairs. (letter 277, pp. 145–146, emphasis added)

A few months later, while *Frankenstein* was being written, Percy
Shelley wrote the following lines to Leigh Hunt: "But thus much I
do not seek to conceal from myself, that I am an outcast from human society; my name is execrated by all who understand its entire
import—by those very beings whose happiness I ardently desire. I
am an object of compassion to a few more benevolent than the rest,
all else abhor and avoid me" (letter 310, pp. 208–209, emphasis
added). These words unavoidably call to mind the monster's plea
to Frankenstein: "Believe me Frankenstein: I was benevolent; my
soul glowed with love and humanity: but am I not alone, miserably
alone? *You, my creator, abhor me;* what hope can I gather from your
fellow-creatures, who owe me nothing? They spurn and hate me"
(p. 95, emphasis added). Other letters are equally suggestive; on
January 17, 1817, Percy Shelley wrote to Lord Byron: "My late wife
is dead. The circumstances which attended this event are of a nature of such awful and appalling horror, that I dare hardly avert to
them in thought. The sister of whom you have heard me speak
may be truly said (though not in law, yet in fact) to have murdered
her for the sake of her father's money" (letter 315, p. 218). Em-
broiled in a fight for the custody of his children, Shelley described
to Jane Clairmont "the malice of these monsters" (letter 316, January 30, 1817, p. 220). Shelley sees himself again in the role of the
outcast and the wretch when he writes to Lord Byron, "As to me, I
can but die; I can but be torn to pieces, or devoted to infamy most
undeserved; and whether this is inflicted by the necessity of nature,
and circumstances, or through a principle, pregnant, as I believe,
with important benefit to mankind, is an alternative to which I cannot be indifferent" (letter 337, September 24, 1817, p. 246). The

monster's departing words have precisely this tone, and they were indeed written by Percy Shelley, but the strange similarities between the novel and the correspondence suggest an intellectual affinity and affective involvement much deeper than the simple role of copy editor would entail.

Certainly any analysis of the novel that would make use of biographical elements should take into account the extraordinary scene that took place on an evening in July 1816, on Lake Geneva, when Percy took his wife for a monster with eyes on her breasts and ran screaming from the room. This is how Emily Sunstein describes the episode in *Mary Shelley:* "Keeping up the 'ghostly' tone near the following midnight, Byron recited *Christabel,* to Mary a poeticization of her own childhood situation, but Shelley suddenly 'saw' Mary as the villainess with eyes for nipples (possibly blaming Mary for seducing him from Harriet) and ran screaming out from the room." (p. 122).[22] Another allusion to the scene was published anonymously: "Frankenstein was hatched—the wretch abhorred, / Whom shuddering Sh——saw in horrid dress."[23] "Last names of women were commonly used in such poems," notes Emily Sunstein, interpreting the verses as a description of the conception of *Frankenstein.* These few lines seem instead to be a direct reference to the scene where Percy saw Mary as a monster and ran away screaming. In *Bearing the Word,* Margaret Homans interprets this episode as a manifestation of Percy Shelley's incapacity to reconcile "the ideal of disembodied femininity" with his real lover. She adds, "Mary's sense of herself viewed as a collection of incongruent body parts—breasts terminating in eyes—might have found expression in the demon."[24] The image of eyes in the place of nipples is also suggested in the frightening conclusion of "The Sandman," published by E. T. A. Hoffmann the same year: "At this point Nathaniel saw that a pair of blood-flecked eyes were lying on the floor and staring up at him; Spalanzani seized them with his uninjured hand and threw them at him, so that they struck him in the chest."[25]

Whereas Percy Shelley spoke in his letters with the very voice the monster would later use, with the same *wretchedness,* the character of Elizabeth offers a female version of monstrosity that may well appear as an echo of the "monster in dress" that he saw that evening. Not that Elizabeth necessarily represents the monstrosity Percy saw in Mary, but she may well stand for the monstrosity Mary may have felt in herself after an incident that deeply upset her. Elizabeth carries death: she is the direct cause of the death of Victor's mother; she is an unwitting but real agent of William's murder, a fact she willingly acknowledges ("O God! I have murdered my darling infant!") (p. 67). Victor is strangely reluctant to approach her and postpones their wedding several times, motivated by the fear that the monster will carry out his death threat, but also moved by a stranger and stronger feeling, perhaps best expressed when he says, "As the period fixed for our marriage drew nearer, whether from cowardice or a prophetic feeling, I felt my heart sink within me" (p. 188). Although Victor believes that the death threat is against him, the victim is Elizabeth, and she is the only victim whose death causes no remorse in the monster: "Yet when she died!-nay, then I was not miserable" (p. 218). It is worthy of note that these words were added to the manuscript by Percy Shelley himself.

We know that Percy Shelley was responsible for the contrast between Victor's character and that of Elizabeth. He also suggested that Victor should travel to England to create a female companion for the monster, a suggestion he expressed as follows in a marginal note: "I think the journey to England ought to be Victor's proposal.—that he ought to go for the purpose of collecting knowledge for the formation of a female." [26] The contrast between Victor and Elizabeth and the suggestion that Victor should create a female are not unrelated. Percy Shelley wrote these lines from Victor's tale: "The world was to me a secret, which I desired to discover; to her it was a vacancy, which she sought to people with imaginations of her own" (p. 30). The notions of "vacancy" and of a mind peopled with "imaginations" thus characterize Elizabeth. They also describe her own feminine monstrosity, which is destroyed in the gruesome scene where Frankenstein drowns the "unborn" body of the female he had planned to create for the monster. This scene of destruction is exceptionally violent: "I thought with a sensation of madness on my promise of creating another like to him, and, trembling with passion, tore to pieces the thing on which I was engaged" (p. 164). "The remains of the half-finished creature, whom I had destroyed, lay scattered on the floor, and I almost felt as if I had mangled the living flesh of a human being . . . I felt as if I was about the commission of a dreadful crime, and avoided with shuddering anxiety any encounter with my fellow creatures" (pp. 167–168). This extraordinarily brutal crime is no more than an explicit comment on the nature of the monster itself, perhaps a lasting metaphor for the entire novel. But it is worth noting that this scene was written at the instigation of Percy Shelley and that he himself chose to describe the monster as "an abortion" rather than a "devil."[27] This grisly destruction thus takes on an additional meaning; it is a double rejection of the very idea of reproduction, the most deliberate description of *repulsion* to be found in Romantic fiction. Thus, it would appear that *Frankenstein* was not just an agonized meditation on motherhood, an exploration of the deeply divided feelings a mother could have for her own children, as Barbara Johnson has persuasively argued, but also a more general repudiation of the idea of human procreation. The case is illustrated not only by the birth of the monster, which suggests a repulsion for sexual intercourse as the means of procreation, but also in the scene of hatred for both the female body and the unborn fetus in which Frankenstein destroys and drowns the parts of an "unborn" female. These themes are familiar to critics. From this perspective, the monster's final words, also written by Percy Shelley, offer the strongest image of the Romantic poet as *sterile* monster: "I shall collect my funeral pile, and consume to ashes this miserable frame, that its remains may afford no light to any curious and unhallowed wretch, who would create such another as I have been" (p. 220). The monster is glorified in its uniqueness, as the only such being, incomparable, unnameable, deprived of the possibility of procreating, and determined that it should never be reproduced, that is, duplicated.

Frankenstein is undoubtedly one of the most intriguing examples of literary collaboration, and with the exception of the 1831 Preface and the changes made by Mary Shelley for the third edition, it is impossible to assign with absolute certainty either to Percy or to Mary Shelley *complete* creative responsibility for any part of the novel. Although Margaret Homans does not question Mary Shelley's authorship of the novel, she notes the important influence of Percy Shelley's poem "Alastor" on the book.[28] The themes of pregnancy, procreation, and abortion are not, as we have seen, the exclusive domain of Mary Shelley's writings. Nor can it be asserted that, even having written the powerful conclusion of the novel,

Percy Shelley had the last word. He wrote the dramatic denoue-
ment on the sea of ice that was, for the Romantics, an image of the
future, the frozen landscape of the times to come. But it was Mary
Shelley, in her truly remarkable—if misleading—Preface of 1831,
who gave the novel its most powerful definition, articulating with
rare acuity the dynamics of monstrous creation as a complex metaphor for literary inspiration.[29]

What is remarkable as well is the way both Percy and Mary Shelley skirted the question of the authorship of *Frankenstein*. Percy
Shelley was only too happy to distance himself when the devastating article in the *Quarterly Review* appeared: in the hierarchy of literary genres in early nineteenth-century England, surely the craft
of poetry ranked higher than that of writing horror prose. In a
similar fashion, Byron had been quick to disown *The Vampyre*, in
which the extent of his own participation and that of Polidori were
unclear.[30] Conversely, Mary Shelley was eager to reveal her secret
to Walter Scott, the author of a very favorable review in *Blackmoor
Magazine*, and above all, to dispel the notion that Percy Shelley was
the author of the novel. She wrote on June 14, 1818, from Bagni
di Lucca to Walter Scott:

> Sir, Having received from the publisher of Frankenstein the no-
> tice taken of that work in Blackwood's magasine, and intelligence
> at the same time that it was to your kindness that I owed this
> favourable notice I hasten to return my acknowledgements and
> thanks, and at the same time to express the pleasure I receive
> from approbation of so high a value as yours. Mr Shelley soon
> after its publication took the liberty of sending you a copy but as
> both he and I thought in a manner which would prevent you
> from supposing that he was the author we were surprised there-
> fore to see him mentioned in the notice as the probable author,—
> I am anxious to prevent your continuing in the mistake of sup-
> posing Mr Shelley guilty of a juvenile attempt of mine; to
> which—from its being written at an early age, I abstained from
> putting my name—and from respect to those persons from
> whom I bear it. I have therefore kept it concealed except from a
> few friends. I beg you will pardon the intrusion of this explana-
> tion. (p. 71).

One can only notice the difference in tone between this humble
claim to a novel Walter Scott liked and thought had been written

by Shelley and the rather triumphant, self-assured declaration of authorship in 1831. By 1818, Mary Shelley had surely been made aware of the slightly disreputable character of the novel she and Percy had devised; but by 1831, she was a recognized writer whose early work had enjoyed considerable success. Whether, in both instances, Mary Shelley was moved to conceal her husband's participation in the novel by consideration of his fame as a poet, by the growing difficulties with Percy Shelley's family, or by increasingly urgent financial needs is of little importance to the modern reader. But the fact that she misleadingly laid claim to *sole* authorship of the novel is crucial.

The Fate of Paternity

However complex and intriguing the story of the composition of *Frankenstein* may be, the history of the criticism of *Frankenstein* is more remarkable still, for it casts new light on Romantic and modern concepts of literary progeny. From the very beginning, critical appraisal of the novel seemed to have been inspired in part by the much-criticized lifestyle of the Shelley group, and focused attacks on the presumed author through a severe assessment of the novel. Indeed, for the early critics, as for many recent ones, it was hardly conceivable to comment on *Frankenstein* without discussing the author as well. This was true when the *Quarterly Review,* in the belief that it was Percy Shelley's life and opinions that were being discussed, published these comments: "Our readers will guess from this summary, what a tissue of horrible and disgusting absurdity this work presents.—It is piously dedicated to Mr Godwin, and is written in the spirit of his school . . . His disciples are kind of *outpensioners of Bedlam,* and, like 'Mad Bess' or 'Mad Tom,' are occasionally visited with paroxysms of genius and fits of expression, which make sober-minded people wonder and shudder" (p. 382).

Without retracing the entire critical history of *Frankenstein* we may isolate a few instances of its singularity. For many years following the decline of its popularity, *Frankenstein* was ignored, and if discussed at all, was taken as evidence of the predictable delusions of a predictably unstable woman of only mediocre talent.[31] Even critics more sympathetic to the novel or to Mary Shelley's accomplishments are quick to point out *Frankenstein*'s literary weaknesses.

Robert Kiely notes, "[Mary Shelley's] prose style is solemn, inflated, and imitative, an unhappy combination of Godwin's sentence structure and Shelley's abstract vocabulary."[32] George Levine writes, "Of course, *Frankenstein* is a 'minor' novel, radically flawed by its sensationalism, by the inflexibly public and oratorical nature of even its most intimate passages."[33] Harold Bloom is equally prudent in his estimation of the work: "I am suggesting that what makes *Frankenstein* an important book, though it is only a strong, flawed novel with frequent clumsiness in its narrative and characterization, is that it contains one of the most vivid versions we have of the Romantic mythology of the self."[34]

Yet *Frankenstein* has been rehabilitated for reasons that may be attributed to a certain perception of Mary Shelley's life and misfortunes. Capitalizing on the brilliant Preface of 1831, critics have reconsidered *Frankenstein* as a book inextricably linked to Mary Shelley's personal experiences with maternity. In a ground-breaking analysis, Ellen Moers wrote in *Literary Women:* "*Frankenstein* is a birth myth, and one that was lodged in the novelist's imagination, I am convinced, by the fact that she was herself a mother . . . Death and birth were . . . hideously intermixed in the life of Mary Shelley as in Frankenstein's 'workshop of filthy creation.'"[35] Ellen Moers's analysis provided the starting point for a provocative series of readings associating the questions of motherhood and monstrosity. In *The Madwoman in the Attic,* Sandra Gilbert and Susan Gubar tried to assess *Frankenstein's* literariness by distancing themselves from a purely autobiographical reading: "In making their case for the work as female fantasy, though, critics like Moers have tended to evade the problems posed by what we must define as *Frankenstein's* literariness." But, while making their case for *Frankenstein* as a self-conscious "book about books," Gilbert and Gubar also perpetuate a reading of *Frankenstein* as autobiography. The monster remains "the child of two authors (Victor Frankenstein and Mary Shelley) whose mothers have been stolen away by death," or "Mary's cadaverous creature."[36] Their lucid examination of the "nameless" nature of monstrosity leads them to an evaluation of Mary's personal experience: "Mary knew of the importance of names too. Perhaps most of all, though, Mary's sense of the fearful significance of legitimate and illegitimate names must have been formed by her awareness that her own name, Mary Wollstonecraft Godwin, was absolutely identical with the name of the mother who had died in giving birth to *her*" (p. 242).

The reading of *Frankenstein* as autobiography, as a privileged metaphor for Mary Shelley's textual motherhood, has been of crucial importance in the recent rehabilitation of the novel and the rediscovery of its author. Even critics not directly concerned with Mary Shelley's traumatic experiences of motherhood have been moved to draw convincing parallels between her life and her fiction. "There are strong reasons why Mary Shelley in particular should so firmly identify the anxieties of parenthood with what Harold Bloom (and following him, Gilbert and Gubar) understands as the anxieties of authorship," writes Chris Baldick. "For Mary Shelley such a double anxiety is overdetermined in the first place by her literary parentage and her association with Percy Shelley and Lord Byron."[37]

In the profusion of critical readings, three main lines of interpretation of the novel have emerged: one is represented by Mary Shelley's own description of the text she conceived following a dream; another maintains the traditional view of *Frankenstein* as a mediocre novel written by a self-dramatizing woman; and the last, most recent one, views the story as a complex metaphor for childbirth. What these three interpretations have in common, despite their varying theoretical perspectives, is that although they all are intent on establishing a connection between the text and its author, they all *obliterate* the participation of Percy Shelley and his legitimate contributions to the novel. Mary Shelley's own "disingenuous Preface," to use James Rieger's words, claimed that she did not owe a single idea to her husband. Traditional literary history would not have the name of a respected poet associated with such a disreputable novel. The view that *Frankenstein* can be read as a text about motherhood and literary procreation precludes Percy Shelley's participation as well. All these readings *erase the role of the legitimate father,* the silent father who does not recognize himself, who is not recognized by others, in his monstrous progeny. In this instance, criticism reproduces the very structure of monstrosity. The monstrous progeny is linked to and claimed by its mother as the product of a deranged imagination ("my imagination unbidden possessed me"). At the same time, the legitimate father is replaced by those illegitimate models that so fevered the mother's imagination that she wrote this extraordinary tale, this literary monster, at the age of only eighteen, a feat Robert Martin deems "almost miraculous."

It is nothing short of remarkable that Percy Shelley's participation in the novel has been so consistently overlooked despite the extensive evidence available to all readers and critics.[38] Further, Rieger has proven that the so-called ghost-story contest presented by Mary Shelley as the origin of *Frankenstein* is nothing but fiction. A series of articles have explored in detail the facts surrounding Percy Shelley's important collaboration and specific examples of his contributions. Yet for all this evidence, *Frankenstein* continues to be interpreted almost exactly the way monstrous progeny themselves were evaluated at the time of the Renaissance, that is, as the uncanny procreation of a monstrous mother. Not only is Percy Shelley's role generally ignored, but it is strongly contested by biographers when they necessarily come across some unavoidable evidence of his contribution. The otherwise reliable Emily Sunstein, to give but one example, goes to considerable length to diminish the role of Percy Shelley: "Not all of Shelley's wording is necessarily for the better. Moreover, Mary made her own, often substantive changes in some six hundred places on the extant drafts . . . That Shelley's editing was in no way vital to *Frankenstein* is why Mary did not mention it in her Preface" (*Mary Shelley,* pp. 430–431). In another footnote she comments: "E. B. Murray claims that both Mary and Shelley were intent on keeping Shelley's 'share' in the novel even more secret than her authorship, adducing her discard of a satiric passage about Oxford, which he had attended . . . Mary properly discarded the passage because it was atonal, discursive, and puerile" (p. 433). Finally, the suggestion has recently been made that any attempt to attribute to Percy Shelley part of the authorship of *Frankenstein* is but a gesture of reappropriation by male critics of a successful female production.

Clearly, for such a position to be remotely tenable there must be some assumption that Percy Shelley's contribution to the novel *diminishes* Mary Shelley's accomplishment and casts a shadow on her precocious talent. By implying that a sole author is more deserving than a co-author, such a view rigorously applies the notion of parental singularity to the structure of literary procreation. Moreover, this view presupposes that it is unthinkable for a book about monstrosity—a book called "my monstrous progeny"—to be other than a woman's work; unthinkable, as well, that the author, as its monstrous mother, might be other than the sole progenitor of this unspeakable creation. There is no doubt that at least two critical views—Mary Shelley's own perception and the interpretation of *Frankenstein* as textual autobiography—also rehabilitate monstrosity. But the fact that *critical discourse reappropriates the very structure of monstrosity* also shows how much we are still indebted to the Romantic idea of imagination and progeny.[39] Romanticism's own reappraisal of the monstrous as a metaphor for the *unique* and its revalorization of the artist as lone genitor have had a lasting influence on our tendency to overestimate the *single* creator and, conversely, on our underestimation of the idea of *co-production*. The Romantic aesthetics of artistic creation effectively reproduces, or duplicates, the lengthy debates on the respective roles of father and mother in procreation, which would endow a *single* parent with the active role and the power to shape the progeny.

Whereas medical discourse had relied on aesthetic metaphors to describe both normal and abnormal births (Nature as sculptor and painter, or the monstrous mother as the poor artist), Romantic discourse uses the aesthetics of literary progeny to reinterpret the monstrous as the unique product of a lone genitor. Susan Gubar and Sandra M. Gilbert's analysis of *Frankenstein* as a text in which Life imitates Art, rather than Art imitating Life, also illustrates the essential reversal of the Aristotelian principles in Romanticism. These principles then appear as an avatar of the classical economy of monstrosity, the view that life modeled after a painting would result in a deformed progeny.

Notwithstanding the economic pressures that burdened her and the complex feelings both she and Percy Shelley had about the novel, Mary Shelley, one could assume, claimed the book as her own because the very structure of monstrosity had been for so long associated with mothers and because this structure *exonerated* the father of all possible guilt. But Mary Shelley's own erasure of the legitimate father could not, would not, have been so successfully and enthusiastically endorsed had it not, in fact, brought to light two elements more fundamental than the existence of a co-author. The erasure of the father relies on a tradition that closely associated monstrous births with the mother, stressing the principle of parental singularity. In this economy of creativity and *worth*, one genitor—and one only—was entirely responsible for the shape of the progeny. Far from constituting the beginning of a new myth, such as one associated with the industrial revolution, *Frankenstein* is the last and perhaps most explicit image of an old myth; a two-thousand-year-old tradition closely tying the birth of monstrous children to their mother's deranged imagination, erasing the legitimate father, and pointing instead to the illegitimate models that had so effectively reversed the natural process in which life should imitate life itself.

But if *Frankenstein* can be read as the concluding chapter of an old myth, the 1831 Preface is without a doubt a perfect manifesto for a new aesthetics that posited the work of art as monstrous and the artist as sole genitor of an inimitable progeny. The duplication proposed by Mary Shelley (this is the story of a monster, and this story is my monster) effectively accounts for the Romantic interpretation of Monstrosity as Art. The uncanny equivalence of this novel of procreation with Mary Shelley's perception of the novel as progeny has provided rich ground for literary speculations and analysis. Mary Shelley may not have pioneered the idea of the artist as a lone genitor haunted by sterility and the thought of abortive creations, but in her 1831 Preface to *Frankenstein,* she gave it its most forceful and definitive formulation.

7

The Artist's Studio

No artistic endeavor fascinated the Romantics more than the art of portraiture. Because it relied on the resemblance between model and canvas, portrait painting emphasized both the artificial quality of resemblance between nature and art and the distrust that necessarily accompanies all uncanny similarities. In 1765, the *Encyclopédie* had unequivocally declared that resemblance existed only as a function of the mind's perception of things and that the identity of two objects was the result not of their shared physical qualities but of the mind's assessment of them. Romanticism stressed the peculiar quality of indisputable similarities: the absolute resemblance between nature and art or, more specifically, between the model and its portrait, became as much an object of wonder as a source of suspicion. Moreover, in few stories is the mother's image at once so strongly evoked and so thoroughly repudiated as in narrative accounts of the painting of portraits. For here the conception of the work of art breaks the laws of nature by asserting in no uncertain terms that procreation is the responsibility of a solitary father. The genesis of art excludes the maternal in favor of a male fecundity whose progeny, the portrait, discloses both art and the hidden monstrosity behind art: its unnatural birth.

The Father's Art

Hawthorne's fascination with the art of portraiture is well known and has received ample critical attention. Millicent Bell cites the following remarks from Hawthorne's 1850 *Note-Book:* "I love the odor of paint in an artist's room; his palette and all his other tools have a mysterious charm for me. The pursuit has always interested my imagination more than any other, and I remember before having my first portrait taken, there was a great bewitchery in the idea as if it was a magic process." Elsewhere, Hawthorne noted, "It is my present opinion that the pictorial art is capable of something more like magic—more wonderful and inscrutable in its method than poetry, or any other mode of developing the beautiful."[1] In Haw-

Jean-Auguste-Dominique Ingres, *Raphael and the Fornarina*, 1812.

thorne's tales, the "magic" and "bewitchery" of art take the shape of a domestic fiction where the role of the painter is immediately transformed into that of a singularly powerful demiurge. Thus Hawthorne writes in "The Prophetic Pictures": "'But this painter!' cried Walter Ludlow, with animation. 'He not only excels in his peculiar art, but possesses vast acquirements in all other learning and science. He talks Hebrew with Dr. Mather, and gives lectures in anatomy to Dr. Boylston.'"[2] This painter—who remains nameless throughout the story—speaks every language, including Mather's tongue, that is, Hebrew. Conversely, the only language he cannot speak is his native, "natural" language: "He will speak like a native of each clime and country of the globe, except our own forests" (p. 54). The image of a mother tongue that is neither native nor natural sheds a peculiar light on the conceptual powers of the painter, which can be compared to those of an aberrant maternity.

"All men—*and all women too*, Elinor—*shall find a mirror of themselves* in this wonderful painter," Hawthorne notes (p. 54, emphasis added). The painter thus appears as a representation: he becomes the specular image of all possible models, male and female. This curious detail is stressed by the cursory description of his physical appearance: "He looked somewhat like a portrait himself" (p. 58). Moreover, the painter's capacity to reflect the female turns him into another vision of the hermaphrodite, one of Romanticism's recurring obsessions. But while tradition considered hermaphrodites to be monsters and often sterile productions of nature, in this case art transcends nature's limitation. The artist as creator claims the role of the father and, more obscurely, reclaims that of the missing mother as well. Further, inasmuch as the painter both mirrors his models and internalizes them, he never paints anything but himself, that which is already inside him, his specular soul. The art of painting, and more specifically the art of portraiture, is mediated by the father's quasi-physiological interiorization: painting is a process of pregnancy and delivery.

The notion of Romantic portrait painting as both genesis and childbirth is further complicated by the fact that portraiture, though it can be described in terms of progeny, nevertheless remains entirely separated from any form of natural conception. For between the model and the painter on the one hand, and between the painter and his canvas on the other, art (*technè*) imposes a form of opacity that makes it impossible to know or experience nature (physis). In the same way that Hawthorne's painter can speak "Mother's tongue" while remaining ignorant of his "natural language," the painter in his art has mastered all the lessons of the past yet remains strangely alienated from the lessons of nature. This paradox is made explicit by Hawthorne when he notes:

> The painter, of whom they had been speaking, was not one of those native artists who, at a later period than this, borrowed their colors from the Indians, and manufactured their pencils of the furs of wild beasts. Perhaps, if he could have revoked his life and prearranged his destiny, he might have chosen to belong to *that school without a master,* in the hope of being at least *original,* since there were no works of art to imitate nor rules to follow. But he had been born and educated in Europe. People said that he had studied the grandeur or beauty of *conception,* and every touch of the master hand, in all the most famous pictures, in cabinets and galleries, and on the walls of churches, till there was nothing more for his powerful mind to learn. Art could add nothing to its lessons, but Nature might. He had therefore visited a world whither none of his professional brethren had preceded him, to feast his eyes on visible images that were noble and picturesque, yet had never been transferred to canvas. (p. 55, emphasis added)

The search for the original, which is essentially the search for the living, for an art modeled after that which never before figured as an object of painting, also reveals the blasphemous potential of the painter's art. The artist, who has been nurtured by the images adorning the walls of non-Reformed churches, clashes with a culture that still condemns image-making. In the Renaissance, the prohibition against images had played a specific role in the dissemination of stories of monstrous births attributed to the mother's imagination, and more specifically to her contemplation of sacred pictures. Romanticism in its own fashion renewed this conflict between art and iconoclasm. Françoise Meltzer has described the effects of this clash in Hawthorne's tale: "The story is successful because it pivots on the clash of the two ideologies: the fear of image-making and the simultaneous overt admiration for the artist's technical proficiency in copying: 'awe' and 'admiration' versus a 'presumptuous mockery of the Creator.'"[3] The foundation of

Hawthorne's iconoclastic argument is explicit on this point: not only does the painter sin by reproducing the sacred, but he violates the concept of the sacred by creating images of the natural so life-like that they are mistaken for their models. His work is unsettling to the eye of the beholder. Hawthorne adds, "Their admiration, it must be owned, was tinctured with the prejudices of the age and country. Some deemed it an offence against the Mosaic law, and even a presumptuous mockery of the Creator, to bring into existence such lively images of his creatures. Others, frightened at the art which could raise phantoms at will, and keep the form of the dead among the living, were inclined to consider the painter as a magician, or perhaps the famous Black Man, of old witch times, plotting mischief in a new guise" (p. 56). Hawthorne's view that the painter's art is tainted with a mysterious challenge to God is reflected also in Balzac's "The Unknown Masterpiece." Balzac remarks that there was "something diabolical" in Frenhofer's face as he busily corrected Porbus' painting *Marie l'Egyptienne*. Frenhofer's transformation discloses the magic character and demonic possession that preside over the art of representation: "It was as if the body of this strange character was inhabited by a demon who magically took control of the movement of his hands against his own will. The unearthly glitter of his eyes, the convulsive movements that seemed like struggles, gave to this fancy a semblance of truth which could not but stir a young imagination."[4]

As Romantic art emphasized the artist's feminine side and linked it to what Hawthorne termed "bewitchery," the painter mirrored the images of his female models before reproducing them on his canvas. Conversely, it is the painter's feminine aspect that allows such a strong affinity for forbidden images and lifelike representations. The Romantic painter represents a new instance of parental singularity, benefiting the father who has openly appropriated the feminine in his art. Such a genesis excludes all other forms of engendering. The total incompatibility between artistic creation and familial procreation is, moreover, at the center of another of Hawthorne's tales entitled "The Artist and the Beautiful." To fulfill successfully his artistic destiny, Owen Warland must relinquish Annie Hovenden. Not surprisingly, the child of Annie Hovenden and Peter Danforth cruelly destroys Warland's creation, the "living" butterfly in all its splendid and fleeting beauty. "While it still hov-

ered in the air, the little child of strength, with his grandsire's sharp
and shrewd expression in his face, made a snatch at the marvellous
insect and compressed it in his hand. Annie screamed" (*Selected
Short Stories,* p. 220). The nature of the artist's creative act is described in the simplest and most forceful terms. When Annie asks
if the butterfly was alive, Owen Warland answers: "Alive? Yes, Annie; it may well be said to possess life, for it has absorbed my own
being into itself" (p. 217).[5] The artist in Edgar Allan Poe's "The
Oval Portrait" is equally alienated from the idea of procreation,
and the completion of his character, his hermaphroditic dream of
parental singularity, is expressed briefly but no less decisively: "He,
passionate, studious, austere, and having already a bride in his
Art."[6] A similar image appears in Gogol's "The Portrait": "Pure,
stainless, lovely as a bride, the painter's work stood before him."[7]

The Canvas and Its Model

The Romantic portrait at once exceeded and betrayed the concept
of classical mimesis. The representation does not imitate nature, it
seizes it. The canvas does not simply mirror the living, it seems
itself to be alive, fantastically and fatally. The living quality of such
a representation resolves the paradoxical dilemma described by
Millot,[8] that is, the difficulty of representing a model that changes
incessantly, that is always *unlike itself* in time and space. As Hawthorne points out somewhat enigmatically: "The originals hardly
resembled themselves so strikingly as the portraits did" (p. 57). In
"The Prophetic Pictures," when the painter's models arrive at the
studio their surprised expressions reveal the amazing qualities of
his work: "Being on the eve of marriage, Walter Ludlow and Elinor
were eager to obtain their portraits, as the first of what, they doubtless hoped, would be a long series of family pictures. The day after
the conversation above recorded they visited the painter's rooms.
A servant ushered them into an apartment, where, though the artist himself was not visible, there were personages whom they could
hardly forbear greeting with reverence. They knew, indeed, that
the whole assembly were but pictures, yet felt it impossible to separate the idea of life and intellect from such striking counterfeits"
(p. 56).

However, if the painter's work consists in producing a counterfeit of the living, this is because, for the painter, the living already are like a portrait. Caught in a ray of sunshine, Walter and Elinor appear to be works of art to the practiced eye of the artist: "A sunbeam was falling athwart his figure and Elinor's, with so happy an effect that they also seemed living pictures of youth and beauty, gladdened by bright fortune. The artist was evidently struck" (p. 58). Hawthorne's tale thus tends to go beyond the already blurred limits of life and representation. In fact, "The Prophetic Pictures" suggests that the conceptual power of the painter lies in his ability not only to create lifelike paintings, but, through his pictures, to affect the nature and course of life itself.[9] That this influence plays a very particular domestic and familial role is made abundantly clear by the events of the story.

The painter's initial project, Hawthorne tells us, was to represent the couple itself; in other words, to portray both individuals on a single canvas: "The painter expressed a desire to introduce both their portraits into one picture, and represent them engaged in some appropriate action. This plan would have delighted the lovers, but was necessarily rejected, because so large a space of canvas would have been unfit for the room which it was intended to decorate. Two half-length portraits were therefore fixed upon" (p. 58).[10] Because the painter insists on a life-size representation the plan for a portrait of the couple together has to be abandoned. His insistence on this point leads to the decision to produce two half-length portraits, thus symbolically separating the couple from themselves and from each other, symbolically castrating them. When the portraits were finally completed, "they hung side by side, separated by a narrow panel, appearing to eye each other constantly, yet always returning the gaze of the spectator" (p. 62).

The artist's execution of the paintings further intensifies the couple's metaphoric separation. The two portraits do not in fact initially resemble their models. Rather, unknowingly, the models end up resembling their painted images. It is not surprising that the couple should fail to recognize each other in this new mimetic mode that betrays their profound, underlying alienation. To their eyes the portraits seem alive, possessed with a changing and subtle life: "'I could fancy that the portrait has changed countenance, while I have been looking at it,' cried Walter. 'The eyes are fixed on mine with a strangely sad and anxious expression. Nay, it is grief

and terror! Is this like Elinor?' 'Compare the living face with the
pictured one,' said the painter. Walter glanced sidelong at his mistress, and started. Motionless and absorbed—fascinated, as it
were—in contemplation of Walter's portrait, Elinor's face had assumed precisely the expression of which he had just been com-
plaining. Had she practised for whole hours before a mirror, she
could not have caught the look so successfully" (p. 60). This
chiasmic effect is crucial to Hawthorne's story because the models'
uncanny resemblance to their portraits becomes obvious not when
they look at their own images, but only when each gazes upon the
other's portrait. It is while contemplating Walter's image that Elinor reveals the tormented expression the painter had caught in his
portrait of her. Thus, resemblance in art does not rely on a mirror-
like effect or even on a reversed one where the model would end
up resembling its projected image. Rather, resemblance to one's
portrait is indirectly realized through the contemplation of the image of another. This also is recaptured in the portraits who seemed
to "eye each other constantly." The painter's art has achieved a
subtle transformation: he paints not a model, but rather a beholder, that is, a model entirely absorbed in the contemplation of
art. Elinor captures the look of her own portrait the way the *Encyclopédie* had described a painter capturing resemblances. But now
the roles are reversed: transformed by the contemplation of art,
the living subject models itself after representation, a representation that is at once obscurely shifting, fluid, and prophetic.

Walter's hidden violence and Elinor's future terror are thus prefigured in their portraits, but the story suggests that these emotions are caused by the portraits as well. Walter's attempt to murder
Elinor seems to be precipitated by his deliberate contemplation of
the artist's work: "Walter remained silent before the picture, com-
muning with it as with his own heart, and abandoning himself to
the spell of evil influence that the painter had cast upon the features . . . and when at last he turned upon [Elinor], the resemblance of both to their portraits was complete" (p. 66). However,
this is not the crux of the story. Unbeknownst to his models, the
painter had done a sketch showing the couple reunited: "The
painter, after saluting them, busied himself at a table in completing
a crayon sketch, leaving his visitors to form their own judgment as
to his perfected labors. At intervals, he sent a glance from beneath

his deep eyebrows, watching their countenances in profile, with his pencil suspended over the sketch" (p. 60). The exact content of the sketch is never revealed to the reader, but Elinor is filled with terror when she is surreptitiously shown the "crayon sketch of two figures." Finally, what comes to the painter's mind when he witnesses Walter's attempt to kill his wife is the sketch rather than the portraits: "In the action, and in the look and attitude of each, the painter beheld the figures of his sketch. The picture, with all its tremendous coloring, was finished" (p. 66).

This modest crayon sketch awaiting its finishing touch—its "coloring"—from the actual murder attempt it no doubt prefigured, throws a curious light on the role and nature of representation in Hawthorne. Although Walter and Elinor end by resembling the painter's prophetic portraits, the portraits seem to be the cause of both resemblance and murder: Elinor is terrified by Walter's portrait, in which she discovers his potential for violence, and Walter is driven to his crime through contemplating the painter's portrayal of their faces. The portraits do not simply reveal a future passion, they are the very agent of the foretold murder. Hawthorne thus says of the painter's art: "Was not his own the form in which that destiny had embodied itself, and he a chief agent of the coming evil which he had foreshadowed?" (p. 66). The painter's intervention places art and reality at the same level: "He had advanced from the door, and interposed himself between the wretched beings, with the same sense of power to regulate their destiny as to alter a scene upon the canvas" (p. 66).

It appears at first that sublimated art serves as a model for the living, but in "The Prophetic Pictures" Hawthorne in fact suggests a quite different vision of artistic creation. Art alone serves as a model for art or any other form of representation. Just as the painter's models were the great European masters "in cabinets and galleries," rather than nature, Walter and Elinor are seen not simply as original living creatures, but rather as "two living *pictures* of youth and beauty." The painter seeks to represent on canvas not living nature, but an already-formed representation embodied by two models. Thus the origin of the paintings and the source of their uncanny resemblance to the living may be not the models themselves but the artist's literal *conception* of a scene that includes murder, the product of his "perfected labors." In other words, the subjects of the portraits are not the unhappy lovers but their image, internalized by a painter who "mirrors" all men and women and transposed into a sketch of terror and violence: a design in every sense of the term. The basis for the portraits is first of all the pencil sketch that awaits only Elinor's murder before it can take on "its tremendous coloring."

Nature is indefinitely repressed in this tale of two lovers who, for having gazed upon an image, are condemned to fulfill a destiny that has been literally traced for them by an artist too enamored of his art and not enough of nature. Total resemblance, that is, the perfect coincidence between art and life, is achieved only with the attempted murder of Elinor (already prefigured as well in the metaphoric castration of her represented self). Romantic art as progeny is then represented as a monstrous project. The painter's ability to capture resemblances is grounded in his ability to foretell a time when the woman, the future mother already separated from her husband by the painter's decision to use two canvases, is reunited with her husband in a scene that frames her murder. The artist's mastery is achieved at the expense of the living; in this case, at the expense of the young bride who, like the legitimate father of the past, is meant to be erased in the conception of a monstrous project. The monstrosity of art duplicates the monstrosity of unnatural progeny, replaying the reversal where life imitates art or, rather, where life is lived as art, already inscribed on the canvas by a murderous hand.

The artist's design to erase the bride in favor of an aesthetic reality that transcends the living is a familiar theme in the work of Hawthorne and other writers of the time. "The Birthmark" also evokes, in even greater detail, a hierarchy demanding the sacrifice of the woman to aesthetic perfection. Hawthorne reiterates Colonna's traditional view that Nature works as a Painter or a Sculptor would, "for our admiration, not in order to show us [their] craft."[11] He writes, "Our great creative Mother, while she amuses us with apparently working in the broadest sunshine, is yet severely careful to keep her own secrets, and, in spite of her pretended openness, shows us nothing but results."[12] In the Classical Age, Nature was described as working like a painter. For Romanticism, however, inasmuch as Nature remained an essentially mysterious maternal force, the painter was seen as working like Nature. By her betrayal of Nature's designs, the monstrous mother was like a bad artist. Now, by his betrayal of art—that is, of art as a "natural," if mysterious, endeavor—the monstrous painter is like a bad mother. Françoise Meltzer notes, "'The Birthmark' can be read as the story of the erasure of difference through the insistence upon mimesis; and through a concomitant attempt to erase gender difference, to masculinize nature. But nature, truth, is so much woman that Aylmer is feminized by the very attempt to lay his hands upon her." [13] Aylmer's attempt to erase the birthmark, the mother's own signature, from Georgiana's otherwise perfect face betrays his desire to take the mother's place and to finish the creation of an almost perfect progeny. In this attempt, Aylmer reveals Georgiana's hidden monstrousness: not the superficial imprint of a hand on her cheek, but, as he tells her, the fact that the "crimson hand, superficial as it seems, has clutched its grasp into your being with a strength of which I had no previous conception" (p. 96). After several "abortive" attempts, Aylmer successfully corrects the mother's defective creation, but in the process he loses Georgiana forever.

Many critics have seen in Hawthorne's tales the expression of a troubled sexuality. Harry Levin describes the stories as "rife with matrimonial fears." [14] Frederick Crews adds, "The hero is facing a matrimonial challenge." [15] More precisely, Crews sees in "The Birthmark" the explicit avowal of sexual revulsion:

> Aylmer's desire to remove his bride's one flaw stems from revulsion against her sexuality. He confesses that Georgiana's crimson birthmark "shocks" him, whereupon she cries, "You cannot love what shocks you!" But Aylmer, true to Hawthornian form, *can* desire the very thing that offends his squeamish mind, and his dream of plunging his knife into the birthmark until it reaches Georgiana's heart reveals a fantasy of sadistic revenge and a scarcely less obvious fantasy of sexual consummation. His "medical" curiosity and his willingness to risk Georgiana's death to remove a harmless blemish are thinly disguised substitutes for his urges to *know* and *destroy* her sexuality. [16]

The only thing we might add is that a birthmark was hardly ever a "harmless blemish," since it was thought to be the very imprint of a mother's unsatisfied desire. [17] Georgiana's birthmark, or "envie," lives and changes color with her every breath, bearing witness to the truth and nature of the "matrimonial challenge": only after all signs of its *maternal* origins have been erased can the progeny be perfect. If anything, the birthmark points to the deficient mother and the unpredictable character of female desire.[18]

The Mother's Image

Edgar Allan Poe's "The Oval Portrait" further illustrates a recurring motif of Romantic art: that an art capable of giving the illusion of life can be achieved only at the cost of life itself; that the model *and* its living portrait cannot coexist; that the Romantic artist unfailingly chooses art over the living and thus sacrifices the living to art.[19] The scene is always portrayed as a domestic tragedy: in the very first lines of the narrative of portraiture, a sacrifice is announced: "Evil was the hour when she saw, and loved, and wedded the painter . . . hating only the Art which was her rival; dreading only the palette and brushes and other untoward instruments which deprived her of the countenance of her lover. It was thus a terrible thing for this lady to hear the painter speak of his desire to portray even his young bride" (p. 189).

Predictably, "as the *labour* drew nearer to its conclusion" the bride wasted away. The birth of art will claim the model's life. "When many weeks had passed, and but little remained to do, save one brush upon the mouth and one tint upon the eye, the spirit of the lady again flickered up as the flame within the socket of the lamp. And then the brush was given, and then the tint was placed; and, for one moment, the painter stood entranced before the work which he had wrought; but in the next, while he yet gazed, he grew tremulous and very pallid, and aghast, and crying with a loud voice, 'This is indeed *Life* itself!' turned suddenly to regard his beloved:—*She was dead!*" (p. 190). Although it is tempting to see art as the simple transfer of "life" from the living model to the lifelike portrait, Poe's description of the creative process suggests a slightly different genesis. As in "The Prophetic Pictures," the painter, similarly nameless, paints not a living or even "present" model, but an abstract, interiorized vision of this model. In Hawthorne's story, the painter paints not so much from life as from his drawing of an imagined scene (a murder) whose resulting effects (violence and fear) are then infused into the two portraits. Nor, in Poe, does the painter look up from his easel to study the model "of the rarest beauty" whose portrait he is presumably painting: "[He] turned his eyes from the canvas rarely, even to regard the countenance of his wife" (p. 190). The hidden monstrosity of the painter—which will be revealed by his work—is that, like the mother's perverted imagination, he creates not from nature but from art: he entirely ignores the legitimate, the "putative" model (much as one might refer to "the putative father" of an offspring of uncertain parentage), to paint but a mental imprint. The same paradox illustrates Gogol's own allegory of creation. In "The Portrait," Chartkov is so taken with his art that he becomes thoroughly oblivious of the women who serve as his models: "He began to paint. The work so fascinated him that he forgot everything else. He even forgot the presence of the aristocratic ladies" (p. 531). As if further to suggest that a portrait's life does not emanate from its model, Gogol adds, "They had so exerted themselves at dancing at balls that they were now like wax figures" (p. 531).

Poe's tale describes with unusual restraint the particular monstrosity of the work of art thus conceived. When the narrator first sees the painting, he *has to* shut his eyes. Attempting to analyze the portrait's astonishing uncanniness, he notes: "As a thing of art, nothing could be more admirable than the painting itself. But it could have been neither the execution of the work, nor the immortal beauty of the countenance, which had so suddenly and so vehemently moved me. Least of all, could it have been that my fancy, shaken from its half slumber, had mistaken the head for that of a living person. I saw at once that the peculiarities of the design, of the *vignetting*, and of the frame, must have instantly dispelled such [an] idea—must have prevented even its momentary entertainment" (pp. 188–189). The beholder's horror does not stem from the idea that the portrait could mysteriously be alive, nor does he believe at any time that art could have superseded life. Rather, he attributes the initial dread the portrait evokes to a significantly different feature. Now able to keep his eyes on the portrait, he notes, "I remained, for an hour perhaps, half sitting, half reclining, with my vision riveted upon the portrait. At length, satisfied with the true secret of its effect, I fell back within the bed. I had found the spell of the picture in an absolute *life-likeness* of expression, which, at first startling, finally confounded, subdued, and appalled me" (p. 189).

The spectator's gaze cruelly contradicts the artist's naive triumph: "This is indeed *Life* itself!" To the beholder, the portrait has nothing to do with the living: its decorative function (underscored by the repeated use of the word *vignette*) and its oval frame both emphasize its status as representation. Thus the horror inspired by the portrait is not that of an art that would supplant the living, but that of an art which at once absolutely resembles the living *while obviously remaining artifice*. The difference is suggestive: the painter succeeds by producing not life, but lifelikeness at life's expense. Artistic creation is not the birth of a work that will live on at the expense of its model. On the contrary, the perfection of art, and specifically of portraiture, is achieved by sacrificing the living to the artificial, or the model's beauty to an image that has never been, and will never be, anything but an inert canvas, a vignette, a marvelous portrait—but no more than a portrait—a contrived resemblance. This is far removed from the theme of Pygmalion or Faust, which has been invoked repeatedly by critics to introduce interpretations of these works. Poe's and Hawthorne's concerns are with repudiating nature, not with imitating it; with dismissing the model, not with representing it. Rather than reproducing the living, they produce art.

However, if the visible model is consistently ignored by the artist, what then is represented on the fateful canvas? The Romantic fascination for portraiture is mixed with a persistent, if at times disguised, iconoclastic motif.[20] As we have seen earlier, the prohibition against image-making is also related to the maternal role.[21] As Jean-Joseph Goux noted in his analysis of Freud:

> The prohibition against making an image of God implies that sensorial perception takes a back seat to the abstract idea. It consecrates the triumph of the spirit over the senses or, more specifically, the renunciation of instincts . . . It is odd that he does not explicitly establish what we find to be the particularly illuminating relationship *between the Judaic prohibition against image adoration and the incest taboo with the mother*. By carving images of gods, one makes a material image of the mother and adores the maternal figures through the senses. By tearing oneself away from the seduction of the senses and elevating one's thoughts toward an unrepresentable god, one turns away from desire for the mother, ascends to the sublime father, and respects his law. It is here that

the Mosaic commandment takes on its importance. The *Jewish Oedipus* is acted out in the prohibition against portrayal.[22]

Following Goux's argument, I would suggest that the Romantics' fascination with portraiture and their simultaneous preoccupation with iconoclasm replay in their own specific ways the taboo of incest with the mother. Marie Bonaparte, along with other readers of Poe, related the creation of Poe's most tragic characters to the haunting memory of his mother's death at the age of twenty-four. Bonaparte interprets the principal characteristics of Poe's work as the outward signs of his sworn fidelity to the young woman. In Bonaparte's view, the oval portrait in the story, the lifelike canvas that creates such a startling effect on the beholder, is no more than the well-known medallion portraying Poe's mother, and Poe reenacts his own domestic tragedy in the scene of the portrait:

> And, indeed, while *The Oval Portrait* was being written, a woman, in fact, was dying at Poe's side: the woman who served as the model for his picture-tales. The depth of the need for a model of this kind, was a main reason why he chose the little Virginia, marked out for phthisis, for his wife . . . With her young, dying body, she resembled Elizabeth: this he did much as a painter would choose a well-made woman for his Venus. And since, once upon a time, when he was small, a woman had to die that he might become Poe the writer so, later, was he irresistibly led to choose one who was doomed to a lingering death, to be the model for his canvases.[23]

One may disagree with Marie Bonaparte's general analysis of Poe's neurosis, but her remarks on "The Oval Portrait" are particularly illuminating in their emphasis on a crucial displacement: how a beautiful young woman is sacrificed in order for the painter successfully to create *another's* portrait—the mother's image. This also explains why the painter has no need to observe his model and never lifts his eyes from the canvas. The sexual, incestuous nature of the portrait is illustrated as well by the beholder's instinctive reaction of covering his eyes when first seeing the painting, the Oedipal gesture of blinding oneself when the truth is revealed. "I glanced at the painting hurriedly," says the narrator, "and then closed my eyes. Why I did this was not at first apparent even to my own perception. But while my lids remained thus shut, I ran over in my mind my reason for so shutting them. It was an impulsive movement to gain time for thought—to make sure that my vision had not deceived me—to calm and subdue my fancy for a more sober and more certain gaze" (p. 188). An explicit preoccupation with metaphorical blindness echoes the Romantic rhetoric of creation. Gogol's "The Portrait" is ripe with suggestions associating the perfection of artistic vision with the artist's capacity to observe what he should never see. And the desire to murder will follow. When the painter's work is rejected by a jury because of "something de-moniacal in the eyes, as though some evil feeling had guided the artist's hand," the painter is seized with uncontrollable anger: "It is impossible to describe the degree of fury in him when he returned home. He almost murdered my mother" (pp. 555–556). Gogol's artist, like those who exceed the natural limits of their art, will be punished in his domestic life. "Three catastrophes which happened afterwards, the sudden deaths of his wife and his daughter and his infant son, he regarded as divine punishment" (p. 558). The conclusion of the tale points to the possibility of a more general form of collective blindness. After the portrait with the diabolical eyes has disappeared, "for a long time those who were present were bewildered, wondering whether they had really seen those remarkable eyes or whether it was merely a dream which had flashed before their eyes, strained from long examination of old pictures" (p. 561).

The Veil and the Canvas

The complex idea of art as monstrous genesis is central to Balzac's philosophical tale "The Unknown Masterpiece." Balzac tells the story of three generations of painters: Frenhofer, the master; Porbus, rejected as court painter by Marie de Médicis in favor of Rubens; and the young Nicolas Poussin, poised at the beginning of his brilliant career. Michel Serres has described this spiritual family as a genealogical tree: "Poussin, the child, is at the base of the tree; Porbus, the adult, is at the middle; and the old Fernhofer [sic] lost among the golden leaves at the top. Or rather, for I am not sure of the direction, Poussin the child is among the green leaves at top; Porbus is to be found at the point where the trunk splits into the main branches; and the old painter is the diabolical figure hiding among the roots' dark shadows." [24] To these three generations must be added a fourth, which provides the key to the meaning of the genealogy of art: "Old Frenhofer is the only pupil Mabuse would take. Frenhofer became the painter's friend, deliverer, and father; he sacrificed the greater part of his fortune to satisfy Mabuse's passions" ("The Unknown Masterpiece," p. 123). Frenhofer explains, "Mabuse alone possessed the secret of giving life to his figures; Mabuse had but one pupil—that was I. I have had none, and I am old. You have sufficient intelligence to imagine the rest from the glimpses that I am giving you" (p. 117).

Thus a unique and sterile domestic circle is gathered around a mysterious painting that Frenhofer refuses to unveil. The original couple Mabuse-Frenhofer engendered each other: Mabuse is the master who bequeaths his knowledge to Frenhofer. Like Hawthorne's painter, Frenhofer is above all art's own creation: he looked "like a portrait by Rembrandt, walking silently and without a frame in the dark atmosphere he had created" (p. 109). Frenhofer in turn becomes both pupil and father, jealously guarding both his artistic secrets and the "unknown masterpiece" to which he has passionately devoted himself for over ten years. But the painters' studios are haunted by women/models/mistresses. In Porbus' studio we find *Marie l'Egyptienne,* a painting intended for Marie de Médicis, the queen, the protectress, and the painting's probable model, who has also rejected her favorite's work. "Your good woman is not badly thrown together," says Frenhofer impertinently, "but she is not alive . . . because you look from time to time at a naked woman who stands on the platform before you, you fondly imagine that you have copied nature, think yourselves to be painters, believe that you have wrested His secret from God" (p. 111). It is not enough occasionally to contemplate the female in order to grasp the secret of life, at least not life as it is conceived by the artist.

Only Poussin lives with a woman, but he is not a painter yet, he is merely an apprentice. His Gillette is beauty, perfection, and youth incarnate. Frenhofer thinks that he too desires her, or rather, that he would like to contemplate her ideal perfection: "Ah! where does she live . . . the undiscoverable Venus of the Ancients, for whom we have sought so often, only to find the scattered gleams of her beauty here and there? Oh! to behold once and for one moment,

Nature grown perfect and divine—in a word, the Ideal—I would give all that I possess . . . Nay, Beauty divine, I would go to seek thee in the dim land of the dead; like Orpheus, I would go down into the Hades of Art to bring back the life of art from among the shadows of death" (p. 123). But the fate of artists' models, even ideal ones, is betrayal and oblivion. Poussin promises to "give," or lend, Gillette to Frenhofer in exchange for one glance at Frenhofer's hidden masterpiece—the courtesan Catherine Lescaut, *La belle noiseuse* of his painting. The hierarchy of art is already made explicit in Poussin's belief that life, understood from an artist's point of view, stems not from the female but solely from the *image* of the female. Poussin's art duplicates the principles already at work in the stories of Hawthorne and Poe. As the model herself is never an image to be copied, the painter's gaze hardly needs to rest on Gillette's beautiful body: "'If you wish me to sit once more for you as I did the other day,' she continued with playful petulance, 'I will never consent to do such a thing again, for at these moments your eyes do not appeal to me. You do not think of me at all, and yet you look at me'" (p. 126). The unseeing eyes rob Gillette of her own identity. The difference between the value of Gillette's astounding beauty and that of Frenhofer's painted ideal is made clear in the exchange between Porbus and the old master, Frenhofer: Porbus remarks, "'Young Poussin is loved by a woman of incomparable and flawless beauty. But, dear master, if he consents to lend her to you, at the least you ought to let us see your work.' The old man stood motionless and completely dazed. 'What!' he cried piteously at last, 'show you my creation, my wife? *tear away the veil* beneath which I have chastely concealed my happiness? This would be a terrible prostitution! For ten years I have lived with her! She is mine, mine alone; she loves me. Has she not smiled at me, at each stroke of the brush I have given her? She has a soul, the soul that I have given her'" (p. 129, emphasis added).

Frenhofer's true passion for his image of a woman contrasts with Poussin's unfaithful love for the beautiful Gillette. Poussin, struggling for a moment with feelings of remorse, "cursed himself in despair that he should have brought his fair treasure from its hiding-place. The lover overcame the artist" (p. 132). But the struggle is short-lived, for Balzac shows the unquestionable supremacy of art over the living. When in the last scene Frenhofer finally agrees to unveil his masterpiece, Gillette herself is entirely forgotten by all three painters. As the famous canvas is finally revealed, Frenhofer in a state of utter exaltation exclaims: "Aha! . . . you did not expect to see such perfection! You find yourselves in front of a woman and you are looking for a painting . . . Where is art? lost! disappeared! Those are the very forms of a young girl" (p. 134). But these words do not refer to the unhappy Gillette, standing disconsolate in a dark corner of the studio. Rather, they describe Frenhofer's supreme achievement. "Have I not caught the very hues of life, the spirit of the living line that defines the figure?" (p. 134), he exclaims triumphantly. Art is lost, claims Frenhofer, and indeed, to Porbus and Poussin's surprise, they see nothing but "confused masses of colour contained by a multitude of fantastical lines that go to make a dead wall of paint" (p. 135). Michel Serres notes that, still fascinated by this startling canvas, "they turned their backs on the living, beautiful young girl. The imbeciles!" (p. 35).

The only recognizable form emerging from the chaos of Frenhofer's painting is a fragment, the form of a bare foot: "In a corner of the canvas as they came nearer, they distinguished a bare foot emerging from the chaos of colour, half-tints and vague shadows that made up a dim formless fog; but a delightful, a living foot! They were petrified with admiration upon seeing this fragment that had escaped such unbelievable, slow and gradual destruction. The foot appeared like the torso of some Venus made of marble from Paros, emerging from the ashes of a ruined city" (p. 135). This scene reveals several secrets without disclosing Frenhofer's ultimate masterpiece. Porbus and Poussin stand transfixed, hypnotized by the beauty of this exquisite foot and at the same time so horrified by what they see as Frenhofer's madness—the chaos of colors covering the canvas—that they speak about him in the third person, as if he were no longer present, no longer alive: "'Sooner or later, he will find out that there is nothing there!' cried Poussin" (p. 136). But a general blindness pervades the scene: Porbus and Poussin's incapacity to see what Frenhofer beholds with passion: "'I see her, I see her,' he cried, 'she is marvellously beautiful'" (p. 137). But at the same time, Frenhofer, like Porbus and Poussin, remains blind to the ideally beautiful Gillette, who cries in horror: "Kill me! . . . I must be a vile thing if I love you still, for I despise you"

(p. 137). This scene establishes a link between two previously separate motifs: First, the dismissal of the woman/model who is repeatedly neglected or rejected, but whose presence remains nevertheless necessary to the production of art; the painter turns away from her, yet she must preside over the birth of art. Second, the idea that a veil must cover what the model, or the painter's view of the model, has revealed. "In course of time," wrote Hawthorne in "The Prophetic Pictures," "Elinor hung a gorgeous curtain of purple silk, wrought with flowers and fringed with heavy golden tassels, before the pictures, under pretence that the dust would tarnish their hues, or the light dim them" (p. 63). The veil may also be metaphoric, as in Gogol's "The Portrait": "He was unable to see through the dark veil that hid the works of the old masters" (p. 516). In Balzac, the veil may be said to be a triple one. A first metaphoric veil protects Frenhofer's secret: "Show you my creation, my wife? *tear away the veil* beneath which I have chastely concealed my happiness?" And later: "Would you have me fling aside ten years of happiness like a cloak?" (p. 129). The second veil is a palpable one, the heavy drapery covering the unknown masterpiece that Frenhofer lovingly puts back in place after having disclosed his secret: "Frenhofer drew a green serge covering over his *Catherine* with the sober deliberation of a jeweller who locks his drawers when he suspects his visitors to be expert thieves" (p. 137). But the final veil cannot be lifted or torn away: it is the ultimate protection for Frenhofer's ideal woman, and it has been painted over the canvas by the master himself. It consists of "the coats of paint with which the old artist had overlaid and concealed his work in the quest of perfection" (p. 135). That this overlay was an afterthought, painted over the image of a presumably perfect Venus, is confirmed by Porbus' startled exclamation: "There is a woman underneath!" (p. 135).[25]

The veil of paint with which Frenhofer chastely covers his perfect creation corresponds to the Oedipal moment when the beholder of Poe's oval portrait closes his eyes. What this indescribable "chaos of colors, tones, blurred nuances, a sort of formless fog" conceals more than anything is that there is no model for *La belle noiseuse*—not Catherine Lescaut, not a courtesan, not any other living woman. "She was born in my studio," says Frenhofer. "She is

not a creature, she is a creation" (p. 129). Resemblance and lifelikeness have finally become superfluous. Art reaches perfection for
Frenhofer precisely because he has ceased to imitate an external
object. The unknown masterpiece represents its own principle of
artistic genesis, the very idea of conception: "This is why I have
studied for seven years the effects of *coupling* light with objects.
Look at this hair, isn't it flooded with light?" (p. 134, emphasis
added).[26] Josué Harari argues that Frenhofer's painting exempli-
fies an "ambiguous sexual destiny": the canvas is "a transformation
of another painting in the story (Marie l'Egyptienne) who emblem-
atizes a figure of sexuality *without biological gestation*. According to
the legend, young girls who feared not becoming mothers would
secretly come to pray for the divine intervention of Saint Marie the
Egyptian . . . This painting raises the ambiguous sexual problematic of a birth that bears the mark of an exclusion, that of the real,
biological woman, the other of male sexuality . . . The secret of art
. . . would thus be the creative principle without sexuality, without
the other, without the woman." [27] Art's object then is that privileged
moment when the artist becomes the lone genitor and represents/
reproduces without a model: in Frenhofer's words "at once father,
lover, and god" (p. 129). Michel Serres, however, sees *La belle noiseuse* as the most perfect example of the tale's theme of fecundity,
the triumphant conclusion to all the previous attempts at representation. Reviewing the gallery of paintings presented to the readers, Serres observes: "Marie l'Egyptienne about to cross the waters,
and the first Adam by Mabuse the father, and the beautiful female
portrait painted in the manner of Giorgione: so many beautiful
paintings, so many beautiful painted women are born from this
beautiful noiseuse: Eve, ocean, mother, womb, fabled uterus, inseminated by Ouranos' sperm-filled and bloody brush" (p. 51). Yet
a veil covers this prolific body. The taboo against images and the
taboo of incest with the mother become indistinguishable in Balzac's tale. Oedipus is once again blinded: that is, he erases what was
there to be seen but must never be seen again, and he sees where
there is nothing more to behold except a marvelously perfect foot,
the fetishist's emblem of the all-powerful mother.[28] In the end, enlightened as to his fateful blindness yet denying his failure, Frenhofer, after burning all his paintings, kills himself.

The Terror of Germany

At different times in their careers, Hawthorne, Poe, and Balzac drew upon, or were accused of having borrowed outright, themes, decor, and characters from other authors. In answer to these accusations they wrote elaborate disclaimers. These various statements, half-confessions or virtuous denials, reenact between the writer and the (often repudiated) author who inspired him a relationship similar to that which existed between the painter and his model. For example, in a note added to "The Prophetic Pictures," Hawthorne readily admitted that the story had been "suggested by an anecdote of Stuart, related in Dunlap's *History of the Arts of Design*,—a most entertaining book to the general reader, and a deeply interesting one, we should think, to the artist" (p. 54). But he vehemently denied having stolen "Dr. Heidegger's Experiment" from Alexandre Dumas: "In an English review, not long since, I have been accused of plagiarizing the idea of this story from a chapter in one of the novels of Alexandre Dumas. There has undoubtedly been a plagiarism on one side or the other; but as my story was written a good deal more than twenty years ago, and as the novel is of considerably more recent date, I take pleasure in thinking that M. Dumas has done me the honor to appropriate one of the fanciful conceptions of my earlier days" (p. 76). Balzac's "L'elixir de longue vie" is preceded by the following comment concerning its genesis: "At the beginning of the author's career, a friend, now long gone, gave him the subject of this Study, which he later found in a collection published at the beginning of the century. He conjectures that this fantasy is the handiwork of Hoffmann of Berlin; it was published in some German almanac and left out of his works by the publishers. THE HUMAN COMEDY is rich enough in invention for the author to confess an innocent borrowing; and like the good La Fontaine, he will in his own way, and unwittingly, have treated a tale that already had been told."[29] Poe, whose tales had often been linked in various ways to Hoffmann's, denied any form of imitation in the 1839 preface to his *Tales of the Grotesque and Arabesque*: "The Truth is that, with a single exception, there is no one of these stories in which the scholar should recognize distinctive features of that species of pseudo-horror which we are taught to call Germanic, for no better reason than that some of the secondary names of German literature have become identified with its folly. If in many of my productions terror has been the thesis, I maintain that terror is not of Germany, but of the soul—that I have deduced this terror only from its legitimate sources and urged it only to its legitimate results." This concern with the writer's originality—whether his stories were invented, copied, or plagiarized—seems to confirm and reinforce a reading of Romantic tales of portraiture as metaphors in which questions of original invention, paternity, and legitimacy echo what Poe called the "terror . . . of Germany," that is, the terror of recognizing one's filiation, the influence and marks of one's father.

In the same preface where Balzac begrudgingly admitted his debt to Hoffmann, he introduced a story of parricide as a meditation on legitimacy and heredity: "As all of European civilization is built upon the mainspring of HEREDITY, its elimination would be madness. But could we not improve this essential cogwheel the way we improve the tools that are the pride of our time?" (p. 82). Balzac was a great admirer of Geoffroy Saint-Hilaire, the founder of teratology, to whom he later dedicated *Le père Goriot.* Here, however, the word "heredity" is used in its primary sense to designate the right to inherit from one's father. In Balzac's tale, heredity, which posits the absolute necessity of the father's death in order for the son to live a full life, drives Don Juan Belvidero to commit a horrible murder. The father must die so that the son may inherit the name, title, and property that are rightfully his. The troubling question of heredity is not essentially different from Balzac's claim of literary paternity in the last lines of his preface to "L'elixir de longue vie." "If the author has kept the old expression 'To the Reader' in a work where he tries to portray every literary form, it is in order to make an observation relative to certain Studies, and especially this one. Each one of these compositions is based on fairly new ideas, whose expression the author thought useful. He may give priority to certain forms and ideas that have since become part of the literary domain, and even quite commonplace. The initial publication dates of each Study will therefore not be indifferent to those readers who wish to give the author his due" (p. 82). Balzac's claim of original paternity, following the admission that Hoffmann had probably been the first to write on the specific subject that had been "given to him" (much as one receives a legacy) by a friend, both states and questions the nature of literary paternity.

Between the confession of a borrowing and the tale of a parricide, Balzac the author simultaneously recognizes a father (Hoffmann) and narrates the necessity of killing him. Balzac's art as well as the ambiguous status of Romantic creation are inextricably linked to the question of inheritance on the one hand, and to the idea of doing away with the father on the other. What Harold Bloom terms "the anxiety of influence" surfaces in Hawthorne's, Poe's, and Balzac's recurring obsession with originals and imitations and their continual fear of being themselves copied and thus stripped of what is rightfully theirs. Like the monstrous mother, they vacillate between acknowledging a father and desiring his erasure. They claim their own form of parental singularity, the sole responsibility for the creation of their peculiar progeny, the *legitimate* terror of the soul. The issue of legitimacy has always been an issue of paternity and filiation, the very definition of the paternal role in genealogy. In the literary lineage described here—Hoffmann, or Stuart, and their heirs, Hawthorne, Poe, Balzac—the rebellious sons are themselves in the reverse position of "recognizing," "acknowledging" a father, accepting a legacy and yet asserting their own and complete independent creativity. In their assertion of original authorship and in the metaphor of art as progeny, the Romantics sought to dismiss the very idea of filiation while being haunted by the desire to procreate without the other. Just as Camille Dareste claimed sole responsibility for the thousands of monsters he created alone in his laboratory, Romanticism claimed unprecedented progeny: art as the offspring of a single artist, one that has already repudiated all forms of filiation. "The Unknown Masterpiece" may be interpreted as the story of such a genealogy.

The practical issues of copyright and protection of authors' rights, the question of sources and influences, the fear of plagiarism and duplication are recognizable threads running through the mysterious tales of portraiture. Does an artist create or copy? Why is the model necessary, yet dismissed, in all tales of portraits? Is art the product of life or of lifelikeness? In an article entitled "Imitation-Plagiarism," Poe noted: "When a plagiarism is detected, it generally happens that the public sympathy is with the plagiarist, and his friends proceed to every extreme in the way of exculpation. But how unjust! We should sympathize rather with him upon whom the plagiarism has been committed. Not only is he robbed of his property—of his fame . . . but he is rendered liable by the crime of *the plagiarist to the suspicion of being a plagiarist himself.*" [30] The Romantics' preoccupation with plagiarism is but one more expression of the question of parental singularity, of the vision of the artist as lone and monstrous father. From this perspective, the plagiarist's crime is not just that of stealing, but of blurring the difference between the original and the counterfeit. Literary creation is all the more precarious in that its nature as a representation fails to distinguish it from other representations of itself, so that originals may be taken for forgeries. [31] This precariousness is the most violent threat to the idea of the creative artist, and it is a threat made explicit in all tales of portraiture: since art is apparent imitation, how can its derivative nature be transcended or erased? How can it conceal the fact that behind every original there hides a model, another image, another imitation, another artist, another progenitor? As interpreted by Romantic writers, the art of portraiture reaches a paradoxical resolution: by emphasizing that the model may never be considered the origin of the portrait, but rather a fecundating—if repudiated—agent, the artist shows himself to be the source of art, putting on the canvas what he carries within himself, as a woman bears a child modeled after an image. In this way, he points to the incestuous nature of the creative process by substituting the mother's image for that of the beleaguered bride; the painter thus offers yet another mode of filiation. The resulting picture, like Frenhofer's chaotic celebration of fecundity, must be covered with a veil. Confessions, claims of authorship, or heavy draperies of purple silk are all variations of literary veils— the shrouds that cover the secret of life, the mother's body.

8

Family Undertaking: Madame Tussaud's Wax Museum

In his introduction to an early edition of John Tussaud's *The Romance of Madame Tussaud's*, Hilaire Belloc remarked, "You cannot conceive of a better medium than wax among all the known mediums for production of effigies of human beings. Yet it is not perfect. And it is precisely *because the likeness is so great*, precisely because the effect is so parallel to that of reality, that we note the minor details in which *illusion is not achieved*." [1] The paradox that a medium is imperfect precisely because it allows for the greatest resemblance had already been formulated by Eugène Delacroix in his evaluation of daguerreotypes. In 1850, he wrote: "One should not lose sight of the fact that the daguerreotype must be considered only a translator whose purpose is to further initiate us to the secrets of nature; for despite its astonishing reality in certain parts, it is only a reflection, a copy of the real *that is false, in a way, because it is so exact*. The *monstrosities* it presents are justifiably shocking, even though they are, literally, those of nature itself." [2]

The relationship suggested by Delacroix between the copy that is "false . . . because it is so exact" and the resulting effect of monstrosity sheds some light on the mixture of fascination and horror that was produced by early wax cabinets (a horror also documented by numerous gothic tales). Unlike the framed portrait, the waxwork is falsified by its very claim to produce a more lifelike *effect* on the beholder. Its claim to life is its true lie, part of its monstrosity. But the wax figure is also perceived as monstrous because of its literal translation of nature's inner monstrosity, its way of seeming to reveal nature's hidden designs. Belloc may have provided the most eloquent formulation of nature's fatal teleology with this

A wax studio. Making anatomical models.

comment: "To put it in extreme terms, the ideal of the modeller in wax would be to reproduce a figure such that one knowing the original could be deceived and think he had found again his friend *dead or sleeping*" (*Romance*, pp. 27–28, emphasis added). It was this monstrosity of nature—that the sleep of the living is but an anticipation of unavoidable death—that gave the wax figure its unbearable realism. In this perspective, nothing could better illustrate the "execution" of a work of art than the properties of the wax effigy. It simultaneously dissimulates its art, erases its technique, eludes the artist's signature, and reproduces the model as *dead*. Yet the waxworker's art establishes a singular relationship between the model/victim and the executioner. Commenting on the historical value of the wax impressions of the guillotined heads that formed the centerpiece of Madame Tussaud's Museum, Belloc added, "The revolutionary figures sometimes look odd to us precisely because their real aspect has been so vividly preserved. The hand that modelled Marat was a hand of Marat's age. It touched the flesh of the dead man. The eyes that received the conception reproduced by the hands, gazed upon Marat himself as he lay back dead" (ibid., p. 31).

This description of the wax modeler's art suggests a relationship between model and artist radically different from that found in Romantic portrait aesthetics. For Hawthorne, as for Poe and Balzac, the success of a portrait—its "lifelike" quality—always involved a risk for the model. That risk could be termed "erasure": erasure of the female image which both inspires and inseminates the artist's mind, yet which must ultimately disappear so that art may thrive—an ambiguous art that veils incestuous desire. Poe's painter hardly raised his eyes from the canvas to consider the beautiful model seated next to him. By contrast, the art of wax-modeling such as that practiced by Marie Tussaud forces the sort of recognition denied to the painter's model. Madame Tussaud's own eyes were said to have gazed upon Marat, her own hands to have touched his face; thus, the distance between model and artist was abolished. The subject, of course, was already dead.

Madame Tussaud's Peculiar Art

In the 1892 catalogue of Madame Tussaud's Exhibition, the famous waxworker is described as having left France for England in

1802, boldly transporting "the idea of her uncle's 'Cabinet de cire,' including the *embryo* 'Chambers of Horrors,' to British shores."[3] This "embryo" was to develop into a full-scale gallery of monsters and one of the most popular attractions of nineteenth-century London. The Tussaud's Museum of wax figures, if not the first one of its kind, certainly became the most successful. Undoubtedly, its success was in part due to the fascination of its gruesome center-piece, the Chamber of Horrors.

Astonishingly little is known about the life of Madame Tussaud. Until 1978, just two books accounted for most of what was told about her remarkable personal odyssey. One recorded Madame Tussaud's own *Memoirs and Reminiscences of the French Revolution;* the other, written by her great-grandson and published in 1919, presented a history of the Museum, appropriately entitled *The Romance of Madame Tussaud's,* which capitalized on Madame Tussaud's own fragmented memories of her life. The *Memoirs* claimed that Marie Grosholtz was born in Berne, Switzerland, in 1760, the daughter of Joseph Grosholtz, a name "which is as renowned in Germany as Percy in England, Montmorency in France, or Vicomti in Italy."[4] Her mother was said to have been the daughter of a Swiss clergyman "of a highly respected class" (*Memoirs,* p. 24). According to the *Memoirs,* Marie was born two months after her father's death, after which her mother went to live with her brother John Christopher Curtius, a practicing physician in Berne. Pauline Chapman's recent account of Madame Tussaud's youth, however, tells a substantially different story. Marie Grosholtz was born on December 7, 1761, not 1760, in Strasbourg, not Berne. Although Chapman does not elaborate on the reasons that led Madame Tussaud to add one year to her age, it is possible that she was actually an illegitimate child. Her mother, who had never learned how to read, was in no way related to John Christopher Curtius. She joined his household as a housekeeper.

Even the character of Curtius is shrouded in mystery. He appears in Madame Tussaud's *Memoirs,* as well as in her great-grandson's history of the Museum, as John Christopher Curtius, but he becomes Philippe Guillaume Mathé Curtius in more recent works on the Tussauds' history. Chapman does not explain the singular discrepancy in names. Could it be that Marie Tussaud was not so well acquainted with the famous Curtius? At any rate, Curtius modeled anatomic limbs in wax and his talents as a modeler soon surpassed his reputation as a doctor. According to Madame Tussaud's great-grandson, Curtius "extended the scope of his labours to the execution of many miniature portraits in that same plastic material, and gained the patronage of many of the leading members of the aristocracy" (*Romance*, p. 56). Curtius followed the Prince de Conti to Paris in 1762, where he found "a handsome suite of apartments awaiting him at the Hotel d'Aligre, hard by the Croix du Tahoir in the Rue St. Honoré" (ibid., p. 59). By all accounts, his housekeeper and her daughter joined him in Paris in 1766. In 1770, Curtius opened a wax cabinet at the Palais-Royal, to be followed thirteen years later by a second installation at the popular boulevard du Temple. According to Chapman, the young Marie Grosholtz learned her trade from Curtius: "She was absorbed and happy as she learned how to oil a sitter's face and flatten any facial hair with pomade, before a mask of fine plaster of Paris was applied. The sitter breathed through quills or straws inserted in the nostrils."[5] Madame Tussaud's life in Paris before and during the French Revolution is largely undocumented, save for her own published recollections. Chapman is cautiously vague about the dramatic episodes that would lead to the success of Madame Tussaud's Wax Museum.[6] But for all its improbabilities and obvious chronological aberrations, Madame Tussaud's tale is not without interest, since it illustrates (like Mary Shelley's 1831 Preface to *Frankenstein*) a genealogy of fame and horror as conceived and described by a woman of exceptional character and unusual talents.

Madame Tussaud claimed to have been acquainted with the royal family of France and to have instructed the king's sister, Madame Elizabeth, in the art of wax-modeling. The young Marie Grosholtz moved to Versailles around 1780. She developed a strong attachment to the royal family and thereafter described herself as a faithful royalist. In 1783, Curtius created the "caverne des grands voleurs," dedicated to famous criminals and housed with his exhibition in the boulevard du Temple: "As soon as Justice has despatched someone [Curtius] models the head and puts him into the collection, so that something new is always being offered to the curious, and the sight is not expensive for it costs only two sous" (*Horrors*, p. 1). With the onset of the Revolution, Curtius asked his "niece" to leave Versailles and live with him. There is some evidence that Curtius participated in the destruction of the Bastille, or at least that he went to great lengths to publicize his devotion to the revolutionary cause. He had a pamphlet printed depicting his role and several times made himself known to the authorities with various patriotic gestures, no doubt to attest to his enthusiastic dedication to the new regime. As a foreigner and a German-speaking subject, he could easily have been suspected and arrested in the political turmoil of the Revolution. In his house, Madame Tussaud tells us, she met all the famous leaders, from Mirabeau to Marat and Robespierre. But it was her claim that she was forced to take wax impressions of the beheaded victims of the guillotine that proved crucial to the creation and stunning success of Madame Tussaud's Wax Museum. This horrible task formed the "embryo" of the Chamber of Horrors. According to her great-grandson, "We have it from her own mouth that it was a task with which she dared not hesitate to comply" (*Romance*, p. 90).

Even before the guillotine claimed the royal family, Madame Tussaud described vividly to her biographer how she was forced to "take an impression" of the Princesse de Lamballe, a victim of the September 1792 massacres, whom she had met earlier at Versailles:

> Her head was immediately taken to Madame Tussaud, whose feelings can be easier conceived than described. The savage murderers stood over her, whilst she, shrinking with horror, was compelled to take a cast from the features of the unfortunate princess. Having known her virtues, and having been accustomed to see her beaming with all the cheerfulness and sweetness which are ever the heralds of "temper's unclouded ray,"—to hear her accents teeming but of kindness, always affording pleasure to her auditors, and then, alas! for Madame Tussaud to have the severed head of one so lovely between her trembling hands, was hard indeed to bear. The features, beauteous even in death, and the auburn tresses, although smeared with blood, still, in parts, were unpolluted by the ruthless touch of her assassins, and shone with all their natural richness and brilliance. Eager to retain a memento of the hapless princess, Madame Tussaud proceeded to perform her melancholy task, whilst surrounded by the brutal monsters, whose hands were bathed in the blood of the innocent. (*Memoirs*, II, pp. 30–31)

This vivid scene complemented perfectly the popular view of the brutal Revolution. But an exhibition catalogue of 1803 describing the decapitated heads of the victims of the French Revolution casts some doubt on this account of Marie Tussaud's initial feelings about the fate of the unfortunate princess. The catalogue describes the Princesse de Lamballe as a woman who perpetrated "a thousand barbarous and indelicate acts" (*Waxworker*, p. 200).

In fact, there is no evidence that either Curtius or his protégée was asked, or even allowed, to take wax impressions of the most famous victims of the revolutionary riots or the guillotine. Recent biographers, reluctant to abandon the legend that still gives a special tragic aura to the Chamber of Horrors, content themselves with speculating that the orders Marie Grosholtz received were secret, and there would have been no traces left: "The strictest secrecy was imposed on Curtius and Marie by those members of the National Convention who issued the orders. The modelled head would not be publicized, nor would it be exhibited in the *Salon de Cire*. Such a thing would cause additional shock and hostility in other European countries" (*Witness*, p. 131). But legends die hard; in a later book Pauline Chapman rewrites the tragic scene in which Curtius is supposed to have modeled the decapitated head of the king's mistress as follows: "There are several accounts of Curtius' visit to the Madeleine cemetery in the chill December dusk where he awaited the arrival of the cart with the bodies. Sorting out the head he needed with practiced fingers he smoothed out the distortion of the still beautiful face of Madame du Barry, oiled the features, applied the plaster mask before the head was tossed to join the others in the common grave. Soon the wax likeness was arousing much interest in Curtius' exhibition" (*Horrors*, p. 17). Eventually, Madame du Barry was "resurrected" as "sleeping beauty." Her lying figure still breathes softly, thanks to an ingenious clockwork, later replaced by an electric system.

The collection of these dreary impressions was to form the nucleus of the original Chamber of Horrors (called the Separate Room until 1846) and its enduring attraction. It included the heads of Hébert, Robespierre, and Fouquier-Tinville. Madame Tussaud also claimed to have been forced to take an impression of Marat soon after his assassination, and a few weeks later, to have been asked to take another of Charlotte Corday. Madame Tussaud, long after she had settled in England and turned her skills and attention to other subjects, maintained a passionate interest in the most gruesome aspects of the revolutionary period. She sent her sons in search of the executioner Sanson or his descendants. They brought back from France what the exhibition catalogues called "the most extraordinary relic in the world": the blade and the lunette of the Paris guillotine used during the days of the Terror, still on view today at the Tussaud Museum.

Curtius died in October 1794, leaving Marie Grosholtz, "my pupil in my art," his sole heir. On October 18, 1795, Marie Grosholtz married François Tussaud, a civil engineer from a family of metal workers established in Burgundy. Marie Tussaud was thirty-four, her husband twenty-six. A daughter was born in 1797, but died six months later. Two sons, Joseph and François, were born in 1798 and 1800. Very little is known about Marie Tussaud's husband. He is said to have been a gambler who offered very little financial support to his family. Marie separated from him in November 1802, when she accepted an offer from one of Curtius' friends, a certain Philipstal, to join him in England, where he had a magic lantern show called Phantasmagoria. After a successful season in London at the Lyceum Theater in 1801, Philipstal correctly estimated that Marie Tussaud's wax collection would add an exciting touch to his own exhibit. Madame Tussaud left Paris, taking along the revolutionary mementos and her eldest son. She left behind the less dramatic wax figures, her two-year-old son and her husband, and never returned. In a letter dated 1804, she announced to François Tussaud that she wanted an official separation and asked him to see to the care of her mother. Her younger son, François, joined his mother in 1822. She never saw her husband again and beyond this date nothing is known about him. Demonstrating an unusual resiliency and remarkable business acumen, Marie Tussaud toured England and Ireland with her show, then settled in London, first on the Strand, then on Gray's Inn Road, and finally on Baker Street, where she established permanent quarters in 1835.

Although doubts linger about Madame Tussaud's activities during the French Revolution and the authenticity of the decapitated heads' wax imprints, Chapman notes that "it was the 'death heads,' models and historic relics that gave Madame Tussaud's exhibition at the Lyceum Theatre its unique flavour" (ibid., p. 22). Furthermore, "It was on account of this special aspect of her exhibition that Madame Tussaud was asked when she had been at the Lyceum

Theatre a couple of months or so to model another decapitated head" (ibid., p. 23). Colonel Despard, found guilty of plotting against the British government, had been condemned to be hanged and decapitated in 1803. Twenty thousand people watched the execution. "The *Times* made a full report on the funeral and noted that 'an artist it is said took a cast of Mr Despard's face a few moments before the lid of the coffin was screwed down' . . . Colonel Despard remained in wax effigy in Madame Tussaud's exhibition for many years to come. He joined Marat and the guillotined heads. Curious crowds showed how right Madame Tussaud had been to perpetuate her 'uncle's' *Caverne des Grands Voleurs*. Henceforward, she would always have a separate section—the public wanted it" (ibid., pp. 27–28). Soon, Madame Tussaud's "skillful fingers," to quote her biographer, would be known for their ability to model with equal expertise from the living and the dead: "She also advertised her willingness to make portraits from life of any visitors who fancied their likeness in wax, and in addition she announced 'the artist can model from the dead body as well as from animated features'" (ibid., p. 28). Yet it would take some time before this new "genre," associated with the most violent aspects of inflicted death, would be fully accepted. Whereas the masks of the French Revolution continued to attract a public fascinated with the revolutionary excesses, the domestic horror of the death penalty did not immediately lend itself to the theatrical effects of the Wax Museum. To quote Chapman: "During twelve years following her departure from Ireland Madame Tussaud was unable to make any additions to her Separate Room. It was a frustrating situation. There were executions for every imaginable crime—murder for gain, jealousy, revenge or illicit passion; child-killing; arson; poisoning horses; etc." (ibid., p. 33). But Madame Tussaud, in spite of her best efforts, could not gain access to the criminals, dead or alive. All this changed, however, when Arthur Thistlewood was hanged and decapitated in 1820. Like Colonel Despard, Thistlewood had been convicted of political crimes. Madame Tussaud "performed her task between Thistlewood's conviction and sentence to be hanged which took place on 12 April and the execution which was carried out on 1 May . . . When Madame Tussaud entered the condemned cell she saw a tall man of military appearance. She spread the plaster over a long sallow face . . . Madame

Tussaud never retained the portraits that no longer attracted public attention and a surviving catalogue of 1822 printed in Manchester makes no mention of Thistlewood or Despard" (ibid., pp. 37–38). Slowly, the Chamber of Horrors was extended and regularly updated during the nineteenth century with new wax figures whose models were infamous for particular criminal atrocities. But in spite of this slightly disreputable aspect of her exhibition, or perhaps because of it, Madame Tussaud, all witnesses agree, led a peaceful existence from her move to England until her death in 1850, devoting herself to the enlargement of the exhibition, which became a family undertaking. Although she maintained the grisly tradition of taking wax impressions of soon-to-be executed criminals and of victims fresh from the gallows, she is pictured in the Museum as a dignified old woman who enjoyed the favor of the great leaders of the time and remained a staunch royalist to her last days. She died on April 15, 1850, at the age of eighty-nine.

The Space of Imagination

Two episodes from Madame Tussaud's carefully crafted legend illustrate the development and continuing appeal of the Chamber of Horrors. The first is described by her great-grandson in these terms:

> As we view to-day the quaint little figure of Madame which stands in the Exhibition she helped to found in France and established in this country, we must imagine her in the full vigour of her young womanhood, sensible to the dangers and terrors of the Revolution in which she was about to be involved. The Exhibition was as yet in its infancy; but stirring times were approaching, and the days were pregnant with meaning for the France that was to be—a time of bloodshed and grim ruthlessness born of a people's desire for freedom, and attended by ghastly scenes in Paris that revealed the extremities to which unbridled human passions could go. (*Romance*, p. 81)

These lines describe Madame Tussaud's activities during her youth in terms reminiscent of childbirth: the "infancy" of the Wax Museum was bathed in the blood of the Revolution and the days were "pregnant with meaning" while the young girl in the bloom of womanhood devoted her talents to creating the Chamber of

The late Madame Tussaud, 1850.

Horrors' first exhibits. The legend of Madame Tussaud's being
forced to take impressions of the freshly guillotined heads of the
Revolution was indispensable to the success of her *oeuvre*. But as
noted earlier, her account of molding the sinister relics that the
tumbril had just deposited at the Madeleine cemetery cannot be
confirmed through any Revolutionary archives. Numerous errors
and implausibilities in this account cast the greatest doubt over
these episodes. Yet that the very history of the Museum's origin
may be a *fiction* throws a peculiar light on the power of the female
imagination that created the lugubrious Chamber of Horrors. At

its origin is the violence the young woman was purportedly made to participate in: "We can hardly imagine her bitter experience when *compelled* to employ her young hands in taking impressions of heads immediately after decapitation . . . she was *compelled to reproduce* the lineaments of Louis XVI, Marie-Antoinette, Hébert, Danton, Robespierre, Carrier, Fouquier-Tinville—the best and fairest, and also the worst and vilest—who met their death on the scaffold. Unthinkable were the *gruesome tasks of faithfully recording their features imposed upon the young woman* who was destined to bring to England that Exhibition" (ibid., p. 87, emphasis added). This tale of violence and fecundity brings forth objects that not only recall the darkest hours of the Revolution or the trials of a young woman, but also illustrate the role and function of the female imagination such as it had been conceived by authors of Antiquity.

The Wax Museum provides a concrete illustration of the very workings of imagination. Cleanthes (331–232 B.C.) believed fantasies, these products of the imagination, to be like "imprints in wax," and described the imagination as being able to perpetuate the imprints in wax long after the mind had perceived them.[7] Avicenna compared imaginatio to wax, since, Murray W. Bundy tells us, "wax . . . retains the impression in good style because its humidity is tempered by dryness . . . This goes on in the organ of common sense and imagination."[8] This illusion of presence—the fact that the "mental imprints" of imagination, like "imprints in wax," can be perceived as if their causes existed here and now, whereas, in fact, they belong already to the past—confirms for many philosophers, from Cleanthes to Malebranche, the danger and weakness of the imagination. The essential difference between imagination and the memory's more rational function was believed to reside in the imagination's inability to differentiate between the present object and the absent object, its way of seeing vividly what is actually removed from the eyes in time and space. Such is also the particular horror connected to the special room of the Wax Museum, the Chamber of the Dead, whose effigies have been made to look so much like the living, an early catalogue tells us, that it "renders it difficult to recognize them from living persons" (*Romance*, p. 110).

The extraordinary tale of Madame Tussaud's taking wax imprints of the newly fallen heads of the Revolution and the stunning creation of the Chamber of Horrors, where the absent and the

Madame Tussaud's Wax Museum, the Separate Room: (left to right) Carrier, Hébert, Robespierre, and Fouquier-Tinville.

dead stand present, offer a powerful metaphor for the classical concept of imagination itself. It is as if Madame Tussaud's heated imagination had directly produced the "monsters" described in the catalogue of the Chamber of Horrors. Like a monstrous womb, the Chamber of Horrors contains a series of figures bearing an uncanny resemblance to objects that did not necessarily participate in their creation. But, more interestingly, the process through which resemblance is achieved—the lifelike wax-modeling—perpetuates the power of imagination to retain the past and mislead the subject into believing that the absent are present. In this perspective, both the Tussaud Wax Museum and the legend surrounding its origin can be said to illustrate the power of imagination and its half-concealed monstrosity. The tale of Marie Tussaud and the conception of the Museum as an embryonic display of monstrous fantasies illustrate once again the workings of the female imagination. Both the horrors of the guillotine and the lingering doubts surrounding the authenticity of the revolutionary "heads" were necessary to this replay of a now-familiar tale of monstrous conception and undisclosed paternity. "No wonder many a heated controversy has waged around these works, for it is hard to realise that they are the actual impressions of those heads that fell under the knife of the guillotine," notes John Tussaud (ibid., pp. 87–88). But therein lay the very attraction of the Chamber of Horrors.

The Hangman's Harvest

When William Corder was executed in front of a crowd of ten thousand in August 1828 for the murder of his mistress "it was not necessary for Madame Tussaud in person to obtain a likeness from Corder's face before or after his execution, nor did she pay the guinea an inch which the hangman is reputed to have charged for the rope. William Corder's body was handed over to Mr George Creed, surgeon at the hospital at Bury St Edmunds where a death mask was taken. Madame Tussaud modelled her portrait on a cast from this" (*Horrors*, p. 40). She thus became closely associated with an area of medical practice that both benefited from crimes by dissecting corpses recently dispatched by justice and created its own criminal field because of its unfulfilled need for more bodies: "In [the] early nineteenth century the supply of bodies for anatomist's

work and teaching was extremely limited," notes Madame Tussaud's biographer, Pauline Chapman. "It was a situation of supply
and demand which led to a steady increase in the gruesome practice of 'body snatching' from graveyards . . . Robbing of graves developed into a profession and those who practiced it for a *livelihood*
were nicknamed 'resurrectionists'" (ibid., p. 41, emphasis added).[9]
It is worth noting that the "Separate Room"—also called "Chamber of the Dead" before becoming the "Chamber of Horrors"—
exemplified a form of resurrectionist practice and was to gain
enduring fame as well from the wax imprints of two criminals condemned for having smothered to death several victims in order to
sell their remains to medical schools. Chapman comments that the
addition of William Burke and William Hare to the wax collection
"resurrected" the centerpiece of the Museum as well: "The trial
and conviction of William Burke provided her with exactly the op-
portunity she needed to bring *fresh life* to the Separate Room"
(ibid., p. 45, emphasis added). Certainly, no figures excited the
public's curiosity more than those of Burke and Hare, which were
added to the Chamber of Horrors shortly after Burke's execution
in 1829, just two years before the prodigiously successful new edition of *Frankenstein*.

By 1833, a placard advertising Madame Tussaud's Exhibition
was already capitalizing on the famous criminals: "The Exhibition
consists of a great variety of Public Characters, modelled with the
greatest care, and regardless of expense, among whom will be noticed the original figures of BURKE and HARE (taken from their
faces, to obtain which the Proprietors went expressly to Scotland);
which have excited intense interest from the peculiar nature of
their crimes, and their approach to life, which renders it difficult to
recognize them from living persons" (*Romance*, p. 110). The curious parallelism between "the peculiar nature of their crimes"
(which alludes to Burke and Hare's murders) and "their approach
to life" (which describes Madame Tussaud's "peculiar art") is not
entirely inappropriate, considering the nature of the murders for
which Burke was executed. A later catalogue describes both their
figures and their life of crime as follows:

> *Burke*. (The model of Burke taken within three hours after his
> execution; and that of Hare from life, in the prison of Edin-

Madame Tussaud's Wax Museum, the Separate Room: Burke and Hare.

burgh). This murderer, with his associate Hare, became notorious for a series of murders, perpetrated for the purpose of
gain. There was a demand in the schools of anatomy for bodies
as subjects for the demonstrations and lectures, and for dissection by the students. Burke and Hare were in the habit of waylay-
ing strangers, suffocating them with a pitch-plaster fastened

tightly over the nose and mouth, and selling the corpses to the professors of anatomy. This practice was carried on for upwards of ten months, during which numbers of persons disappeared in a manner that could not be accounted for. A discovery was at length made; Burke was convicted on the evidence of Hare, and executed at Edinburgh, January 27, 1829. Hare, in consideration of his having turned King's evidence, was again let loose upon the world.[10]

There is an uncanny mirror-effect in this tale: Curtius had started his waxworks by producing anatomical models; Burke dispatched the living to produce corpses for schools of anatomy, and would himself end up as a wax figure, one of the most notorious, in Madame Tussaud's Chamber of Horrors.

Burke's crimes greatly stirred the popular imagination and gave rise to a new expression now only rarely used, but defined as follows in the *Oxford English Dictionary:*

> *Burke* v. [f. *Burke,* the name of a notorious criminal executed at Edinburgh in 1829, for smothering many persons in order to sell their bodies for dissection.]
>
> l.*trans.* To murder, in the same manner or for the same purpose as Burke did; to kill secretly by suffocation or strangulation, or for the purpose of selling the victim's body for dissection.
>
> 1829 *Times* 2 Feb. 3/5 "As soon as the executioner proceeded to his duties, the cries of 'Burke him . . . Burke him—give him no rope' . . . were vociferated . . . 'Burke Hare too!'"

The expression was later extended to include other forms of "smothering," for example, "a book suppressed before issue was popularly said to have been burked," or again, one could also use the expression "to burke a parliamentary conscience." Burke's crimes recall Frankenstein's initial preoccupation with obtaining bodies from dissecting rooms or charnel houses. A few "excellent verses" quoted by her great-grandson even bestowed on Madame Tussaud the subtitle of *Frankenstein:* "Modern Prometheus! who can'st give, / Like him of old, to human form / All *but* the life;— here THOU wilt live / And triumph o'er the "creeping worm" / That sullies all things—pale Decay! *Thy features* ne'er can pass away!" (*Romance,* p. 117). For in this case Madame Tussaud herself played the role of Frankenstein, and Burke's crimes reveal one of the essential principles at work in the creation and the success of the Wax

Museum. Like Frankenstein, Madame Tussaud found, or claimed to have found, her models among soon-to-be-executed criminals, or in mass graves, such as the cemetery of the Madeleine. The raw material of her art and the embryonic object of her Museum are the dead. And what is the nature of her "peculiar art," if not to reenact on the dead the very act of suffocation that Burke practiced on the living? The "plaster fastened tightly over the nose and mouth" is also the preliminary step in casting a mask, whether a death mask or not. To take an impression is also to "burke" a victim, to smother the mask of death in the short time between execution and burial. The technique for wax imprints certainly evoked the idea of "smothering" and its use with a live subject required a special apparatus: "Curtius had taught her to take life and death masks with fine plaster of Paris," notes Chapman, "when submitting to the former the semi-recumbent sitter breathed through straws or quills inserted in the nostrils" (*Horrors,* p. xiv). Unlike Burke, whose smothering caused death, Madame Tussaud, using her plaster casts, brought her famous victims back from death to an illusion of life. But the two proceed along strangely similar lines: Burke's victims disappeared and then were produced as corpses for anatomy schools; Madame Tussaud's subjects were quickly smothered before their burial and were produced later as wax figures (like the earlier models found in anatomy schools).

The monstrous imagination, as shown earlier, produces figures that are a perversion of the original Aristotelian principle that art should imitate nature. The perversion inherent in Madame Tussaud's peculiar art, and not so different from that of Frankenstein, is that this art imitates death and that the product of this imitation of death is an imitation of life, which explains the strange attraction of the Wax Museum. Yet, this imitation of life is strange only because of the accompanying certainty that one is seeing nothing but an imitation. In the Chamber of the Dead, the illusion of life never brings the dead back to life. On the contrary, one could say of Madame Tussaud that she brings the dead back to death.

Burke's character and figure played a special role in Madame Tussaud's exhibition during the nineteenth century. She decided to dispatch her own son to the place of execution to take an imprint of his face. Although Madame Tussaud was shrouded in respectability and her creation enjoyed continuous success, Burke may be seen as her somber double, her criminal alter ego: Both profited from crime, the latter illegitimately, the former with public success. Both attracted crowds, Burke when he was finally executed, Madame Tussaud when she again staged the character waiting to be executed. As Hilaire Belloc noted, "It was [Madame Tussaud's] own talent and industry, the *work of her own hands*, that laid the foundation of it all" (*Romance*, p. 31, emphasis added). We also know that in her wisdom, Madame Tussaud remained supremely conscious of the fact that although passing celebrities supplied both fashionable subjects and a form of respectability, it was the Chamber of Horrors that produced the enduring fascination of her museum of wax figures.

The Artist as Executioner

One of the earliest catalogues of Madame Tussaud's exhibition (1833) outlines the spatial organization of the Museum, which opened with a scene of royal splendor, the coronation of His Majesty William IV, and concluded with a section entitled "Separate Room, Admittance Six-Pence." The coronation of the king of England was given full treatment, with the following description of the group:

> HIS MAJESTY dressed in the magnificent costume of the occasion, is seated on the Throne, holding in his right hand the Orb and Cross, and in his left supporting the Sceptre. His Grace the Archbishop of Canterbury, standing behind the King on his right hand, with his eyes uplifted to Heaven, is in the act of placing the Imperial Crown on the King's head, assisted by the Right Reverend the Lord Bishop of Norwich. On the platform below the King stands Her Majesty, Queen Adelaide, in her State Dress; opposite to her, Lord Brougham, in his Robes; below, his Grace the Duke of Wellington, and opposite to him, Earl Grey, in their Robes of State. Behind the Throne are three figures, representing Britannia, Caledonia, and Hibernia, surmounted by a Canopy.[11]

At the other end of the Museum, after viewing additional royalty, including Louis XVI, his queen, and the Dauphin "taken from life," a few men of letters, and some notorious characters, one reached the Separate Room. The additional entrance fee, six pence, was justified as follows: "The following Highly Interesting Figures and Objects in consequence of the peculiarity of their appearance are placed in an Adjoining Room and form a Separate Exhibition well worthy the inspection of Artists and Amateurs." [12] Added to the heads and relics of the French Revolution were the "original casts" of Burke, Stewart, his wife, Holloway, and Corder, all recently condemned murderers. A postscript of 1837 added: "The above casts are introduced to assist the admirers of Phrenology," the new scientific method that deduced behavioral tendencies from the shape of heads. [13]

Marat was there, "taken immediately after his Assassination, by order of the National Assembly," "one of the atrocious leaders of the French Revolution," an "execrable wretch," "disagreeable and ferocious." Robespierre's head, "taken immediately after his Execution, by Order of the National Assembly," stood next to those of Carrier, Fouquier-Tinville, and Hébert, all victims of the guillotine. Robespierre rated the longest entry, "a sanguinary Demagogue . . . such was the influence of this monster, that France forgot her honour and her religion at his command . . . Of all the monsters who figured in the French Revolution, none have descended to posterity with a name so abhorred as Robespierre." Carrier is described as "an infamous republican . . . After perpetrating every crime of cruelty, lust and avarice, he was recalled, and at last condemned to a deserved death." Fouquier-Tinville, "a Frenchman of infamous memory . . . the most vindictive character . . . The fall of Robespierre checked not this monster . . . At length, punishment came, though late—Fouquier appeared before that tribunal, where he had exercised such bloody tyranny." Hébert, who exhibited a "character of brutality and cruelty . . . died like a coward." The more recent heads, those of Burke, Stewart, and his wife, all bear the note "Taken from their Faces three hours after their Execution." [14] Stewart, executed in Edinburgh in 1829, was a robber and murderer responsible for the deaths of nine persons. Finally, Holloway is said to have murdered his wife "in a manner too horrible to describe." The characters presented in the Separate Room stood out as remarkable monsters whose executions were justifiably demanded by society. From its inception, two features distinguished "the separate room's" models from those presented outside: most of its original characters had suffered a violent end and their impressions had often been modeled *after their death,* either by Madame Tussaud, a few hundred feet away from the guillotine (although the note "by Madame Tussaud's own hands" does not appear until later) or by her associate (in Burke's case, by her son), who had traveled expressly to Scotland to take the criminal's impression "within three hours after his execution."

The Chamber of Horrors also served as the privileged scene of crime and punishment. In the beginning it was reserved exclusively for the great criminals, the "monsters" of the Revolution and their contemporary equivalents. Historical inaccuracies (including dates of birth and dates of execution) had not been entirely corrected even by the end of the nineteenth century. But it was clear from all entries that the violent deaths so forcefully "displayed" in the Separate Room were no cause for sorrow. Robespierre's entry concluded with these words: "Well does he deserve the following epitaph; 'Passenger, lament not his fate, for were he living, thou wouldst be dead.'" [15] Initially, the royal victims were not included in the Chamber of the Dead. But their effigies, "taken from life" like those of contemporary royalty, graced the rooms to be visited before arrival at the Separate Chamber. The internal organization of the Tussaud Museum described a space of political utopia, so to speak, a space where the king's majesty would be glorified and exposed to public scrutiny, but a space also sustained by scenes of the punishment awaiting all those guilty of *lèse-majesté.* In *Discipline and Punish,* Michel Foucault invokes Kantorowitz's analysis of the King's Body as double and suggests that this dual body also requires a somber and necessary double: "At the opposite pole one might imagine placing the body of the condemned man; he, too, has his legal status; he gives rise to his own ceremonial and he calls forth a whole theoretical discourse . . . In the darkest region of the political field the condemned man represents the symmetrical, inverted figure of the king." [16]

A tour of Madame Tussaud's Wax Museum in 1830, opening with the coronation of His Majesty William IV and concluding with the decapitated heads of the regicides, gave a literal illustration of the king's majesty, from the glory of his officially crowned body to the "inverted figure" lodged at the opposite end of the Museum—that of the criminal. As if to emphasize that all crimes are crimes committed against the person of the king, Ravaillac, the assassin of

Henry IV of France, had been added, the only character from the past to be represented in the Chamber. His figure was "taken from a Statue, in the Hall of Statues, in the Louvre," and his punishment was described in great detail:

> Francis Ravaillac . . . was a gloomy fanatic, and conceiving that Henry IV., King of France, had given him offence, he in 1610, mortally stabbed him, while in his coach, and surrounded by his guards. The act was one of very great wickedness; but the punishment inflicted on him was a disgrace to his Judges. His right hand was consumed in a cauldron of boiling brimstone; his flesh was pulled from his bones with red hot pincers; boiling oil, resin, and brimstone, were poured on his wounds, and melted lead on his navel. To put an end to his miseries, four horses were fastened to the four quarters of his body, and being whipped, the animals literally tore him to pieces. Though he denied having any accomplices, his parents were banished from France; and every person bearing his name was compelled to renounce it, that the name of Ravaillac might never more be heard in France.[17]

The Chamber of the Dead thus testified to the king's absolute power and his inescapable justice. The splendor and authority of the monarch was both completed and sustained by the final attractions of the Separate Room, its additional entrance fee, and its lifelike representation of capital punishment: decapitated heads, death masks of criminals, and a model of the guillotine. By the late nineteenth century, a full figure of the executioner had been added, and with the symbol of royal retribution now dominating the room, the decapitated heads of the royal family of France had also found their place. The success of Madame Tussaud's Museum lay primarily in its figuration of historical redress: it was the place where crimes of historic proportion (regicide and parricide) were explicitly denounced and their punishment reenacted for all to see and ponder. This is also why it was so important that the first room one visited was dedicated to various living figures and their effigies taken from life with royal permission, all dominated by a coronation scene—that of the reigning monarch. These scenes gave legitimacy to Madame Tussaud's Museum, and perhaps also contributed to public acceptance of the curious role Marie Tussaud claimed for herself at the time of the Revolution.

Speculating on why the National Assembly, or more precisely the Convention, would ever have wished to order casts of the beheaded victims of the guillotine, John T. Tussaud writes, "The casts were undoubtedly taken under compulsion, either with the object of pandering to the temper of the people, or of serving as confirmatory evidence of execution having taken place—perhaps both" (*Romance*, p. 88). These lines shed light on the aesthetic function of the death masks of the Chamber of Horror. Not only is their purpose to represent the faces of victims or their executioners, not only must they show an undeniable resemblance, but they also serve to prove that *death had taken place*. The idea of executing a work of art, the expressions "to catch a resemblance," "to take a portrait," or, in Madame Tussaud's catalogue, the descriptions of masks "taken from life," of course all suggest that something of the models has been spirited away when their likenesses have been transferred onto a canvas or a piece of plaster. From Poe to Balzac, the Romantic portrait always implied a threat to the model. At Madame Tussaud's, the execution of the death mask reproduced and duplicated the execution by guillotine or, later, by hanging. In the Separate Chamber, the masks confirmed the crime, authenticated death, and manifested the implacable justice of monarchs.

John Tussaud's second justification for the young Marie Grosholtz's somewhat sordid role in the Revolution, as well as for the secret motives that the Convention may have had in seeing reproduced a parricide whose execution it had ordered, is summed up by the words "pandering to the temper of the people." This justification excludes the royal heads which, we are told, were never exhibited in Paris, but may allude to an anecdote describing the Parisian crowds invading Curtius' museum in the early days of the Revolution in order to take famous heads and parade them in the streets. These demonstrations were followed by parades of a more grisly nature in which real decapitated heads were promenaded throughout Paris. Nevertheless, in all likelihood Marie Tussaud's wax heads from the Revolution began their career in England, although they also "pandered" very successfully to "the temper of the people" by testifying to an execution, by demonstrating that justice had been served, and by reproducing the punishment the beholder had not actually seen.

Over the years, many of the instruments and symbols of the

penal system of the time were added to the Chamber of Horrors. These included not only instruments of death—the guillotine's blade and lunette, for example—but also emblems of incarceration: "The Old Toll Bell from Newgate Prison"; "A Cell Door from Old Newgate"; "A Key to the Principal Gate of the Bastille"; and a life-size figure of the executioner. The Chamber of Horrors thus came to signify an exemplary genealogy of crime and punishment. Toward the end of the century a series of scenes depicting the fall toward evil were added: "*The Six Stages of Wrong;* a Graphic Record of a Downward Career Depicted in a Series of Tableaux. I. Temptation. II. End of the Game. III. Ruin. IV. Revenge. V. Guilty or not Guilty. VI. His Last Journey."

"The lure of Horrors," to use John Tussaud's words, lay in their ability to stir the popular imagination by the spectacle of a great crime committed against society; the people found in the Chamber of Horrors an assurance that the crime had indeed been punished.[18] Tussaud illustrates his theory with the following anecdote:

> Referring back to the days before the advent of the daily illustrated papers with their portraits of all kinds of people, a very affecting story was once told by a well-known author.
>
> It related to a very pretty and plaintive young woman who visited the Chamber of Horrors early on the morning that a certain criminal with many *aliases* was executed.
>
> She was accompanied by her father, who, with his arm around her waist to steady her faltering steps, led her up to where the figure of the murderer stood. The poor woman remained gazing at it as though fascinated; then, with a nod, she burst out crying and buried her head in her hands.
>
> Her father gently drew her out of the place, and as he did so whispered in her ear: "Free, my child; free at last!" (*Romance*, p. 306)

This scene, another contribution to the legend that was to envelop both the life of Marie Tussaud and the history of the Chamber of Horrors, brings to light several crucial points. The merging of the spectator with the real or potential victim of the criminal being contemplated suggests a judicial relationship between the beholder and the wax figure of the murderer. In entering the Chamber of Horrors one becomes implicated in a crime as the hypothetical victim of the criminal episode whose final outcome is so tragically depicted. At the same time, one is delivered from the criminal, who has been identified, portrayed, and, in the fullest sense of the word, executed. The spectator is at once victim, judge, and executioner. The beholder's gaze encompasses a symbolic narration that guarantees the just punishment of crime (presided over by the king in the opening rooms or by the victim's father in John Tussaud's story). What distinguishes the Chamber of Horrors is that punishment is double, as the case of Burke illustrates: the murderer always dies twice. Burke was both hanged for his crimes and "smothered" by Madame Tussaud's son in just retribution for the choking of his many victims. The Chamber of Horrors offers, in a single space, the spectacle of crime and punishment, supplemented by the catalogue's narratives. The penal organization it describes affirms as well the victim's rediscovered freedom: "free at last."

Waxworks

Although by far the most notorious, the Chamber of Horrors was not the only attraction of Madame Tussaud's Museum. Her wax model of the great singer Malibran had been extremely well received:

> The sweet, kindly and charitable nature of Malibran, no less than her wonderful genius and capacity, had endeared her to the whole people of England; and crowds flocked to Baker Street to gaze at the counterfeit presentment of the great *cantatrice*. The experience was not lost on Madame Tussaud, then in her seventy-sixth year, but as sharp and clearsighted as ever. She laid it down as the canon in the scheme of her enterprise that celebrities strictly "up to-date" should be continuously added to *every* department of her exhibition. If the Hour brought with it a Man—or a Woman—famous or infamous, the personage of that Hour was forthwith modelled, coloured, dressed, and given an apportioned place in the Baker Street Galleries.[19]

Ironically, another form of death stalked the "living" wax effigies: when their celebrity waned or their popularity declined, they would be melted down to make way for new favorites. One of Madame Tussaud's models is said to have described the dilemma: "I feel very frightened indeed . . . and more than that, exceedingly sorry that I ever promised to become a waxwork, for I have been told since that if the public grow weary of your presence, or the Tussauds get offended with you, they melt you down, and build up a more popular fellow out of your dripping" (*Romance,* p. 250). After the disappearance of his wax figure from the Museum floor, one model queried, "What do you think they have made of me? Perhaps Marshal Foch, perhaps President Poincaré, perhaps President Wilson. I only hope my figure has not been melted down to something in the Chamber of Horrors" (ibid., p. 244). And yet, the Chamber of Horrors alone seemed to guarantee lasting fame.

Insofar as the first step in a waxwork is the death/life mask, one can hardly speak of creative art; rather one must speak of method, the literal application of Burke's technique, that is, of smothering. The technique of waxworks also anticipates the technique of fingerprinting, which would play such an important role in the judicial system at the end of the nineteenth century. Like fingerprints, the death mask testifies to a truth, an authenticity that will always elude the Romantic view of artistic representation by directly connecting reproduction to its referent by the very element of physical contact or imprint. Hilaire Belloc noted that "when a man sees a bust of marble he does not expect to find illusion. The greatest portrait statuary can never be more than a symbol. But the wax effigy aims at exact reproduction" (ibid., p. 27). Contrary to the marble bust or the portrait, which fall into the category of symbols inasmuch as they are interpretations of a model entirely mediated by the artist's gaze and talent, the death mask is first and foremost an impression. The relationship between impression and death (found at every level of the judicial system) is revealed and exhibited at Madame Tussaud's, along with a full display of its origin, the monstrous "embryo" of the Chamber of Horrors, which was to give long life and prosperity to the Museum. This origin, marked by monstrosity and death, is echoed by the illusion the Wax Museum creates in the beholders: that they have just come across a friend or an acquaintance, but *dead or asleep.*[20]

In his remarks on the daguerreotype, Eugène Delacroix stressed the monstrous quality of the relationship between image and model, false for being so exact. Conversely, Walter Benjamin observed, one of the advantages of photography over portrait painting was that photography did not require the long posing sessions

214 Metaphors of Procreation

that were so constraining for the model.[21] The monstrous truth of photography would seem to emanate from its capacity to catch a resemblance that would not, that could not, be mediated by the lengthy sessions during which both the painter and the model stood waiting for a form of revelation. Wax imprints could be seen as a medium halfway between portraiture and photography. If one considers the creation of the Chamber of the Dead in light of Roland Barthes' essay on photography, *Camera Lucida,* it then appears that waxworks owed more to the technology being invented at the time than to the art of portraiture it was trying to emulate. Barthes remarks, "What the Photograph reproduces to infinity has occurred only once," and he adds, "It always leads the corpus I need back to the body I see."[22] For Barthes, the referent is obsessively present in the photograph he contemplates: "It is as if the Photograph always carries its referent with itself, both affected by the same amorous or funereal immobility, at the very heart of the moving world: they are glued together, limb by limb, like the condemned man and the corpse in certain tortures."[23] From this perspective, the Chamber of Horrors, with its striking capture of a "funereal immobility," its identification of the subject and model as the very "condemned man and corpse"—what Barthes recognizes in the photograph—made visible the implicit work of the camera obscura. The adherence of the photograph to the referent is illustrated as well in the death masks of Robespierre, Collins, or Burke. The status of the dead and the condemned, whose impressions would become a feature of Madame Tussaud's own camera obscura, her Chamber of the Dead, is described again by Barthes when he analyzes what he calls the "simulacrum," the "eidolon": "The person or thing photographed is the target, the referent, a kind of little simulacrum, any *eidolon* emitted by the object, which I should like to call the *Spectrum* of the Photograph, because this word retains, through its root, a relation to 'spectacle' and adds to it that rather terrible thing which is there in every photograph: the return of the dead."[24]

The relationship, one could say the "affinity," between the wax mask and the photograph (and, conversely, the opposition between the portrait and the waxwork) is made even more explicit in the following lines, in which Barthes attempts to define more precisely what separates the photograph from the portrait: "The first man who saw the first photograph (if we except Niepce, who made it) must have thought it was a painting: same framing, same perspective. Photography has been, and is still, tormented by the ghost of Painting (Mapplethorpe represents an iris stalk the way an Oriental painter might have done it); it has made Painting, through its copies and contestations, in the absolute, paternal Reference, as if it were born from the Canvas . . . At this point in my investigation, nothing eidetically distinguishes a photograph, however realistic, from a painting. 'Pictorialism' is only an exaggeration of what the Photograph thinks of itself. Yet it is not (it seems to me) by Painting that Photography touches art, but by Theater." [25] Thus, we see outlined in Barthes' work a double referent that appears each time between the model and its photograph: on the one hand, the referent is portrait art, perceived (importantly so) as paternity—albeit a somewhat *repudiated paternity*—in favor of theatricality, a staging that literally frames the subject; on the other hand, the subject's image is the referent it carries—"carries" perhaps the way Diderot's soldier carried his dead fetus, a referent seen as the "return from the dead."

The same theatrical effects Barthes perceives in photography are the explicit object of Madame Tussaud's Chamber of the Dead. These effects offer another illustration of what Walter Benjamin called the "exhibition value" of the modern work of art at the same time that they anchor the objects, decapitated heads and penal symbols, in a specific space, a Separate Room, meant to retain the "cult value" associated for Benjamin with the beginnings of art. [26] As in photography, the plaster mask bears the image (apparently unmediated by the artist's imagination) of an object to be gazed upon. But, as in a photograph, the mask is framed theatrically, staged in a dramatic setting that celebrates punishment by death and keeps alive the moment of execution. The idea of photographic centering, or framing, is anticipated by Madame Tussaud's Museum, this complex area where spatial ideology combines with either pedagogical or purely spectacular needs, for "cult value does not give way without resistance," as Benjamin remarks. [27] Behind this explicit frame—this separate space accessible only upon payment of an entrance fee—is another space, another frame also anchored in the ideology of spectacle: the guillotine. [28] If the revolutionary legend has survived with such intensity in the most famous of wax museums, if the image of Marie Grosholtz taking impressions of victims' fallen heads a few hundred yards from the guillotine is so necessary to the concept of the Chamber of the Dead, it is because death is staged, ritualized, and authenticated there. Barthes says that the photograph continues to signify what he calls the *ça a été* (the *that-has-been*) of the object. Similarly, the Wax Museum and, more particularly, the Chamber of the Dead, with its relics, funeral props, itemized catalogues, and the legend of its beginnings originating somewhere between death and the tomb, testify to the *ça a été* of executions—executions guaranteeing in the penal universe of the Museum that all masks are death masks.

Barthes himself is aware of the relationship between the mask and the photograph. Playing on the double function of the mask— its ability to dissimulate (the individual) and to reveal (a general quality)—Barthes writes, "Photography cannot signify (aim at a generality) except by assuming a mask. It is this word which Calvino correctly uses to designate what makes a face into the product of a society and of its history . . . The mask is the meaning, insofar as it is absolutely pure (as it was in the ancient theater). This is why the great portrait photographers are great mythologists."[29] In the portrait as mask, that is, as global portrait, as historical truth (whose best examples, Barthes suggests, may be Nadar's images of the French bourgeoisie and Sander's of pre-Nazi Germans), Barthes detects a photographic effect "critical enough to disturb" and yet "too discreet . . . to constitute an authentic and effective social critique." He adds, "What committed science would acknowledge the interest in Physiognomy?"[30] Here the photographic mask as defined by Barthes and the death mask—"introduced to assist the admirers of Phrenology" (Tussaud's catalogues, 1830's)—differ suggestively. The ideology expressed by these words from the older Tussaud catalogues is directly intended for those concerned with developing a science that would uncover the secrets of the criminal brain, its natural determination. In Tussaud's project, the masks enter into a mythology of crime organized as a teleology of punishment.

Madame Tussaud's masks confirm. They confirm death and a penal system that guarantees and makes visible the punishment of the guilty. But at Madame Tussaud's the mask is *masked,* so to speak.

There are, after all, three distinct stages in the preparation of the wax figures. First is the traditional "death mask" of fine plaster of Paris smothered over the model's face. From this mask is taken a "clay squeeze," which serves as a model for the wax "imprint." Thus the spectators never see the mask that was liberally plastered over the victim's features; they see only its "negative." In this respect, the waxworks of the Tussaud Museum, while metaphorically anticipating the photographic process, also echo the art of portraiture. It is in the third stage that the modelers, Marie Tussaud and her sons, assert their talents and give a face to death with their own "skillful fingers." It is the material underlying the mask itself that is offered to the spectators' gaze. The mask proper, the agony of labor, has been "burked."

While portraiture, as dramatized in the literature of the period, was defined as a specifically masculine art, what obscure ties link the female to the Wax Museum or to the "embryo" of the Chamber of the Dead? Madame Tussaud did not invent the wax museum. She was preceded by Curtius in Paris, and two other women were already operating wax galleries in England when Marie Tussaud arrived in 1802. What Madame Tussaud "invented," in a manner of speaking, was the origin of the wax museum as mausoleum, in the ancient sense of the term. She created a monument to the dead where the king's glory and the criminal's punishment were played out. While portraiture for the Romantic imagination hides behind its veil an incestuous desire that results not in the death of the father but in the concealment of the maternal inseminating element (its incestuous perversity), the Tussaud Museum expresses and exhibits in its own way the latest metamorphosis of a maternal imagination diverted from its legitimate object. It displays works of art whose models are recognizable but dead, whose criminal fathers have been surreptitiously pushed aside. The posthumous progeny stand in the shadow of the living king, the redeeming father. The majesty of the king's image at the entrance of the Museum might also be seen as an erasure of Marie Grosholtz's possibly illegitimate birth. At any rate, it is probably because the penal system underlying royal majesty is portrayed in the Wax Museum with such determination that Conan Doyle chose to lodge his most famous detective, Sherlock Holmes, at 221B Baker Street, the very street where the Wax Museum had gained fame and respectability.[31] The bachelor of crime and the mother of the Chamber of Horrors may be said to have created for the beholder a fictional phrenology of art, a space of investigation halfway between the monstrous womb and the "detective's rooms," between the executioner's gaze and the drug-addicted private eye.

9

Idumea

The most faithful interpretation of the theory of imaginationism may be found in Villiers de l'Isle-Adam's *L'Eve future* (1886). The author, an impoverished French aristocrat, was a close friend of Stéphane Mallarmé, an avid reader of Hegel, and an occasionally sarcastic observer of new scientific developments; he had previously published a series of *contes cruels* rivaled only by Poe's tales in their horrifying suspense and dark melancholy. *L'Eve future* retains much of the somber quality of Villiers's earlier works. Set in Menlo Park, New Jersey, in the 1880s, the story opens in a house surrounded by deep and lonely gardens, where Thomas Edison, "the man who made a prisoner of the echo," meditates. He imagines the sounds that might have been recorded for posterity had he invented his phonograph thousands of years earlier: Adam and Eve expelled from Eden, the trumpets of Jericho, Memnon's melancholy greeting to Aurora. And he ponders another creation, a mysterious experiment he intends to keep secret until its time has come. Edison is dreaming of creating an "Imitation Human Being," far removed from the automata produced by "those artisans of former days . . . Poor fellows, for lack of the proper technical skills, they produced nothing but ridiculous monsters. Albertus Magnus, Vaucanson, Maelzel, Horner, and all that crowd were barely competent makers of scarecrows. Their automata deserve to be exhibited in the most hideous of wax museums."[1] Edison is developing a technique of reproduction, "of *identification*" rather, that allows for the creation of "mysterious presences *of a mixed nature*" (p. 61). His project has not yet reached fruition when the arrival of an unexpected visitor precipitates Edison's plan for his new

creation. Lord Ewald, a long-time friend of the scientist, has come
to bid Edison a last goodbye before carrying out a suicide plan.
Ewald, the last son in a long aristocratic line, has fallen in love with
a supremely beautiful singer: she is, indeed, the incarnation of the
Venus Victorious.[2] Unfortunately, Ewald cannot bear the awful contrast between her splendid appearance and her mediocre soul.
"Her beauty, I assure you," Lord Ewald reports, "was beyond re-
proach, defying the subtlest analysis. From the outside, and from
the brow to the feet, a sort of *Venus Anadyomene;* within, a personality absolutely FOREIGN to this body. Imagine, if you will, this ab-
straction brought to life: a bourgeois Goddess" (p. 36). Unable to
bear his passion for this paradox, "an animated dualism who repels
and attracts me" (p. 46), and unable to renounce her, Ewald has
resolved to die. Edison listens to this remarkable story and, after a
brief hesitation, suggests his latest invention as the ultimate remedy for Lord Ewald's despair.

Genesis II

In a room filled with "various objects, like monsters risen from a
scientific underworld" (p. 53), Edison reveals his secret project, as
marvelous as it is frightening. In the underground world of his
laboratories he has begun to create the Ideal Woman, a new Eve.
She lacks only a specific physical body, and thus first appears
shrouded in veils and jewelry, an animated frame of precious
metal: "Standing on this dais, a sort of BEING appeared, its form
suggestive of nothing so much as the *unknown*. The vision seemed
to have features compounded of shadow; a string of pearls across
her forehead supported a dark veil which obscured the entire
lower part of her head" (p. 57). Edison proposes to complete his
creation by giving her the classical beauty and flawless appearance
of Alicia Clary, Ewald's mistress. This woman-to-be will possess, he
says, Alicia Clary's superb, inspired voice and elegant gestures, but
she will also be pure intelligence: her body and mind will be in
perfect harmony. However mad this enterprise may appear to
Ewald, Edison offers to explain, with cool precision, the complex
mechanisms of his projected android:

> Since this woman [Alicia Clary] is precious to you—I AM GOING
> TO STEAL HER OWN EXISTENCE AWAY FROM HER! I'm going to show

you, with mathematical certainty and on this very spot (the demonstration may freeze your soul, but you cannot refute it), I'm going to show, I say, how, making use of modern Science, I can capture the very grace of her gesture, the fullness of her body, the fragrance of her flesh, the resonance of her voice, the turn of her waist, the light of her eyes, the *familiarity* of her movements and her step, the individuality of her glance, all her traits and characteristics, down to the shadow she casts on the ground, everything *she appears to be*—her reflected Identity. I shall be the murderer of her stupidity, the assassin of her triumphant animal nature. (p. 63, translation modified)

This superb creature will be made of precious materials: two solid gold recording machines will reproduce Alicia Clary's melodious voice; her carriage, her step, the texture of her skin will be copied with the greatest exactitude by unique and unprecedented methods. After listening to Edison's lengthy and precise technical explanations, Lord Ewald observes with some irony: "The problems of creating an electro-magnetic being were easy to solve, *the result alone was mysterious*" (p. 157). Only one element in this mystery has a name: Sowana, an enigmatic woman whose story emerges later and who seems to communicate under hypnosis with Hadaly, Edison's android.

Lord Ewald, though highly skeptical, accepts the inventor's fantastic offer and agrees to delay carrying out his suicide plan for three weeks, the time Edison will need to complete the android and cure Ewald of his desperate passion for the too human Alicia Clary. One evening, Ewald receives a telegram from Alicia Clary inviting him to join her as a house guest at Menlo Park. Meeting her once again, the young man is dazzled by her beauty, hauntingly evocative of the *Venus Victorious*. He renounces the ideal but improbable creature that Edison had promised him and discovers new charms in his mistress. His change of heart, however, comes too late. This woman who has seduced him anew is not Alicia. It is her shadow—Edison's android, Hadaly. Terrified, then seduced forever, Ewald takes Hadaly and sails for Scotland. A fire breaks out on the ship and Hadaly "dies" in the flames. Unable to go on living without her, Ewald announces his own impending death to Edison.

L'Eve future provides an exemplary demonstration of the nineteenth-century aesthetics of resemblance and monstrosity. In a

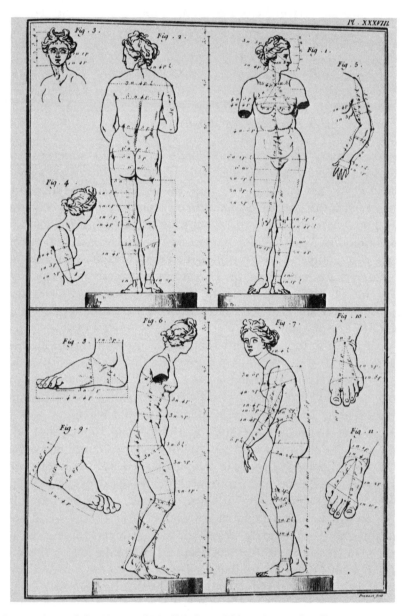

Proportions of the Venus of Medici, from Diderot's *Encyclopedia*.

strange sequence of extraordinary similitudes, Hadaly appears exactly like Alicia Clary, herself the living embodiment of the statue of the *Venus Victorious* in the Louvre. These two cases of resemblance, however, derive from an entirely different order of things. When Alicia Clary makes her first appearance in Edison's parlor, the shock is tremendous: "The woman was stunning; a living evocation of the presence of the *Venus Victorious*. Even at first glance, her resemblance to the divine statue appeared so striking, so incontestable, as to give one an indefinable shock" (p. 169). Edison, although struck like Ewald by the likeness between the singer and the statue, recognizes the monstrous origin of this similarity and exclaims: "For all his intelligence, that nice young lord simply doesn't see that her resemblance to the statue (and one can practically see the imprint of the stone in her flesh) that this resemblance, yes, is nothing but a *sickness;* it must be the result of some *envie* in her bizarre lineage. She was born that way, as some children are born speckled or with web-feet; in a word, she is an anomaly as odd as a giant! Her resemblance to the *Venus Victorious* is nothing but a kind of elephantiasis of which she will die. A pathological deformity, with which her wretched little nature is afflicted" (p. 181, translation modified).

Alicia Clary's beauty is an *envie,* notes Edison. As in the theory of earlier times, this beauty can be attributed to her mother's fascination with a statue. It is nothing but the visible imprint of a mother's unsatisfied desire. Once again, we are faced with the order of monstrous similitude, the result of a maternal desire and fascination for an object that did not participate in the progeny's conception. Alicia Clary is monstrous in the perfection of her likeness to a statue, monstrous because the model that struck her mother's imagination is the product not of nature but of art. Despite her beauty, she remains an unnatural deformity. Her monstrosity betrays itself as well in the marked disparity between her sumptuous beauty and the mediocrity of her mind. Such is the essential heterogeneity of the monster, that heterogeneity which appeared in the monsters of Greek antiquity: composite beings which unite, in a single body, the qualities of those disparate categories that spawned them, but to which they do not belong—harpy, mermaid, sphinx, Minotaur, Medusa. "Between the body and the soul of Miss Alicia, it wasn't just a disproportion which distressed and upset my understanding; it was an absolute *disparity*" (p. 31), notes Lord Ewald; and he adds, "Yes, on occasion I was tempted to think *quite seriously*, that in the dark spaces of Becoming this woman had somehow strayed by accident into this body, which did not belong to her at all" (p. 31). She is "one of the darker and more sinister anomalies" (p. 31), and Lord Ewald comments that "the non-correspondence of the physical and the intellectual made itself felt constantly, and in the proportions of a paradox" (p. 36).

Alicia Clary's monstrosity thus manifests itself in two ways: On the one hand, her striking resemblance to the *Venus Victorious* both betrays a mother's aberrant passion and abolishes the figure of the legitimate father. On the other hand, her essential duality points to the heterogeneity hidden beneath her uncanny perfection: a gaping chasm in representation, the price of perfect likeness, the indelible manifestation of the "unnatural" character of a monster inspired by a representation rather than its living model. And this monstrous side of nature in turn justifies Edison's mad undertaking. "It is mysterious," he says, "that this sublime monstrosity should appear in the world just in time to provide legitimacy [*légitimer*] for my first android!" (p. 181, translation modified). Legitimacy, as Edison sees it, stems from several possible sources. By taking over the mother's role in reproduction, Edison assumes in turn the parental singularity fed by the heated imagination that was thought to cause monstrosities in earlier times. But at another level, the model he chooses for his android creation, Alicia Clary, is herself identified as a monstrosity unnaturally modeled after a statue whose original and living model is lost in ancient times.

Representing, or recreating, a monster, however, requires one to reverse the already unnatural order of its original production. Hadaly both represents and represses Alicia Clary. She duplicates all Alicia's physical attributes to perfection, but she has successfully erased the paradoxical duality that also signaled Alicia's teratological nature. And it could be said that in the line of descent from the *Venus Victorious* to Alicia Clary to Hadaly there is only the representation of a model that is already represented; the origin remains forever dissimulated: a genealogical descent of cold marble, marked by the immobility of a statue, the vacuity of the soul, a series of animated mechanisms and disparities. But to invent Hadaly—to reproduce Alicia Clary's features with a fidelity as perfect as that with which the mother's wandering imagination models the fetus—is also to reproduce the monstrous phenomenon that Edison recognized in the beautiful singer. This process is a modern version of teratogeny. Edison, the father figure, envisions, plans, and executes what would have resulted previously in some monstrous malformation. But this is not the only aspect of her creation that sets Hadaly's genesis apart from previous monstrosities. Hadaly reproduces, but exactly in reverse, the reproduction that is already Alicia Clary. For one thing, unlike Renaissance or seventeenth-century monsters, Hadaly has a very visible and powerful father-signatory, as well as an extraordinarily detailed genesis. No particular of her creation is hidden from us; the entire book V, the space of a pregnancy, reports in the minutest details the making of her physical appearance: flesh, "rosy mouth, pearly teeth," eyes, hair, and epidermis are all coolly explained, as if during a dissection, by the father/scientist. Hadaly is Edison's explicit progeny, his most glorious creation, which he has every right to claim as a work of art. Also, just as the monster's mother made life from art, the artist makes art from life modeled after art itself. By modeling his progeny on Alicia Clary, Edison reconstructs a hypothetical natural order; it can never be said, nor is it said, that Hadaly looks like the *Venus Victorious*. She resembles only the statue's living portrait, Alicia Clary. Furthermore, representation derives from, and the hidden protocols of artistic paternity point to, new and unthinkable limits. The high stakes of creation seem about to betray both the creator *and* his audience. During the stormy evening when Ewald believed himself to be again seduced by Miss Alicia Clary, "he forgot the long arid and despairing hours he had undergone; his love revived . . . He was reborn! Like ghosts from an enchanter fleeing, Hadaly and her empty mirages disappeared completely from his thoughts" (p. 192). Yet Ewald remains vaguely troubled:

> At that moment, the obsessive notion returned to him, that Edison was even now waiting in his lifeless caverns to show him the black monstrosity of the Android.
>
> "Ah, no," he said to himself, "was I out of my mind? I was dreaming of a sacrilege, a plaything, a puppet, the mere sight of which would have made me laugh, I'm certain! A ridiculous, senseless doll! As if, in the face of a living young woman as beautiful as this one, all that madness would not vanish on the spot!

Electricity, hydraulic pressure, cylinders, and so on—ridiculous!
. . . I know you, you exist, truly, as a creature of flesh and blood,
like me! I feel your heart beat! You wept for me! Your lips stirred
under the pressure of mine! You are a woman whom love can
render as ideal as your beauty!" . . . As his kiss melted on her lips,
he caught a vague scent of amber and roses. A deep shudder
shook his frame from head to foot, even before his understanding was able to grasp the thought which had just struck his mind
like a thunderbolt.

At the same time Miss Alicia Clary rose from the bench and,
placing on the young man's shoulders her hands *glittering with
many rings*, she said to him in a melancholy voice—in that unfor-
gettably melodious, supernatural voice that he had heard before:
"Dear friend, don't you recognize me? I am Hadaly." (p. 192)

Ewald is initially terrified: "The young man felt as if he had been
directly insulted by Hell itself . . . Aghast at the horror of the trap
sprung on him, he stared at the Android. His heart, gripped by a
frightful sense of bitterness, burned within him like a lump of ice
. . . He took her hand; it was the hand of Alicia! . . . He looked
deep into her eyes; they were the very same eyes . . . only her
expression was sublime! . . . it was the woman herself . . . but trans-
figured! Become at last worthy of her own beauty, her real identity
finally brought to life!" (p. 193).

The success is complete. At first, Lord Ewald is seduced by Hadaly because she is like her model, because she lets illusion take the
upper hand and allows her own identity to be mistaken for that of
another. The very perfection of the imitation creates a misrepresentation. Fraud and error suddenly shift to the side of representation, precisely because it is flawless. Hadaly's astonishing likeness
to her model enables her not only to appear as the "living" portrait
of Alicia Clary, but also to take her place—no longer as a monster,
but as the Ideal. The replacement of the model by a perfect duplicate undoes the very function of representation, and this is where
L'Eve future differs from so many Romantic texts on automatons:
Edison's android has an explicit, if monstrous model; it first claims
to duplicate nature. The original—the living—and the represented—the artifice—are joined in dangerous proximity. That *naturalness* should lose its role as model and origin is yet another aspect of the deceptive violence that accompanies the making of

artifice. "The false Alicia," notes Villiers, "seemed far more *natural* than the true one" (p. 194).

In legal terminology, the word "representation" refers to a delegation of power, and "delegation" in turn implies a distance between the seat of power and the place where it is exercised "in the name of." Hadaly's success amounts to a usurpation of that power, an illicit fusion of the source—the origin, or its image—with its field of action—art, or artifice. This operation, moreover, involves another transgression—the very one that the monstrous set in motion in previous centuries: the final dissimulation of genesis, the exile of the father. The misrepresentation achieved here erases with a single stroke the model and the signatory, the genitor. What disappears at the moment when Hadaly, as Alicia Clary, triumphantly seduces Ewald is Edison's mediation, the long hours in the laboratory and the extraordinary explanation of the android's conception. In the tradition of artistic representation, there is always a visible gap between the original and its replica—a flaw in the work, or a deliberate "phantastic" reorganization of proportions—that amounts to an author's signature, that signals the respective locations of the model, the copy, and the mediator in a work transformed by the dictates of art. Beyond the iconoclastic suspicion that images *as* images could supplant the models that inspired them, there is a long tradition that strictly forbids any representation *not labeled as such*, any image whose iconic character is not immediately recognizable, due either to a flaw in its execution or to the presence of an author's signature. At another level, a similar prohibition forbids any reproduction of an existing work of art not labeled as such. Art and forgery converge in the uncertain realm where a quest for perfect reproduction subverts the status of art and the fate of the model. In an essay on forgery in art, Michael Wreen notes that "the norm of authenticity is a historical norm concerned with the *origin* and *genesis* of a painting."[3]

Although the story of Hadaly's genesis and Edison's role are well known to the reader, the father's mark is ultimately erased once more. In any representation absolutely identical to its model, in any convincing duplication, there is no room for a signature, for the name of the artist as father. By replacing Alicia Clary, if only for a moment, Hadaly successfully dismisses Edison's labor, his power, and his knowledge. The work of art is erased, and in its place appears a subject. The emancipated subject abolishes the father's mark and his very identity, in a move which shifts the play of uncanny resemblances to the domain of monstrosity. The subversive quality of this perfect imitation lies in its ability both to replace the model, whatever the model's ontological status might be, and to efface the maker. For the effect of this perfection is to replace the original model; it is not a near perfection that invites comparisons. Hadaly's mysterious identity raises a slightly different question. This is a case of successful substitution never achieved by portraiture or waxwork: Ewald will never see Alicia and Hadaly side by side, although by extraordinary coincidence newspapers report that the singer died in the same shipboard fire that also destroyed Hadaly. As with forgery, the idea is not simply to imitate but to replace. The master forger, capable of reproducing a signed masterpiece so skillfully that the experts are fooled, wishes to see his work hung not next to the original, but rather in its place. If the two were to be juxtaposed, the challenge would be not to judge their respective merits, but to detect their legitimate origin or, as the French expression emphasizes, "rendre chaque oeuvre à qui de droit." When examining the aesthetic value of originals and copies, Nelson Goodman remarks, "Rembrandt paintings are in general much better than copies by unknown painters. But a copy of a Lastman by Rembrandt may well be better than the original . . . The fact that we cannot tell our two pictures apart merely by looking at them does not imply that they are aesthetically the same—and thus does not force us to conclude that the forgery is as good as the original." Later Goodman adds: "The popular conviction that there can be no aesthetic difference between two pictures if they cannot be distinguished by merely looking at them is undermined by challenging the very notion of 'merely looking.'"[4] Hadaly's challenge might similarly be said to be a challenge to the beholder.

Hadaly's second victory, that of seducing Lord Ewald as herself and not while passing for Alicia Clary, goes beyond a successful substitution and illustrates the power of illusion and art. "You will have to be careful, when you compare the two and listen to them both, *that it isn't the living woman who seems to you the doll*," Edison gravely warns Ewald (p. 64). This is, strictly speaking, a misrepresentation, because neither Lord Ewald nor the reader will ever see

Alicia Clary and her duplicate side by side. But Edison's point, and his triumph, consist in making artifice compelling *as* artifice. Once Hadaly has identified herself, Ewald's newly revived passion for Alicia Clary is completely forgotten. Hadaly overcomes Ewald's final reservations—his fears—precisely *because* she is not Alicia Clary; there is a depth in her dark eyes which, in its very deceptiveness, is more fascinating than the living singer's compromised beauty. This is the apotheosis of art.

Is this the moment when paternity is restored and Edison vindicated? Once Lord Ewald acknowledges his passion for Hadaly rather than for Alicia Clary, once Hadaly has seduced Ewald through her own depth and beauty—mysteriously superior to that of the model she so faithfully reproduces—Edison's paternity should be fully acknowledged. But this is hardly the case, for Edison too is startled by his handiwork. He is astonished to hear Hadaly speak words that he had not recorded on the two golden phonographs which serve as her lungs. And this is when Hadaly's other genitor, Sowana, emerges from the subterranean shadows.

Who is Sowana? Her legal name is Any Anderson; she is the mother of two, abandoned by her husband and so shocked by his loss that she has contracted an incurable disease—sleeping sickness. When Edison hypnotizes her, another personality emerges from the sleeper: "She used to be a simple woman, perfectly honorable, even intelligent, but, after all, of very limited views—and so I knew her. But in the depths of her slumber another person is revealed to me, completely different, many-sided and mysterious! So far as I can tell, the enormous knowledge, the strange eloquence, and the penetrating insight of this sleeper named Sowana—who is, physically, the same person—are logically inexplicable. Isn't this duality a stupefying phenomenon?" (pp. 210–211). The aspect of this duality called Sowana, a duality reminiscent of monstrosity, asks Edison to let her participate in the creation of his android: "Sowana, as if subject to some demonic spirit of exultation, forced me to explain all [the android's] most hidden secrets— until, when she had studied every last detail, she was able, *occasionally*, TO INCORPORATE HERSELF WITHIN IT, AND ANIMATE IT WITH HER 'SUPERNATURAL' BEING" (p. 211). Sowana's purely spiritual being communicates with Hadaly and is in some way incarnated by what the inventor calls "the Human Sphinx." The first results of Sowana's influence on Hadaly are so striking that Edison is moved to say, "The workman was aghast at his own work" (p. 211). And looking at Hadaly one last time he then admits, *"not everything about this creature is an illusion!"* (p. 211).

The play of representation, and representation as progeny, is falsified once more. Edison's sublime creation is also the mysterious work of Sowana: as if Sowana, the maternal figure, had enabled the work to escape its signatory once again, as if the maternal element had once again eclipsed both the father, Edison, and the model, the monstrous Alicia Clary. In a dramatic reversal of the tradition that credited the mother with the material shape of progeny and the father with the living principle, in *L'Eve future*, Edison provides no more than an intricate metal frame and a superficial likeness to a living being. Hadaly's soul is Sowana's work. The maternal principle is vindicated at the very moment when Edison's creation escapes his control. In the end, this adventure at the boundaries of life and art will be sanctioned by death. Having transferred her spiritual being to Hadaly, Sowana dies; and after Hadaly has been burned "alive" in the manner of witches of old, and Alicia Clary drowned, Ewald writes to Edison, "My friend, only the loss of Hadaly leaves me inconsolable—I mourn none but the shadow" (p. 219, translation modified). A graven image is put to rest.

L'Eve future prolongs and transforms the aesthetics of creation already illustrated in romantic tales of portraiture. At first, Villiers appears to *unveil* the work of art so carefully shrouded by Balzac's Frenhofer. In a singular scene, the only one where Hadaly in her potential form appears next to Alicia Clary, the physical model she will reproduce, Villiers describes a conversation between Ewald, Edison, and his mistress:

> "What's that?" she said, laying down her liqueur glass and stretching out her hand.
>
> Even as she spoke, Edison rose from the table and strolled over to open the great window looking out over the park. The moonlight was superb. He leaned against the railing, smoking, his back turned to the stars.
>
> "It's a beautiful make-believe flower," she said with a smile; "isn't it for me?"

"No, my dear; you are too true for it," the young man replied simply.

Suddenly, in spite of himself, he closed his eyes.

There, on the steps of her magic alcove, Hadaly had just appeared. She pushed aside with her glittering arm the draperies of deep red plush.

Motionless in her armor and under her black veil, she stood there like a vision.

Miss Alicia Clary, having her back turned in that direction, could not see the Android.

Hadaly had no doubt been present, and had overheard the last few phrases of the conversation. From her fingertips she blew a silent kiss to Lord Ewald, who abruptly rose to his feet.

"What is it? What's the matter?" cried the young woman. "You frighten me!"

She turned to look but the draperies had closed, the apparition had disappeared.

Meanwhile, profiting by this momentary distraction of Miss Alicia's, Edison had stretched forth his hand before the face of the frightened woman.

Softly, gradually, her lids closed over her lustrous eyes; her arms, as if petrified into Paros marble, remained motionless, one resting on the table, the other, still holding its bouquet of pale roses, resting on a cushion. (p. 178)

Ewald, faced with the veiled, seductive image of Hadaly, repeats the Oedipal gesture of blinding: he closes his eyes. Poe's narrator in front of the oval portrait had similarly acted. The painters of Hawthorne's and Balzac's tales, as we have seen, covered their masterpieces with draperies of precious materials, as if removing from sight a blinding piece of evidence. Hadaly's veils are the object of many detailed descriptions. Surrounded by "curtains of black moire dropped elegantly from an arch of jade," she appears with her forehead supporting "a dark veil which obscured the entire lower part of her head . . . The trailing ends of the veil twined around the neck over the metal gorget, then, tossed back over the shoulders, were knotted behind her back; thence they fell to the waist of the apparition like a flowing head of long hair, finally dropping to the ground, where they were lost in shadow. A scarf of black batiste was knotted about her waist like a loincloth, and trailed across her legs a line of black fringe into which brilliants had been sewn" (p. 57). In "The Unknown Masterpiece," when Porbus and Poussin stood in front of Frenhofer's canvas finally unveiled they saw nothing but a wall of paint from which emerged a bare foot, a fragment that "seemed to them like the torso in Paros marble of some Venus emerging from the ashes of a ruined town."[5] A strange repetition takes place. When Hadaly disappears, shrouded in dark veils and mystery, Alicia Clary is hypnotized by Edison and her uncanny resemblance to the *Victorious Venus* is enhanced by her arms "petrified into Paros marble." In both cases, we must believe we see the "unknown masterpiece" by the same effect of temporary unveiling. Alicia Clary asleep, reduced to a being of exquisite beauty, is none other than her mother's desires unveiled and none other than Hadaly unveiled; conversely, Hadaly removes her veils only to assume Alicia's physiognomy. But Alicia's physical beauty, so *separate* from her soul, is but a veil, a last curtain for Hadaly's mysterious unknown being. Thus are their own monstrosities, the secret of their births, shrouded from the public gaze. When faced with Hadaly, either veiled in black drapery or shrouded in Alicia's appearance, Ewald reacts with the same instinctive gesture of averting his gaze. When he finally recognizes Hadaly beneath the form of Alicia Clary, "wholly incapable of controlling himself, he closed his eyes" (p. 193). Later on, Hadaly interrupts herself to ask him: "Why do you put that bit of glass in your eye? Don't you see perfectly well, even without its help?" (p. 200).

Hadaly, however, means to tear away the veil and to reveal to a degree the nature of her unfathomable being. Pleading her cause, eager to seduce Ewald as *herself* (a complex notion at best), she speaks of those moments when "the spirit is still half-veiled in the midst of sleep" and discovers a new dimension of space, a "living ether," which is Villiers's own version of the Mallarmean *Azur.* "The path joining these two kingdoms leads through that domain of the Spirit which Reason . . . calls, in hollow disdain, MERE IMAGINATION" (p. 195). Through Hadaly's mystical discourse, Villiers fully rehabilitates the power of imagination as that which alone gives access to the Infinite. Although imagination as described in the last pages seems far removed from the capacity to imprint striking visual effects on progeny, it nevertheless answers for all forms of creation, even monstrous ones. Hadaly's "life" now depends on

Ewald's own desire, on his willingness to imagine, to procreate a being, although we already know the peculiar nature of this procreation. She says, "The man who has looked on an Android as you looked on me *has killed the woman within him*" (p. 203, emphasis added).

Image of a Sterile Father

In his analysis of Hoffmann's tale "The Sandman," Freud briefly considers the theoretical status of Olympia, Professor Spalanzani's beautiful, silent daughter. Nathaniel falls hopelessly in love with her, only to discover in a particularly harrowing scene that she is an automaton. As Freud relates the scene, "Olympia was an automaton whose works Spalanzani had made, and whose eyes Coppola, the Sandman, had put in. The student surprises the two men quarrelling over their handiwork. The optician carries off the wooden eyeless doll; and the mechanician, Spalanzani, takes up Olympia's bleeding eyeballs from the ground and throws them at Nathaniel's breast, saying that Coppola had stolen them from him (Nathaniel). Nathaniel succumbs to a fresh attack of madness, and in his delirium his recollection of his father's death is mingled with this new experience. He . . . then falls upon the professor, Olympia's so-called father, and tries to strangle him."[6]

Despite the importance that Freud attaches to this scene, he by no means considers it the most important one in the story. And for him the motif of the living doll is neither the source nor the cause of the text's uncanny effect. Olympia, the perfect representation of a hypothetical model for Spalanzani's daughter, is nothing, according to Freud, but "a personification of Nathaniel's feminine attitude towards his father in his infancy . . . Olympia is, as it were, a dissociated complex of Nathaniel's which confronts him as a person, and Nathaniel's enslavement to this complex is expressed in his senseless obsessive love for Olympia. We may with justice call this love narcissistic."[7]

Reading Hoffmann's text as an illustration of the theory of repetition compulsion, which he had recently formulated, Freud dismisses the disquieting power of Olympia and her two fathers. But as long as Olympia passes for a living being, the identity of *one of her fathers*, Coppola, is obliterated, leaving only the benevolent, apparently "natural" father, Professor Spalanzani. Indeed, Coppola alone is a source of terror in the story. Olympia, the perfect representation, conceals Coppola's contribution: the fabrication of the eyes, the strangest as well as the most lifelike aspect of the automaton. The tragic scene that devastates Nathaniel serves to uncover this deception and reveal it as monstrous by exposing a double paternity. This revelation could not have occurred without the murder of representation as fraud and the restitution of Olympia as oeuvre. At the same time, the two infanticidal fathers reinstate the heterogeneous character of a monster: the optician carries off the body, which he did not make, and leaves behind the eyes, which are his work. This spectacle ought to open the eyes of the hero-spectator to the nature of his love; on the contrary, it plunges him into darker blindness as to the nature of Coppola, the other father figure.

This scene announces the demands of the signatory: Coppola, the Sandman who alternates between throwing sand in people's eyes and unveiling the naked truth, restores representation to its own character. Freud's analysis of the story can be read with the following modification: "A morbid anxiety connected with the eyes and with going blind is often enough a substitute for the dread of castration,"[8] but only to the extent that the castration complex is already present in the relation between Coppola and Olympia as *representation,* and insofar as the dissimulation of the signatory, the repression and abolition of the father by his monstrous creation, also amounts to a form of castration. Olympia the illusion, the briefly convincing counterfeit, reveals at the moment of her destruction a previously repressed connection with the father that duplicates the tie between the signatory and his work.

This detour to the unthinkable limits of perfect representation suggests, in counterpoint, that all legitimate representation (that is, that which offers itself as such), any acknowledged and recognizable line of descent, ought to involve a degree of imperfection with respect to the model, a derivation, and especially a signature. Not that imperfection should be regarded as an aesthetic criterion; but perfection abolishes the very space that enables the spectator to compare the model—even if it be eccentric or hypothetical—with its image. Not that recognizable derivation should be considered an indispensable element of the beautiful; but it eludes that absolute resemblance which alone can allow a representation to replace its model. Not that the signature determines worth; but it bears conclusive witness that the representation is nothing more than that, an opus.

All these elements, which do not in the last analysis belong to the criteria of aesthetic judgment, are nevertheless implicit in any theory of representation or aesthetics. The monstrous or fantastical character of a representation that does not offer itself as such— and that consequently takes the model's place—would stem from its hypothetical abolition of everything that might contribute to the definitive status of the work as imago: that is, the abolition of the frame, within which the momentarily repressed signature of the artist is also acknowledged in its proper guise. That such an abolition is destined to fail, in more ways than one, was already perceptible in the confusion between *anomalos* and *a-nomos:* an irregularity returned to the norm and considered a variation of the norm, in other words, returned to its frame and thought of as a category grounded in the *parergon*. The monstrous is no longer anything but an accident. This is when the father and signatory, momentarily repressed, lends himself to representation, no longer as the origin of art, but as imitation.

In the end we have to consider the possibility that the *artist* as representation (as, for example, in a series of paintings showing the artist's studio from Velasquez to Courbet) implies a form of castration, as the signatory becomes his own model and his mark is completely absorbed by the canvas; the artist's visibility as the object of representation competes with his duplicate, the progenitor who signs. The feminization of the artist's self-portrait, manifest at times, or at times disguised, echoes the Romantic tradition of portraiture discussed earlier. What are the different functions of the painted image of the artist in his studio and of his name applied to the lower part of the canvas after the painting has been completed, as the name of the one who produced the painting? These separate identities visibly illustrate two separate claims and belong to two different modes of recovery: one a representation, a descriptive claim of paternity that we know cannot be separated from a repudiated—albeit necessary—feminine model; the other an attribution, a claim of paternity that alone gives the painting, its origin and production, any form of validity. This case of double paternity has often been reenacted in the Literature of the Uncanny. *L'Eve future* maintains the eradication of the father, inasmuch as he too is subject to representation, a floating signature. At the beginning of the novel we are told: "Everyone knows nowadays that a most distinguished American inventor, Mr. Edison, has discovered over the last fifteen years a prodigious number of things, as strange as they are ingenious ... In America and in Europe a LEGEND has thus sprung up in the popular mind regarding this great citizen of the United States ... Henceforth, doesn't the personage of this legend—even while the man is still alive who inspired it—belong to the world of literature?"[9] *L'Eve future,* then, tells the story of another monster: Edison himself.

Edison's hidden monstrosity is linked to the general fear of sterility that haunts the creative artist. Monsters were traditionally thought to be sterile either because Nature, in its wisdom, did not allow the infinite reproduction of deformities, or because it refrained from allowing legitimate issue to a mother's illegitimate desire.[10] Alicia Clary feels fortunate not to have borne any children; Hadaly, of course, is barren. She tells Ewald, "My fatal womb is not even worth calling sterile ... if you dismiss me, I will go to the desert without Ishmael" (p. 202, translation modified). But Hadaly only displaces the question of sterility, just as she has displaced the question of monstrosity since the beginning of the story. For another question emerges from the tale, not that of Hadaly's nature but rather that of Edison's. A revealing answer is given in the following lines:

> Edison is forty-two years old. A few years ago his features recalled in a striking manner those of a famous Frenchman, Gustave Doré. It was very nearly the face of an artist *translated* into the features of a scholar. The same natural talents, differently applied; mysterious twins. At what age did they completely resemble each other? Perhaps never. Their two photographs of that earlier time, blended in the stereoscope, give this intellectual impression that certain effigies of the superior races are *only fully realized as images* stamped on coins and scattered through Humanity. When one compares Edison's features with those of ancient engravings, they offer a *living reproduction* of the Syracuse medal representing Archimedes. (p. 7, translation modified, emphasis added)

Left: Thomas Edison at thirty-one, by Matthew Brady (1878); right: Gustave Doré, by Paul Nadar. "The face of an artist translated into the features of a scholar . . . mysterious twins. At what age did they completely resemble each other? Perhaps never." (Villiers de l'Isle-Adam, *Tomorrow's Eve*).

Edison's striking resemblance to Gustave Doré's *photograph* and to Archimedes's *representation* on an antique coin suggests that Edison himself bears the marks of a feverish maternal imagination, that he too has been fashioned, like the monsters of old, after portraits and effigies. He bears the stigmata of monstrosity. It now appears that the living portrait of a misguided maternal desire is, first of all, the artist himself. There is no portrait *of* the artist, but always, *in* the artist, the portrait of a monstrous desire. The artist is an emblem of monstrosity, the signature of the *envie*. His obsessions with a fatal sterility make creation the supplement to an impossible filiation. Like the original Eve, *L'Eve future* will be created, not engendered. Unlike the original Eve, however, she will bear no children. The act of artistic creation thus appears as the imitation of a monstrous genetic process: painted models, errant passions, striking resemblances, sterility. *L'Eve future,* this other "enfant d'une nuit d'Idumée," both discloses and conceals a Mallarmean sterility. In Mallarmé's *Le don du poème,* Idumea evokes the country of Esau, the disinherited and monstrous elder son of Isaac and

Rebekah (also alluded to in Hadaly's revelatory speech). Denis
Saurat explains: "For the Jewish Kabbalah, God first created a
monstrous mankind. He replaced it with our own mankind. Jacob
replaced Esau: the kings of Idumea were pre-adamic men; they
were sexless beings, and reproduced without women, but they
were not hermaphrodites in God's image . . . the poet makes his
poem alone, without a woman, like a king of Idumea, a monstrous
birth. This monster will be humanized if woman welcomes him." [11]
This sheds some light on Sowana's mysterious role, the fecundating mother, although we know that neither Sowana nor Hadaly can
be saved. We know as well that both are merely Edison's reflections,
his own image as consumed artist.

From the beginning of *L'Eve future,* the symbolist artist, Edison,
is simultaneously seen as father and as monster. Both dissimulation
and erasure of his sterility, both object and result of a fascination
with the obscure works of mimetic monstrosity, every creation is
the *tombeau* of a misguided desire.[12] Just as the artist as monster
had successfully abolished the image of a legitimate father, the
work of art always contends with, and tends toward, the erasure of
the artist. This may also account for the artist's signature as the
mark of a double project. On the one hand, it signals the presence
of a father so that the maker may never again be erased by an unfaithful and monstrous creation; outside the work of art but insep-
arable from it, it offers the paternal inscription. On the other hand,
if the work of art is only the repetition of a monstrous birth that
excluded the father in the first place, what is the signature, if not
the futile reinscription of an already abolished artist?[13]

In a work thus negated and reclaimed *(aufgehoben),* the labor of
the maternal imagination is unequivocally present; the maternal
desire that presides over the creation and the desire for the mother
that haunts the creation's beholder and last creator are finally unveiled. As Hadaly (or Edison) says, quite simply, "Femme, j'eusse
été de celles que l'on peut aimer sans honte": "As a woman, I would
have been one of those who can be loved without shame" (p. 202).

10

Misconceptions

The oldest tale of ex-utero procreation is the Jewish legend of the golem. The word *golem,* which appears in the Bible and numerous rabbinical texts, refers to an unformed mass without a soul.[1] "At a certain stage in his creation Adam is designated as 'golem,'" writes Gershom Scholem. "'Golem' means the unformed, amorphous . . . In the philosophical literature of the Middle Ages it is used as a Hebrew term for matter, formless *hylé* . . . In this sense, Adam was said to be 'golem' before the breath of God had touched him."[2] Scholem quotes a Talmudic passage describing the creation of Adam: "In the first hour the earth was piled up; *in the second he became a golem,* a still unformed mass; in the third, his limbs were stretched out; *in the fourth the soul was cast into him.*"[3] Legends in the Talmud suggested that the creation of Adam could be repeated, to a limited extent, by enlightened rabbis. It was possible to give life to a golem, to make an artificial man, by using a combination of letters from the Hebrew alphabet. Emily Bilski and Moshe Idel observe that in the twelfth century, which saw "a virtual explosion of discussions on the golem," several techniques for giving life emerged: "To create a golem you recite combinations that begin with the first eleven letters of the Hebrew alphabet; to undo this act of creation (render a golem lifeless) you recite letter combinations beginning with the second half of the Hebrew alphabet. Another technique involves the spreading of dust in which three letters spelling *adam* (man) are written, followed by the recitation of letters. A golem is supposed to emerge from the unformed dust on its own, such is the power contained in Hebrew letters. In a third technique that appears at this time, though its origins are probably much earlier, the golem appears with the three Hebrew letters that spell *emet* (truth) inscribed on his forehead. When the first letter is erased, leaving the word *met* (he is dead), the golem is destroyed."[4] Furthermore, limbs were associated with specific letters, and as a thirteenth-century Kabbalist warns, "One has to be very cautious not to change a letter or a vowel from its place because the limb created by the means of this letter will change its natural place in [the] body."[5]

Enriched by important commentaries of the *Sefer Yezirah,* or *Book of Creation,* a mysterious text written between the third and the sixth centuries, and by the writings of the Kabbalists, the idea of the golem provoked much speculation on the nature of life and the possibilities of creation. In most traditions, the golem was not given the power of speech. Moshe Idel notes that "although the techniques proposed to create an anthropoid are substantially linguistic, the result—namely, the artificial man—is considered to be a speechless being" (*Golem: Jewish Magical and Mystical Traditions,* p. 264). According to Idel, this apparent "dissonance between the nature of the technique and that of its result" is less surprising than it might at first seem, if one considers that the linguistic tools used in the creative process "do not form a communicative language. It is not the regular Hebrew that is intonated by the creator of the Golem in order to animate him, but mathematical combinations, which only accidentally mean something, and even then the context is meaningless" (ibid., p. 264). This description thus challenges the observer to conceive of a purely performative speech act, entirely devoid of descriptive or remotely recognizable elements, one that would carry no meaning other than that of its own performance. There was speculation about the golem's ability to reason as well, although it was acknowledged that because it was created by man it could not have a soul. And since the golem had no soul, it was possible to destroy it without actually committing a "murder." But the only way to destroy a golem was to "undo" the linguistic act of creation, since a golem could not be physically hurt. Although texts on the possibility of creating a golem are very ancient, the first tale to report a rabbi's actually giving life to a statue of clay dates only to the seventeenth century. Bilski and Idel quote an anonymous manuscript in Oxford, ca. 1630, which tells the story of how R. Eliahu of Chelm created a golem by means of the

Sefer Yezirah. According to this tale, the golem grew so large that he had to be destroyed "by erasing the *aleph*, the first letter of *emet* (truth)."[6]

In my discussion of the golem I will not address the complex and highly theoretical discussions of the Kabbalists or the interpretation of the golem in the context of religious dogma. Rather, I shall consider a "secular" version of the golem, derived from the legends circulating in the nineteenth century around the idea that it was possible to animate a statue of clay by using one of the secret names of God or other sacred words. By that time, tales of the golem had spread throughout Europe and become part of popular culture. In 1808 Jakob Grimm wrote a version of the golem tale directly borrowed from Christoph Arnold's 1674 account of the creation of R. Eliahu of Chelm. Published in the *Journal for Hermits*, it noted:

> After saying certain prayers and observing certain fast days, the Polish Jews make the figure of a man from clay or mud, and when they pronounce the miraculous Shemhamphoras (the name of God) over him, he must come to life. He cannot speak, but he understands fairly well what is said or commanded . . . On his forehead is written *emet* [truth]; everyday he gains weight and becomes somewhat larger and stronger than all the others in the house, regardless of how little he was to begin with. For fear of him, they therefore erase the first letter, so that nothing remains but *meth* [he is dead], whereupon he collapses and turns to clay again.[7]

Many of the spiritual questions related to the act of creation are missing from Grimm's tale, which emphasizes instead magic elements traditional to folktales. Following Grimm, Achim von Arnim, Heinrich Heine, and others popularized the legend, and toward the middle of the nineteenth century, according to Bilski and Idel, there was "a proliferation of popular stories on R. Leow and his creation of a golem."[8] The Kabbalist Leow, or Lowe, was a famous rabbi who had played an important role in sixteenth-century Prague and had personally intervened with Emperor Rudolf II on behalf of the Jews at a time of heightened persecution. An enduring legend recounted his creation of a golem to protect the Jewish community of Prague. Variations on the theme ranged from portraitures of the golem as friendly and helpful to stories of

Rabbi Löw, Town Hall, Prague.

an uncontrollable creature, closer to a monster, bent on revenge and senseless destruction.

At the end of the nineteenth century, Edison, the real-life scientist and fictive father of Villiers de l'Isle-Adam's *L'Eve future*, made a short film entitled *The Golem*, a meditation on the power to give life. The popularity of golem tales at that time reflects the nineteenth-century obsession with the idea of artificial creation and the fascination with the possibility that *man* could give birth to another human being. Although *Frankenstein* may not have been directly influenced by the tale of the golem, a hundred years later the movie versions of the Shelleys' novel integrated the tale with elements of the popular legend surrounding the statue of clay. Isaac Bashevis Singer, who was so taken by the legend that he wrote his own version of the golem story as a magic tale of love and hope, sees the myth as metaphor for both the mysterious question of life—"[The golem] was understood as an embryo"—and artistic creation. Commenting on the numerous writers who have become attracted to the legend, he notes, "I am sure that none of those worldly writers like Leivick, Gustav Meyrink, Arthur Holitscher, Johannes Hess and others believed that a golem existed and worked all the miracles ascribed to him. But I am convinced that these writers felt in the legend of the golem a profound kinship to artistic creativity."[9]

In the course of its rich history, the legend of the golem embodied different beliefs and represented several forms of mystic conviction. At one time, the possibility of animating a man, as imitation of the divine power of creation, dominated the legend; at other times, the creature assumed various social and symbolic roles. Bilski describes the modern perception of the golem as follows: "The notion that the golem is a more primitive version of ourselves was developed in the early nineteenth century by the German Romantics, who used this figure as a doppelgänger or double, to represent the co-existence and conflict of reason and unreason in the human condition. With the advent of psychoanalysis, the golem, in turn, came to represent the Id. Drawing on both these traditions, twentieth-century artists gave the golem new life as doppelgänger and alter ego in the Expressionist and Neo-Expressionist movements."[10] For all its versatility, however, and for all the different beliefs it was meant to represent, the legend has maintained several invariable elements: it describes the creation of a man, and this gesture of giving life is accomplished through the use of letters. One could call it a *symbolic* birth, entirely determined by the father, in opposition to the rich maternal imagination that had produced the monsters of earlier times. The creation of a golem by means of letters, recitations of letters, inscriptions of letters on the creature's forehead, or, in other popular versions, by means of a scroll inserted in the mouth of the statue of clay could serve as a powerful image of giving birth in the symbolic, the linguistic order. Not only does the father of the golem give life, but he does so through a linguistic feature, relying either on the alphabet or on one of the secret names of God, the ultimate symbolic father associated with the power of the word and the omnipresence of the Law. The Name-of-the-Father literally inscribed on the forehead of the inanimate statue brings the human shape to life.

The golem and all its variations in nineteenth-century popular literature also function as the double image of another, as a specular representation of the human, of a self created through language but not yet born to language. This aspect is abundantly illustrated by the commentaries on whether a golem can speak or, in nineteenth-century tales, by the inability of the automaton to express itself (one thinks of Hoffmann's Olympia, whose speech was limited to a frightening "Ha! Ha!"). The golem as double creates for the beholder the troubling figure of the uncanny. As double, the golem is a perfect *simulacrum,* and it exists side by side with the other, the model it duplicates yet at the same time fails to represent. According to the Jewish tradition, a golem can be either male or female. In a way, Edison's future Eve is reminiscent of a golem, animated through the small golden phonographs placed in her lungs. Villiers's golem is an imago, both the duplicate of a desired object and the projection of one's changing desires.

The question of the golem as *subject,* however, remains unanswered, its mystery intact both in legend and in more recent adaptations. In his short story, Isaac Bashevis Singer does not rule out the possibility that the golem might live his own life, animated for the second time by the young Miriam's love. "Others believed that the golem was waiting for her in the darkness and took her with him to a place where loving spirits meet. Who knows? Perhaps love has even more power than a Holy Name. Love once engraved in the heart can never be erased. It lives forever."[11] Thus, in Singer's story a woman is the agent of the golem's second birth. The golem is made a complete human being, capable of feelings and thoughts, through Miriam's love. The phenomenon of parental singularity is ultimately erased, and the golem is given hypothetical life through the intervention of a woman. What Singer's conclusion also suggests is that, while the legend of the golem is a powerful illustration of the father as lone genitor, it also acknowledges the incompleteness of the creature thus begotten. Inasmuch as the creation of the golem emulates God's creation of the first man rather than the principle of human procreation, it must remain incomplete. The artificiality of the golem has to be preserved; otherwise the golem is sacrilegious.[12]

The golem thus stands as the oldest and most successful story of paternal singularity. In this act of procreation, sexuality is erased and replaced by a linguistic pronouncement, first meant to duplicate God's act of creating man, and meant also as an illustration of the magical and cryptic power of words and the mysterious origins of life. Although they are not all explicitly linked to the golem, nineteenth-century tales of artificial creation share some common themes: the idea of a man giving birth and the all-important question of speech on the one hand; and the nature of the progeny and its undefined status as either artifact or human being on the other. The progeny as artifact is usually illustrated by long discussions on the production of the creature, and Villiers de l'Isle-Adam's *L'Eve future* remains the best example of artificial genesis. But the ultimate question of the creature's humanity can be tested only at the moment of its destruction. In Hoffmann's "The Sandman," Spalanzani and Coppola's fight over Olympia's body drives Nathaniel to madness, and the fire that destroys Hadaly makes Ewald commit suicide. But is the golem a subject? Early in the twentieth century, Gustav Meyrink attempted to rewrite the legend from the point of view of the creature being animated through the power of words. The result was an extraordinary tale of wonder and horror that fascinated the Vienna of 1915.

Meyrink's Der Golem

Between 1906 and 1914 Gustav Meyrink wrote his own version of a "birth myth" in *Der Golem,* a free adaptation of Rabbi Lowe's legend.[13] Meyrink was born Gustav Meyer in Vienna in 1868, the illegitimate son of Maria Meyer, a famous actress who won the emperor's favors, and an older Austrian nobleman, Freiherr Varnbuler von und zu Hemmingen. His father abandoned him, and Meyrink maintained a life-long hatred for the mother who gave him neither affection nor a stable childhood. Meyrink's illegitimacy would plague him his entire life and undoubtedly played a fateful role when he was accused of fraud and embezzlement in 1902 and jailed in Prague for several months. Although he was eventually cleared of any wrongdoing, Meyrink came out of jail in ill health and with his reputation destroyed. He left Prague for Vienna and Munich and made his living writing and translating Dickens' novels into German. Meyrink was interested in all forms of esoteric knowledge, and he later attributed the miraculous recovery of his health to the practice of yoga. Meyrink's active dislike of Germany, linked to the political situation of the time, led him into more difficulties. His books were banned and he finished his life a semi-recluse on Lake Starnberg, in Bavaria. Financial problems plagued him to the end, and shortly before his death in 1932, he had been forced to sell his house. His works were later burned by the Nazis. To this day, Meyrink remains a controversial writer, his life and beliefs extolled by some and vilified by others.[14]

Gustav Meyrink's *Der Golem* borrows its main motif from the Jewish legend: the power to animate a creature through the mysterious use of words and the theme of the artificial man, half benevolent, half terrifying, who was said to have haunted the streets of the Prague ghetto in earlier times. But Meyrink did not seek to rewrite the legend in any conventional form: "The alleged Kabbalah that pervades the book suffers from an overdose of Madame Blavatsky's turbid theosophy," comments Gershom Scholem.[15] Certainly, Meyrink tried to combine various forms of esoteric knowledge and to fuse diverse traditions into a spiritual common ground. But for all his fascination with occult sciences "it would be a mistake to regard [Meyrink] as a gull," notes E. F. Bleiler, "for he was a difficult man either to satisfy or deceive. He attended séances together with magicians in order to catch trickery . . . He was usually disillusioned, as he freely admitted, and he came to regard occultism as the 'religion of the stupid,' but he gradually worked out an independent, eclectic position of his own that dominated his later life."[16]

Meyrink borrowed imagery and words from Kabbalistic traditions as well as tantric wisdom and Egyptian mythology. In *The Golem*, the wise Hillel comments:

> Has it ever occurred to you that the game of tarot contains two and twenty trumps—precisely the same numbers as the letters of the Hebrew alphabet? Don't our decks have card after card of which the painted pictures are obviously symbols—the fool, death and the Devil, the last judgment? My good friend, how loud do you want life to shout her answers in your ears? There is no need for you to know, of course, that the word "tarot," bears the same significance as the Jewish "Tora," that is to say, "*The Law*," or the old Egyptian "Tarut," "*Questions asked*," and the old Zend word "Tarisk," meaning, "*I require an answer.*" But learned men ought to ascertain these little facts before they give out with such certitude that tarot dates from the period of Charles the Sixth. And, just as the *Pagad* comes first in the game of cards, so is a man the first figure of all in his own picture book—his own doppelgänger, so to say.[17]

The result of this strange convergence of traditions is an overdetermined tale of creation and doom, where nothing is left to arbitrariness or chance. But in Meyrink's universe, dominated by the conviction that a higher meaning gives sense to the commonest details of everyday life, knowledge seems forever out of grasp, and this belief is illustrated powerfully through the novel's particular narrative conceit: to describe an artificial birth *from the point of view of the creature being brought to life;* to describe consciousness from the point of view of the subject grasping for a sense of self; and finally to describe filiation from the point of view of the hateful son.

The book is organized in nineteen chapters, all bearing monosyllabic titles. The narrator leads the reader through the discovery of his troubled identity as he emerges from sleep without memory; when someone calls him from outside his door, he recognizes his name, Athanasius Pernath, only vaguely. Then he remembers: "Once, long, long ago, it is in my mind that somehow or other I took the wrong hat by mistake; at the time I was surprised how well it fitted me, for the shape of my head I always thought peculiar to myself. I had glanced at that time, down at the lining of the hat, and there had observed, in letters of gold in the white silk: ATHANASIUS PERNATH. And, for some reason I did not understand, the

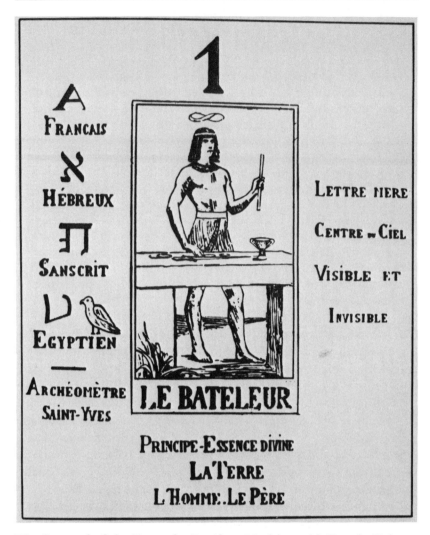

The first card of the Tarot, the *Pagad,* or Magician, with French, Hebrew, Sanskrit, and Egyptian symbols. From volume 1 of *The Encyclopedia of Tarot,* 1978.

hat had filled me with fear and dislike" (p. 10). The narrator's first (and borrowed) identity is, thinly disguised, one of the names of the golem. Athanasius evokes *athanasia,* immortality. But just as the removal of the letter *aleph* from the word *emet* left *met* (he is dead) in the Jewish legend, the removal of the first letter *A* from the name Athanasius leaves thanasius, which recalls the Greek *thanatos,* death.[18]

The power of Meyrink's tale lies primarily in the troubled consciousness of the narrator grasping for more knowledge and a better understanding of his own identity. Athanasius Pernath, as he learns he is called, discovers by overhearing a conversation that he has been in a mental hospital and has lost all memory, all knowledge about himself or his past. As he "wakes up" in a somber room in the Prague ghetto, he receives a visitor, who leaves behind a book in need of restoration. The illuminated letters needing repair form the Hebrew word *Ibbur,* meaning "impregnation," the reincarnation of a soul from a previous body, a soul in search of a new existence. Thus is Pernath's awakening begun. This it takes place in the third chapter, appropriately entitled "I," the first letter of the mysterious word *Ibbur,* as well as the first letter of the first-person pronoun, *Ich.* In a sense, Pernath examines the materialization of his soul when he looks at the title letter of the book brought for restoration: "The letter did not adhere to the parchment in the way I was familiar with in old books, but appeared to consist of two strips of thin gold, soldered together in the centre, and fixed to the edge of the parchment at each end" (p. 11). This floating signifier leads Pernath to more discoveries: "Involuntarily, I read the page through, together with the one that followed. I read on and on. The book spoke to me as had my dream, only clearer and more coherently. Like an interrogation, it pierced straight to my heart. From an invisible mouth words were streaming forth, turning into living entities, and winging straight towards me" (p. 11). A series of visions, some like a carnival, fill the room and then dissipate, leaving Pernath with the sense of an emerging life, which he also experiences as alienation:

> Yet now it was the thing happened, quite other than the way I had imagined. My skin, my muscles, the whole of my body, remembered suddenly, without telling my brain. They made movements I had neither willed nor desired. It was as though my limbs belonged to me no more . . .
>
> It was *his* way of walking! Yes, it was! Yes, it was!
>
> I knew now for certain that he was like that.
>
> My unfamiliar face was now clean shaven, with prominent cheek-bones, my eyes were slanting.

I could feel it, even though I could not see it.

"That is not my face!" I wanted to cry out. I wanted to feel it, but my hand did not obey my will; instead, it crept into my pocket, and pulled forth a book . . .

All of a sudden I was sitting down, without my cloak, without my hat, at my own table. I—I—Athanasius Pernath . . .

I knew now who the stranger was, and that at any moment I could feel his personality within me at my will; yet still was I unable to conjure up his actual presence before me, face to face. I knew I never should be able to.

He was like a negative. (pp. 13–14, emphasis added)

In this passage—and this factor distinguishes Meyrink's golem from all others—birth is described as *dispossession,* as a physical and mental imprint, or rather the negative of an imprint, that is, a life inflicted on the narrator against his will and in the terror of alienation. Pernath is born of a ghost carrying a book and some damaged letters, an unreachable father, a fleeting model whose despicable appearance he inherits against his will. The golem is described as "a spiritual disturbance . . . rising in the form of a wraith that appears to our senses in the guise of a human entity that once, centuries ago, maybe, lived here, and is craving materialisation" (p. 28). He is said to reappear every thirty-three years, still another example of Meyrink's incorporation of different religious symbols. Pernath's transformation into the immortal golem is completed in a series of scenes of relentless terror and rebirth, during which Pernath is told of the legend of the golem, his "agonised quest for materialisation" (p. 30), and is finally subjected to one last trial: experiencing the touch of the hand that, as some traditions had it, put the scroll in the mouth of the inanimate statue to awaken it. "Cold fingers seem to seize my tongue, pressing it back from beneath my teeth, rolling it into a ball, and filling my whole mouth with it. I cannot see those fingers; I know them to be invisible, but none the less I can feel them—the cold substance of them . . . [Hillel] moved his lips, and seemed to be muttering a phrase, though no sound came. Immediately the grip of the fingers upon my tongue was loosened, and my limbs were paralysed no more" (pp. 43–45).

After the rape-like scene that completes his awakening, Meyrink's golem, Pernath, is condemned to a hallucinated search for his life and his past. "As knowledge comes, so comes also recollection," Hillel had said. *"Knowledge and recollection are one and the same thing."* (p. 47). We may remind ourselves that imagination's feminine propensity to imitate memory, because it is unable to make the distinction between present and absent objects, only induces error and is linked to monstrous births; conversely, memory is imagination's rational double, its *masculine* other, the agency of knowledge, and, primarily, knowledge of the self. Pernath's story from then on is imbued with his efforts to reconstruct his hypothetical childhood, when he "would fumble through the alphabet backwards . . . to arrive at the place where they had been teaching us in school" (p. 49). But the quest is never completed, and after a harrowing tale of murder and nightmarish visions, Athanasius Pernath returns the hat bearing his name to its legitimate owner, surrendering his borrowed identity. He is allowed to glance briefly at his double from afar: "Athanasius Pernath turns slowly towards me, and my heart stops beating: *So like is he to myself, it is as though beholding my own face and figure in the glass!*" (p. 190). But the narrator is not allowed into the wonderful garden, whose wall "is all covered with decoration in mosaic, a beautiful Turkish blue background, set with gold, highly stylised frescoes depicting the Egyptian cult of the god Osiris. The swinging door is the God himself: a hermaphrodite in two halves, the right female, the left male. The figure is seated on a flat, radiant throne of mother of pearl, in semi-relief, and its golden head is in the form of a hare. The ears of it stand up high and close together, giving the semblance of two pages of an open book" (p. 189). The golem/Athanasius Pernath thus reclaims his past, but only as a mystic vision of the Origin as hermaphrodite, the pre-Adamic being and bearer of life, whose head is like an open book. But to reach such knowledge, all claims of individual happiness, all desires for an individual identity, must be relinquished. And the hero is left standing forever outside the garden gate.

Athanasius Pernath's experience as wearer of the hat is itself slightly separated from his experience of being the golem, of having been given life through the reading of the book *Ibbur* and the pronouncements of the wise Hillel. His face assumes several independent physiognomies: one with a beard, that of Pernath; and one clean-shaven and with the peculiar slanted eyes associated with the golem. In a particularly frightful episode, Pernath crawls through subterranean corridors, a labyrinth of musty and dark stairways, "one of these innumerable passages that wind beneath the Ghetto, apparently without rhyme or reason, until they reach the river" (p. 62), and finally comes to "a room with no entrance . . . only a barred window . . . The house into which the supernatural Golem had been known each time to vanish" (p. 66). In this metaphoric womb, Pernath finally confronts his ultimate double, the golem, who initially appears as the first card from the tarot game, the *Pagad,* or the Magician, lying on the floor. Then the card begins to take a human shape, to a sound like a heartbeat: "It was crouching in the corner over there—*and looking at me with my own face!* . . . I . . . he . . . I . . . Not a sound. Not a movement. We stared one another in the eyes: the hideous image one of the other" (p. 67). Pernath covers himself with old rags found on the floor, and when he finally emerges from the mysterious labyrinth, he is "surrounded by a surging sea of death-white faces, distorted by terror . . . they were taking me for the Golem" (p. 69). The golem reappears to Pernath during one of his visions, which also illustrates his spiritual genesis: "Slowly, human faces passed before me in endless procession. Dead masks all, with eyes fast closed; my own flesh and blood . . . my own ancestors! . . . century after century lined up before me, till the features, bit by bit, became more and more familiar, culminating at long last in one hideous countenance—the face of the Golem, and none other! With that my chain of forebears broke off short" (p. 97). The narrator's dual experience, that of being inhabited simultaneously by the golem and by the identity of Athanasius Pernath, a gem-cutter, deprives him of all hope of recovering an identity or identifying a father, let alone a mother. Hillel, who has freed his tongue and given him life as a golem, remains mysterious and distant.

In his personal interpretation of the golem legend, Meyrink, by changing the emphasis from the father's giving life to the son's being born in anguish, hatred, and fear, once more transforms the problematic of filiation. One of the book's secondary plots helps illuminate Meyrink's visions of paternity. It concerns the character of Aaron Wassertrum, a pawnbroker with a hideous harelip, jealously protective of his antique bric-a-brac, a rich man living in poverty, full of hatred and resentment, engaged in the relentless pursuit of the man responsible for his son's death. His son, who had repudiated his father's name and called himself Dr. Wassory, had made a fortune in Prague by falsely identifying a disease of the eyes called "green cataract," or glaucoma. Wassory would operate on perfectly healthy patients who, as a consequence of the surgery, would lose half their vision, but remain eternally grateful to have been saved from total blindness. "Time and again—especially with women—he would diagnose glaucoma in cases where there were only harmless visual conditions, simply and solely so that he could advise an operation which would involve him in no difficulties and bring him in lots of money. His patients were as wax in his hands" (p. 19).[19] Wassory's systematic blinding of the rich women of Prague is finally revealed by Charousek, a medical student and (as we learn later) himself an illegitimate son of Wassertrum. Charousek exposes Wassory, who then kills himself.

Two tales of revenge are then intertwined with the golem story: Wassertrum's hunt for Dr. Savioli, the man he thinks is responsible for his beloved son's death; and Charousek's implacable pursuit of Wassertrum, his own father, but a repudiated and abhorred genitor. The theme of blinding—a recurrent motif of Romantic aesthetics—is of particular importance in Meyrink's novel, where all knowledge is acquired through visions. Wassory's trade makes explicit the power of a certain form of knowledge and serves as a metaphoric castration, another form of a more general and violent dismissal of women in the tale. Parallel to Pernath's quest for knowledge about his own identity are the slow revelation of the destructive quality of knowledge and the discovery that all crimes are obscurely linked to a paradoxical Oedipal wish: the desire simultaneously to possess and destroy the mother. Pernath soon admits: "Intangible, the spirit of crime walks through these streets day and night in its quest for human lodgment . . . In a flash I had solved the riddle of all those fantastic beings in the midst of whom I dwelt. I had penetrated their secret; they were being driven, willy-nilly, through this life of theirs by some magnetic, invisible stream just as the bridal bouquet had been swept along the reeking gutter" (p. 22). This last image of the bridal bouquet thrown into a gutter also serves as the emblem of the extraordinarily violent fate

of women/mothers in the novel. Charousek's mother had been sold
to a brothel by Wassertrum, who replaced her with a life-size wax
doll he jealously kept among his antique bric-a-brac. Wassory's
mother died soon after giving birth, and finally, Hillel's own wife,
the mother of the ethereally beautiful Miriam, was "erased" from
her daughter's memory. Miriam tells Pernath: "When my mother
died . . . I thought the pain of it would kill me, and I ran to [Hillel],
and buried my face in his coat, and wanted to cry out, but could
not, as everything in me seemed to be choked up; and—and—it
makes me shudder even now, to think of it—he looked at me, smiling, kissed me on the forehead, and passed his hand over my eyes.
From that day to this all the pain caused by the loss of my mother
vanished. The day she was buried I could not shed one tear . . . My
father walked close to me behind the coffin, and each time I looked
up he smiled at me softly" (p. 90). This image duplicates almost
perfectly Frankenstein's "sacrilegious smile" soon after his own
mother was buried. Wassory, the image of evil, and Hillel, the image of good, both share the uncommon power of blinding women.
The mothers are forgotten, and Miriam lives on in a "blessed state
of sleep."

Filiation is thus experienced as what could be called the fate and
burden of the son. For Charousek, the hated blood of Wassertrum
and the haunting image of his mother as a prostitute poison his life
and body: "Later on," he tells Pernath, "I came to know everything—what my mother was and—and still must be . . . if she still
lives . . . and that my own body . . . was full of his foul blood . . .
Sometimes I think it is more than a coincidence that I am con-
sumptive and spit blood; it's my body probably, revolting against
everything that pertains to *him,* and rejecting him with loathing"
(p. 83). Charousek, who, it turns out, may be but another double
of Pernath, will in turn attempt to kill his father while cursing him
"to all eternity" (p. 132). For Pernath, the unrelenting anxiety over
his identity, the search for his lost childhood, the memory of his
past, all stumble against the wall of the golem's mysterious dwelling
and Hillel's refusal to assume paternity. Meyrink's characters form
a monstrous progeny, full of anger and fury at the fathers who
begot them, both longing and fearing to find a mother/prostitute
too soon deprived of her bridal bouquet.

Images of the Son

In nineteenth-century tales in which fathers give birth to artificial creatures, the question of representation assumes a double urgency. Considered from the point of view of filiation, the creature thus awakened should reproduce something of its father's traits, showing the resemblance that alone had established filiation and legitimacy for so many centuries. To a great extent, Frankenstein's monster does emblematize Frankenstein's soul, his hidden self and desires. But there is also the danger that the creature thus begotten might erase its model, take its place, eradicate the father and assume complete autonomy. The golem legend shifted the question of resemblance to the question of identity by positing strict limits to the power of creation and to the potential of the creature artificially animated. Above all, the limitation applied to the danger of idolatry. Gershom Scholem quotes an excerpt from a thirteenth-century manuscript where the newly created man warns his makers: "God alone created Adam, and when he wished to let Adam die, he erased the *aleph* from *emeth* and he remained *meth,* dead. That is what you should do with me and not create another man, lest the world succumb to idolatry as in the days of Enosh."[20] Meyrink attempted to evaluate the being thus created and, at the same time, to speculate on the specific nature of such a genealogy. In other words, what would be the model for such a creature? Meyrink answers the challenge with a curious array of artistic creations, scattered throughout the novel as peculiar warnings about art and idolatry.

Pernath is by profession a gem-cutter. His activity in the course of the story consists of trying to cut a remarkable stone that had fallen into his hands:

I once more turned my attention to the precious stone upon my table. The preliminary wax model I had made of Miriam's face should really look a thing of beauty when cut into that radiant moonstone, palely blue. I rejoiced thereat; it was a piece of rare good fortune, my finding something so eminently fitting amongst my stock of stones. The deep-black matrix of hornblende, in which it was imbedded, gave just the right light on the moonstone, and the lines fitted remarkably, as though nature

had succeeded in perpetuating a lasting likeness of Miriam's
clear-cut profile. My intention had been at first to cut from it a
cameo of the ancient Egyptian deity, Osiris, together with the vision of the hermaphrodite from the book *Ibbur,* still such a lasting
and memorable image on my mind. From an artistic point of
view the idea appealed to me most strongly, but, by degrees, I
realised such an unmistakable likeness between my initial cutting
and the daughter of Schemajah Hillel that I abandoned my project. (pp. 75–76)

As artist, Pernath reappropriates certain Romantic concerns,
duplicating in his creation an idea of giving birth obscurely tied to
a form of death: this idea is expressed in the contrast between the
wax model—a recurrent suggestion of death in the book—and the
womblike stone in which Miriam's naturally drawn profile is
embedded. Pernath's desire to cut the figure of Osiris, the hermaphroditic representation of the origin as completeness and fertility,
recalls as well the Romantic obsession with the idea of reproducing
alone. But here Nature defeats the artist: the stone's resemblance
to Miriam effectively erases Pernath's earlier goal to represent that
which eludes all representation: the ultimate vision of the origin.
Miriam herself shares the artist's aspiration when she confides that
"one of my dreams . . . is to prefigure to myself as an ultimate ideal
the complete fusion of two human beings into what—have you
never heard of the old Egyptian cult of Osiris?—into what the hermaphrodite stands for in the language of symbolism" (p. 115). But
most of all, the stone is substituted for Miriam as the only form of
possession allowed Pernath. It then embodies a double limitation:
Pernath's inability to sculpt his ideal, the hermaphrodite, because
nature has already produced in the stone matrix a slightly different
face, that of Miriam; and the artist as only a medium, an almost
mechanical performer, the agent of other powers. The stone also
reminds Pernath of the distance between Miriam and himself. It
stands as a beautiful but ultimately useless possession.

Other strategies of substitution and fetishization appear in the
novel. Wassertrum, having "bartered" the woman he loved to a
house of prostitution, buys a wax doll that resembles her from
a traveling wax-show and keeps it locked in his mysterious shop. "A
wax figure, large as life, stands in the corner where he sleeps, on a
sack of straw heaped round with every possible kind of rubbish"

(p. 114). Zwakh, a friend of Pernath, makes his living with a puppet show, and Jaromir, a deaf-mute, "cuts silhouettes of the customers" (p. 126). In another portentous scene, Zwakh's friend Vrieslander carves a curious wooden face while listening to the golem's tale in a cafe. Pernath remembers:

> Stonily, I stared at that little wooden face.
>   The carver's knife seemed to hesitate a little, then suddenly made a strong, decided cut, informing the wooden head, all at once, with terrifying personality. I recognised the yellow countenance of the stranger who had brought me the book . . .
>   *It was myself . . . I and none other . . . and I lay there on Vrieslander's lap, gaping . . .*
>   All of a sudden I was aware of Zwakh's face distorted with excitement. I could hear his voice: "God! It's the Golem!"
>   A short struggle ensued, while they had tried to wrest Vrieslander's work from his hand. But he fended them off, and crying, with a laugh: "All right! I've made a mess of this job," had opened the window and flung the head into the street below. (p. 34)

Again, the carver's art is not an autonomous gift capable of accomplishing a masterpiece; it is only an agency. Objects shape themselves, the same way Pernath/the golem is born, from multiple events/objects: a book, a word, a vision, a statue, a playing card, and a few old clothes. Ultimately, art is no longer possible, and there is no such thing as individual gift, inspiration, or talent to create. The erasure of the artist echoes the erasure of the father, and the objects created stand not as works of art, but always as *reminders,* as distant echoes of a lost memory. Wassertrum's wax doll, Pernath's stone, Vrieslander's wooden figure all point to the loss of something from the past, something whose return would be so dreadful and overwhelming, like the image of Osiris, that it would be impossible to behold and thus to represent. In this way, Meyrink's work illustrates the demise of the father as lone genitor or that of the artist as creator, a demise made all the more murderous for the desire it continues to betray.

Serial Murders

An additional key to the status of representation in the novel is given in one of the many tales that punctuate the story. The puppeteer Zwakh tells of Babinski's celebrated crimes one evening in the Pig and Whistle tavern. Babinski, one of Prague's best-known criminals, had been arrested and condemned to death for the serial murders of young women. But the rope gave way on the day he was to hang, and Babinski's sentence was commuted to life imprisonment. Benefiting from a general amnesty, the murderer was then allowed to lead a peaceful life as a gardener. "It was just about then," continues Zwakh, "that certain wax modellers bethought themselves of making little wax effigies of Babinski, and of being sufficiently tactless as to display them in their windows, dressed, each of them, in little red cloaks. Such an object was soon to be found in the house of each one of the afflicted families. But in still greater profusion were they to be seen in the shop windows, beneath glass cases, and nothing put Babinski in such a fine state of frenzy as to behold one of them" (p. 124). The wax effigies here stand as reminders of, and punishment for, the murder of young women. Babinski dies, presumably in part from exasperation at seeing so many images of himself as a criminal, and the police soon after forbid the display of the statuettes. This is the most effective use of thematized representation in the book. But here also, successful representation, in the conventional sense of a recognizable image of a real-life model, is born of murder and death. The effigies represent not Babinski, but rather the murderer of young women, a murderer miraculously alive and successfully punished through these apparently harmless effigies displayed all around the city. Babinski, Wassory, Wassertrum, even Hillel are participants in the systematic erasure of the female element in the novel.

In a way, every image modeled, every vision beheld, has its origin in death. The culmination of Pernath's terrifying experience comes when he is sent to jail for a crime he did not commit and meets there a young man accused of rape and murder. Pernath fears, and his fears are never dispelled, that Laponder's victim may be none other than Miriam, horribly tortured and burned beyond recognition, as we are told by another convict: "The lamp got knocked over, and the house was burned out. The girl's body was so charred that they still don't know who it was" (p. 171). Laponder, however, although he is condemned to death and eventually executed, is also shown to be deeply innocent: "When I committed my crime," he confides to Pernath, "it was so hideous, I think the mere remembrance of it would kill me to live through again. But I had no choice in the matter. I *had* to commit it, though I was fully conscious at the time of what I did. Something inside me, of which I had had no previous knowledge, came to life, and was stronger than I was. Do you suppose I'd have committed a murder like that, if it had been left to me to choose?" (p. 167). Laponder attributes both to a vision and to the mystical choice of having taken "the path of death" his impulse to commit murder and his aspiration to die himself in order finally to become free.

Pernath is released from jail several months after his innocence has been ascertained because, as he is told by the magistrate: "The reading of the statement had to be postponed till to-day in consequence of your name beginning with a 'P.' Naturally, the cases have to be dealt with in alphabetical rotation" (p. 173; "P" being, not by chance, the initial of the playing card *Pagad* that "gave life" to Pernath as well). Returning to the ghetto, Pernath finds it in ruins and, although it seems he has spent no more than a year in jail, twenty-five years appear to have elapsed since he roamed the streets of Prague. Upon asking a billiard maker if he remembers a certain Pernath, the other replies, "If I'm not mistaken, they used to say that he was mad. Pernath once said, yes I believe he once said his name was—let me think—Laponder—and at other times he'd give himself out for a certain . . . Charousek!" (p. 187).

The reader is thus left with the suggestion that the murderer Laponder is yet another of Pernath's innumerable identities. Pernath would have had to murder the very woman he sees as ideal in order to fulfill an obscure destiny, one of his pre-inscribed lives. Pernath's final double, the owner of the hat bearing that name, his other self shown in the vision of splendor reunified with Miriam, leaves the narrator in a state of complete dispossession. He suffers a deprivation worse than the amnesia that opened the story. All his subsequent, or concurrent, identities have been destroyed, executed, or reclaimed after he has crossed the Moldau (the symbolic river of death where the ferryman bears a Tibetan name), without a self, no longer with a destiny. Meyrink's golem can be seen as a privileged symbol of the postmodern subject, the transient holder of multiple identities and conflicting desires, and, above all, a subject free of any form of stable filiation. "In Meyrink's novel, the golem occupies both the position of double and that of ghost; he

symbolizes the return of the repressed and fully corresponds to
the Freudian definition of the Uncanny (das Unheimliche)," writes
Jean-Jacques Pollet, who interprets the episode of Pernath's wan-
derings in subterranean Prague as a "plongée" into the uncon-
scious.[21] For Manfred Lube, Meyrink's golem is no longer the "Jewish collective soul of the ghetto" but the "Other," referring here to
the reconciliation between rational and irrational forces.[22] Seductive as they may be, these explanations leave aside the troubling
question of images and the fact that Pernath himself is nothing
more than a few magic letters, *Ibbur*, given a temporary life, or a
playing card, the *Pagad*, given a human form. Ultimately, for Meyrink, signs, images, and letters, rather than humans, yield a transi-
tory life, giving monstrous birth to an agonized, half-mad being, a
serial killer.

Palimpsest

Meyrink's *Der Golem* may have found its best commentary in the
works of fiction written a little later by Jorge Luis Borges, another
writer fascinated by Kabbalist writings and a great admirer of Meyrink. In a short essay on *Der Golem,* Borges noted: "Gustav Meyrink
used the golem legend in its minutest details in his unforgettable
tale, adding a palpable horror to the scope of *Through the Looking-
Glass* that I have not forgotten after so many years. There are, for
examples, dreams within other dreams, nightmares lost in other
nightmares. The table of contents itself fascinated me; the name of
each chapter being composed of a single monosyllable."[23]

Borges himself added an essential footnote to the tale of the
creature unknowingly born of a lone father, an artificial creature,
the fragile product of a mystical meditation. In "Las ruinas circu-
lares," Borges writes of a solitary magician, a *Pagad*, hoping to
dream a man: "The purpose which guided him was not impossible,
though supernatural. He wanted to dream a man; he wanted to
dream him in minute entirety and impose him on reality. This
magic project had exhausted the entire expanse of his mind; if
someone had asked him his name or to relate some event of his
former life, he would not have been able to give an answer."[24] After
days and nights of fruitless attempts, the magician's creature takes
shape: "In the Gnostic cosmogonies, demiurges fashion a red

Adam who cannot stand; as clumsy, crude and elemental as this Adam of dust was the Adam of dreams forged by the wizard's nights. One afternoon, the man almost destroyed his entire work, but then changed his mind. (It would have been better had he destroyed it)" (*Ficciones*, p. 60). After having solicited the help of a "multiple God" whose name is Fire, the magician completes the making of a son and sends him away to his own destiny, erasing, however, the son's memory of his birth, so that he would not know he was "a projection of another man's dream—what an incomparable humiliation, what a vertiginous deception!" (p. 62, translation modified). But by fire alone would the creature know it is not human, since fire could not destroy him. As a roaring blaze reaches the circular ruins where the magician sits wondering about his son's fate, he soon realizes that he himself is immune to the flames as well: "With relief, with humiliation, with terror, he understood that he also was an illusion, that someone else was dreaming him" (p. 63). In this short story, Borges questions the status of the progeny born from a single father's magical dream of lone procreation. But Borges also makes the point that the possibility of "fathering" is no more than another dream, a projection, an artificial conceit whose origin is forever lost in a vertiginous repetition of the Same.

It is one of Borges' recurring themes that no act of creation is original, but instead repeats an earlier thought, itself the echo of an earlier creation. Thus in "Pierre Ménard, author of *Don Quixote*," Pierre Ménard "invents" word by word Cervantes' masterpiece, an "invisible" work that is composed of chapters IX and XXXVIII of the first part and a fragment of chapter XXII of the *Quixote*. Pierre Ménard is himself "a symbolist from Nîmes, essentially devoted to Poe, who engendered Baudelaire, who engendered Mallarmé, who engendered Valéry, who engendered Edmond Teste" (p. 50). This filiation illuminates the nature of authority and paternity as well: writers born of other writers. (One is reminded of Balzac's genealogy of painters: Mabuse, Frenhofer, Porbus, and Poussin; of Poe's terror of Germany; and again of the mysterious filiation between Edison and Doré.) The question of the "nature" of Ménard's *Quixote* faithfully duplicates the question of the nature of the golem as subject: "I have thought that it is legitimate to consider the 'final' *Don Quixote* as a kind of palimpsest, in which should appear traces—tenuous but not undecipherable—

of the 'previous' writings of our friend" (p. 54, translation modified). Ménard's palimpsest very specifically covers, but does not disguise, its own traces. Ménard's work thus erases Cervantes' *Quixote*, leaving the palpable genesis (though most of it has been burned) of his own *Quixote*, an unquestionable work of *creation*, inasmuch as creation is ultimately subsumed by repetition.

The notion of repetition in both Meyrink and Borges renews the question of resemblance and its role in filiation. In earlier times, the indisputable link between father and child was one of resemblance. Resemblance established legitimacy and, conversely, the lack of resemblance defined monstrosity. In the ultimate version of the nineteenth- and twentieth-century preoccupation with the idea of a solitary father, of a genitor entirely absorbed by the idea of procreating alone, it becomes clear that the act of genesis produces not a resemblance, or even a double, but rather a repetition.

The acts of procreation are themselves so complex that fathers and sons, lost in their own nightmarish dreams of self-reproduction, may never come to meet. Sons resemble fathers only because they hope in turn to repeat the monstrous act of reproduction that begot them. Repetition does not apply to physical features; it escapes iconography, limiting its sphere to the mechanical reproduction of ritualistic gestures and linguistic pronouncements. The iconoclast can breathe freely in a world where creation is made possible by letters rather than images, and where invention consists in repeating the writings or actions of earlier times. Pictorial resemblance is measured across space, repetition across time. Repetition implies a previous act, a prior instance. The model is not visible in a simultaneous gaze, but resides in a past that can be uncovered only when the ritual gesture of procreation is repeated. Pernath's amnesia, or the strange ignorance of Borges' magician, can be overcome only when the very gesture they hope to remember and reproduce is accomplished anew. Thus creation's paradoxes are clear: How to repeat that which remains unknown until the repetition has taken place? How to find the father before one has proven that he is his father's son by repeating the same blind gestures that produced an amnesiac creature in the first place? What is the status of repetition when the initial model is lost? Monstrosity does not reside then in the physical appearance of the progeny born from a palimpsest father; rather, it reappears in the series of rituals necessary to reproduce the act of paternal procreation. And this ritual is accessible only through words, a book, a letter, an alphabet, the symbolic father, the agency of a law that also requests, always, in one way or another, the erasure of the mother. Thus Pernath, also Wassertrum's son, repeats Wassertrum's bartering of his beloved mistress, Pernath's own mother, by raping and killing Miriam under the name of Laponder.

What Meyrink makes explicit, Borges also suggests. In a short story entitled "The Aleph," the narrator visits the house where once lived a passionately loved woman, Beatriz Viterbo. The sitting room is replete with portraits: "Beatriz Viterbo in profile and in full color; Beatriz wearing a mask, during the Carnival of 1921; Beatriz at her First Communion; Beatriz on the day of her wedding to Roberto Alessandri; Beatriz soon after her divorce, at a luncheon at the Turf Club; . . . Beatriz, front and three-quarter views, smiling, hand on her chin . . ."[25] Beatriz's house also has a secret: it contains an "Aleph," "the only place on earth where all places are seen from every angle, each standing clear, without any confusion or blending" (*Aleph,* p. 23). Seeing the Aleph carries a double price. First is the experience of the limits of language: "I arrive now at the ineffable core of my story. And here begins my despair as a writer," writes Borges. "All language is a set of symbols whose use among its speakers assumes a shared past. How, then, can I translate into words the limitless Aleph, which my floundering mind can scarcely encompass?" (p. 26). If all letters, alphabets, words, and languages are contained in the Aleph, the vision of this ultimate symbolic world demands the sacrifice of all images and—not surprisingly—that of the woman herself. In "the unimaginable universe" the narrator *recognizes* "the rotted dust and bones that had once deliciously been Beatriz Viterbo" (p. 28).

As a conclusion, Borges notes, "I want to add two final observations: one, on the nature of the Aleph; the other, on its name. As is well known, the Aleph is the first letter of the Hebrew alphabet . . . For the Kabbala, that letter stands for the *En Soph,* the pure and boundless godhead; it is also said that it takes the shape of a man pointing to both heaven and earth, in order to show that the lower world is the map and mirror of the higher" (p. 29). Borges is describing here the first card of the tarot game, the card that bears the letter Aleph and represents the magician or *Pagad.* This card also served as Pernath's double and gave its shape to the golem. Borges' second observation is related to his suspicion that the infinite Aleph he briefly beheld might have been a *false* one, and he wonders in conclusion: "Does this Aleph exist in the heart of a stone? Did I see it there in the cellar when I saw all things, and have I now forgotten it? Our minds are porous and forgetfulness seeps in; I myself am distorting and losing, under the wearing away of the years, the face of Beatriz" (p. 30). This description of the Aleph, the mysterious letter symbolizing the place of man between heaven and earth, is achieved and the story concluded at the cost of Beatriz's remembrance. The face that had been recorded in so many portraits, the "innumerable Beatriz," is lost with the "false Aleph." As the story ends, amnesia begins.

Meyrink and Borges tell tales of palimpsests and monstrous filiations, tales of creations handed down from unknown sources, of fathers and artists as helpless agents of mystical forces. To conclude, one could point to a passage in Meyrink's novel where Pernath has a vision of an unidentified speaker who mentions the name "Henoch": "But the rest of it I could not catch," notes Pernath. Although the biblical texts are far from simple on the subject, Enoch, Adam's grandson, seems to have symbolized wisdom and, having written down the signs he saw in heaven, he is also credited with the invention of writing: writing, that is, as transcription. Further, when the *Book of Enoch*, an early example of apocalyptic writing inscribed by a *different* bearer of the same name, was translated into German in 1833–1838, one of the commentators noted in a truly Borgesian fashion: "There is also much probability in [the] supposition that the author of our Book of Enoch had another and older book before him."[26]

Meyrink and Borges both express birth in terms of dispossession: one is born into the world through a series of traumatic revelations, each disclosing that every creation is a repetition. Resemblance is no longer a sign of filiation or the confirmation of lineage; rather it becomes the symptom of the impossibility of ever asserting one's own identity. Past theories of monstrosities all tried to answer the question "Where do resemblances come from?" In these theories, resemblances (mediated by imagination) betrayed the secret desires of the mother, producing a child that would either conform to the norm by resembling the legitimate father, or else be a monster. Imagination and resemblance thus framed two forms of identity: a legitimate and recognizable identity modeled after the father; and an illegitimate identity that revealed the power of passions along with a usurpation of the father's role in procreation. Until the eighteenth century, resemblance played a role in genealogical descent. It consolidated the family tree. When theories of heredity effectively excluded visible resemblance as an acceptable criterion for filiation and Romantic aesthetics stressed the ominous character of all similarities, resemblance came to be seen as generating chaos and disasters: living portraits that cost the life of young brides or lifelike automata doomed to sterility. As resemblances no longer reflected genealogical descent, they yielded a new birth myth in which all forms of filiations were disrupted, in which the model did not anticipate the work of art, nor the father his progeny. Contemporary art has produced many reflections on the blurring of reproduction and duplication. A study of this aspect of our culture would take a book in itself. I will simply conclude with a few remarks on Philip Kaufman's 1978 remake of *Invasion of the Body Snatchers*,[27] perhaps the most exemplary postmodern vision of the relationship between monstrous reproduction and the birth of the work of art.

On the Remake

Don Siegel's 1956 film and Kaufman's remake tell a substantially similar story: an alien agent from outer space—first seen as giant seedpods—takes over the human species. "There is no difference you can actually see," as one of Siegel's characters puts it, except for "something missing": the emotions that both plague the human species and make life bearable.[28] Kaufman's version deliberately emphasizes the birth myth already implicit in Siegel's work: when liberating the human-like "seeds," the pods are transformed into contracting uteruses that expel their fetuses to the sound of labored breathing. Many scenes are accompanied by the soundtrack of an embryo's heartbeat. But no genealogical model can account for the birth of adult embryos perfectly resembling *not* their parents but the bodies they have not yet. become, their predestined victims.

The resulting beings, a mixture of species, are undoubtedly monstrous, although their deepest monstrosity may not lie in the act of dispossession whereby humans lend the aliens their shape and memories. What makes these births so frightening is the suggestion that resemblance does not reveal an identity, but hides a principle entirely alien to it: a monster. Resemblance strikes fear in the beholder in two ways: once the body snatching has taken place, the absolute physical identity between the human being and the alien makes it impossible to "recognize" anyone except for an undefinable sense of something lacking: resemblance disrupts all possibility of knowledge. At another level, resemblance is displayed in the uniformity of the new beings, the promise of an untroubled world, free of pain and despair, free of aging and illness, but deprived of love, sexual desire, and emotions. A dystopic version of Eden.

Kaufman's remake is close enough to Siegel's original film to fully warrant its label as remake. It claims a filiation through its title and the recognizable names of the main characters (Miles Bennell becomes Matt Bennell, and Becky Driscoll is given the name of Elizabeth Driscoll). Some scenes can be viewed as direct "quotations" from Siegel's film: duplicate shots that are not always essential to the plot itself, but create in the spectator a uneasy sense of déjà vu. Crucial parts of the dialogue are repeated almost word for word: "At first glance everything looked the same. It was not."

If anything, Kaufman's personal contribution seems to be his explicit interpretation of the story as the fate of modern procreation. More specifically, in this case of monstrous birth, the mode of generation is reversed and "fecundation" actually follows the birth of the humanlike but incomplete alien. Kaufman's film shows the spectator how procreation, resulting from the encounter between human and pod, takes place. To the agonized question of one of Siegel's characters: "Where do the humans *go* after being taken over by the aliens?" Kaufman responds with a scene depicting the transformation of Elizabeth into one of the new beings. While Bennell is holding her in his arms, professing his love, Elizabeth's body shrivels and her face is shown distorted by a death rictus that may be a direct reference to the passage in *Frankenstein* where Victor dreams that he is embracing Elizabeth: "As I imprinted the first kiss on her lips, they became livid with the hue of death; her features appeared to change, and I thought that I held the corpse of my dead mother."[29] A few feet away a naked Elizabeth emerges, an explicit vision of a Renaissance Eve, tempting Bennell to join her in her newfound Paradise, one without sin, or pain, or pleasure, or sex.

Kaufman's distinctive work also separates itself from its model in other ways: the small-town innocence of Santa Mira has been replaced by the uncanny setting of San Francisco, naturally shrouded in fog. There are elements of uneasy playfulness: in one of the first sequences, Robert Duvall, dressed as a Catholic priest with a long black cassock, sits incongruously on a swing, never to be seen again. Only much later does the spectator—remembering the dead-pan face—realize that the swinging priest may have been one of the first victims of an alien takeover. The dehumanization process deplored by Miles Bennell in Siegel's movie is amplified in Kaufman's film by a depiction of urban decay. In an early scene, Bennell, a health inspector, finds rat droppings in a restaurant's stock; recurring images of garbage trucks punctuate the movie. The city is screened through Bennell's shattered windshield. From the beginning we are told that the beautiful flowers from space that produce the monstrous seeds can grow "on devastated ground." The dehumanization process is compounded by the physical degradation of the environment. The ending marks the most visible difference between the two works: Kaufman's hero is himself taken over by the aliens and the film closes with his screaming denunciation of the last woman to have successfully resisted the invasion. The spectators who have been deluded into believing that Bennell was only faking being a fake human for the last few scenes then realize the horrifying truth. With Bennell's demise and betrayal the fate of the last human female is sealed as well.

But the most interesting aspect of the 1978 version of *Invasion of the Body Snatchers* may lie in the fact that its story also duplicates the relationship between an original film and its remake. Indeed, a remake, the emblem of modern art in more ways than one, is also a form of body snatching, of "burking" as Madame Tussaud would have it. The remake takes over the original, impersonating the model while preventing total assimilation: "It is the same . . . but changed." The remake differs from other forms of imitation such as replays or adaptations by its simultaneous recognition of parentage and erasure of filiation. It claims and negates a genitor. In one of Kaufman's portentous scenes, Don Siegel appears as a taxi driver. In this affectionate tribute to the director of the original movie, the artist as father is portrayed, seized, and framed by the dutiful son. But this tribute is hardly innocent. In Kaufman's movie, Don Siegel plays an alien who coldly runs over and kills a pedestrian, who is none other than Kevin McCarthy, the hero of Siegel's own film, last seen at the end of the first *Invasion* desperately fighting the alien takeover.[30] This vision of the father as murderer also emphasizes that there is no parental reprieve, no genealogy, no descent. A dazzling array of resemblances, of repetitions, of fake humans faking being fakes, and other illusory practices thus cancels all sense of chronology or genealogical identity.

The remake is the perfect screen memory. How fitting that the false memory, the actual product of an easily misled imagination, be illustrated by these metaphors of monstrous births, deluding the viewer with their own specular identities. Malebranche had emphasized the dangerous power of imagination to make things appear that are no longer there, blurring the functions of memory and one's capacity to evaluate time and presence.

Recalling the beautiful opening scenes of Kaufman's film, somewhere in space where new forms of life are born, soon to be humanlike but not human, one can speculate that the long tradition that credited the female imagination with the birth of monstrous beings has now entered a new phase. The father-artist has again been erased in this alien takeover of procreation. The womblike pod has left the female body; the woman is free of blame but also desexualized while monsters proliferate, like so many mirrors of ourselves. As technology once again transforms the dynamics of procreation and the Romantic repudiation of the mother now extends to a more general idea of filiation, we are witness to a new aesthetics that repeatedly evokes the metaphor of its own birth. It is fully disclosed in the concluding shot of Stanley Kubrick's *2001:* the motherless, free-floating embryo, the time and space of a modern odyssey.

Notes

Index

Notes

Introduction

1. The Ravenna monster is first described by Joannes Multivallis in 1512. Its image is reproduced in all the major Renaissance treatises on monstrosity. See Jean Céard's edition of Ambroise Paré, *Des monstres et prodiges* (Geneva: Droz, 1971), pp. 153–155.
2. *Supplément à l'Encyclopédie* (Amsterdam: Rey, 1777), III, p. 566. The article is signed by Marmontel.
3. Aristotle, *Generation of Animals,* trans. A. L. Peck (Cambridge, Mass.: Harvard University Press, 1963), IV, iii, pp. 401–403. For an analysis of Aristotle's theory and influence, see Peck's introduction; Joseph Needham, *A History of Embryology* (New York: Abelard-Schuman, 1959), more specifically pp. 37–60; and Jacques Roger, *Les sciences de la vie dans la pensée française du XVIIIe siècle* (Paris: Armand Colin, 1963), pp. 63–91.
4. In his recent *Making Sex: Body and Gender from the Greeks to Freud* (Cambridge, Mass.: Harvard University Press, 1990), Thomas Laqueur argues that, until the end of the Enlightenment, a "one-sex model" accounted for both the male and female anatomies. Certainly the Galenic model emphasized anatomical similarities, yet in the specific study of procreation, the roles of males and females could never be entirely accounted for by a symmetrical model. See my discussion of Diderot in Chapter 4.
5. Quoted in Jean Rostand, *La formation de l'être, histoire des idées sur la génération* (Paris: Hachette, 1930), p. 38. Unless otherwise indicated, all translations are my own. Empedocles' idea was probably disseminated in Western Europe at the time of the Renaissance through Amyot's translation of Plutarch. His theory was mentioned in many treatises on generation and in almost all the essays written on the specific question of progeny and monstrosity.
6. André du Laurens, *Oeuvres,* trans. Théophile Gelée, médecin ordinaire du roi, (Paris, 1634), pp. 409–410 (first ed. Rouen, 1621). André du Laurens taught medicine at the University of Paris until he was named "ordinary physician" to King Henry IV of France in 1598. In 1603, he became "first physician" to Queen Marie de Médicis and in 1606 "first physician" to the king. See Pierre Darmon, *Le mythe de la procréation à l'âge baroque* (Paris: Seuil, 1981), p. 249.

7. Benjamin Bablot, *Dissertation sur le pouvoir de l'imagination des femmes enceintes* (Paris: Croulleboy and Royez, 1788), p. 10. Bablot, conseiller-médecin ordinaire du roi in Châlons-sur-Marne, near Paris, quoted from *Oeuvres morales de Plutarque,* trans. Amyot, Valcosan edition, V, p. 457. On Bablot see Chapter 3.

8. This theory had the authority associated with traditions from Antiquity. It had also received additional credibility from a passage in Genesis 30, where Jacob outwitted his father-in-law, Laban, by influencing his ewes' imagination at the time they bred: Laban had promised to give Jacob those among his newborn lambs and goats that would be striped or spotted; Jacob peeled rods of poplar and brought them where the flocks came to drink and breed. As Ambroise Paré retold it in 1573: "Jacob deceived his father-in-law, Laban, and enriched himself with his livestock by having rods barked and putting them in the watering trough, so that when the goats and ewes looked at these rods of various colors, they might form their young spotted in various colors, because the imagination has so much power over seed and reproduction that its influence and character remain [imprinted] on the thing bred." In Paré, *On Monsters and Marvels,* trans. Janis L. Pallister (Chicago: The University of Chicago Press, 1982), p. 38, translation modified.

9. In his *De Divinatione* (1567), for example, Pomponazzi refers to Augustine's *City of God,* XXI, 8, to justify his interpretation of monsters as prophetic signs. See Jean Céard, *La nature et les prodiges, l'insolite au XVIe siècle, en France* (Geneva: Droz, 1977), p. 104.

10. Fortunii Liceti, *De Monstrorum Caussis, Natura et Differentiis libri duo* (Padua, 1616). I quote from *De la nature, des causes et des différences des monstres* (Leyden: Bastiaan Schouten, 1708), p. 2.

11. Claude de Tesserant, *Histoires prodigieuses* (Paris, 1567), p. 282, quoted in Jean Céard, *La nature et les prodiges,* p. 320.

12. Paracelsus, quoted in Walter Pagel, *Paracelsus: An Introduction to Philosophical Medicine in the Era of the Renaissance* (New York: S. Karger, 1958), p. 122.

13. François-Marie-Pompée Colonna, *Les principes de la nature, ou de la génération des choses* (Paris, 1731), p. 230.

14. Dubuisson, *Tableau de l'amour conjugal, édition remise à la hauteur des connaissances d'aujourd'hui* (Paris, 1812), IV, p. 11, quoted in Pierre Darmon, *Le mythe de la procréation,* p. 44.

15. Johann Wolfgang von Goethe, *Elective Affinities,* trans. James Anthony Froude and R. Dillon Boylan (New York: Frederick Ungar, 1962), p. 224.

16. E. T. A. Hoffmann, "Mademoiselle de Scudéry," in *Tales of Hoffmann,*

trans. Sally Hayward, with an introduction by R. J. Hollingdale (London: Penguin Books, 1982), p. 63.

17. Alfred de Musset, *Lorenzaccio* (1834), IV, 3.

18. Oliver Wendell Holmes, *Elsie Venner* (Boston and New York: Houghton, Mifflin, 1861), p. 434. I thank Eric Rabkin for bringing this novel to my attention.

19. See M. H. Abrams, *The Mirror and the Lamp: Romantic Theory and the Critical Tradition* (New York: W. W. Norton, 1958). Abrams emphasizes the importance of the biological model in German and English aesthetics at the end of the eighteenth century. Herder's essay "On the Knowing and Feeling of the Human Soul" (1778) represents for Abrams "a turning point in the history of ideas . . . the age of biologism" (p. 204). See Paul de Man's analysis and criticism of the "genetic pattern" in Romanticism in "Genesis and Genealogy (Nietzsche)," *Allegories of Reading* (New Haven: Yale University Press, 1979), pp. 79–102.

Chapter 1

1. *The Complete Essays of Montaigne*, trans. Donald M. Frame (Stanford: Stanford University Press, 1958), I: 21, p. 75. Montaigne discusses monstrosity as well as the monstrous character of his writings, "so many chimeras and fantastic monsters," in several essays: "Of Idleness," I, 8; "Of the Power of the Imagination," I, 21; "Of a Monstrous Child," II, 30; and "Of the Resemblance of Children to Fathers," II, 37. On Montaigne's metaphor of the *Essays* as monstrous, see Mary B. McKinley, *Words in a Corner: Studies in Montaigne's Latin Quotations* (Lexington: French Forum, 1981), and Gisèle Mathieu-Castellani, *Montaigne: De l'écriture de l'essai* (Paris: Presses Universitaires de France, 1988). On the exemplary value of monstrosity in Montaigne, see John D. Lyons, *Exemplum: The Rhetoric of Example in Early Modern France and Italy* (Princeton: Princeton University Press, 1989).

2. Ambroise Paré, *On Monsters and Marvels*, trans. Janis L. Pallister (Chicago: The University of Chicago Press, 1982), p. 38, translation modified. *Des monstres et prodiges* was originally published in Paris in 1573. See Jean Céard's critical edition (Geneva: Droz, 1971). Born in 1517 in Laval, France, Paré is considered one of the most brilliant surgeons of the Renaissance. He was physician to Kings Henri II and Charles IX and owed his life to the king's protection during the Saint Bartholomew's massacres, ordered at the instigation of the queen, in which thousands of Protestants were killed. Paré also served Henry III, but despite his growing reputation, he was denied permission to teach

certain topics at the Faculté de médecine of Paris and was ridiculed
for having chosen to write in French rather than in Latin, as was customary for learned subjects. For an extensive analysis of Paré's book
and a complete examination of his sources, see Céard's introduction,
pp. ix–xlviii.
3. Aristotle, *Generation of Animals,* trans. A. L. Peck (Cambridge, Mass.:
Harvard University Press, 1963), I, xxi, p. 113.
4. Katharine Park, "The Imagination in Renaissance Psychology" (Master of Philosophy diss., University of London, 1974), p. 79. I wish to
thank Katharine Park for having kindly sent me her work.
5. L. J. Rather, "Thomas Fienus' (1567–1631) Dialectical Investigation
of the Imagination as Cause and Cure of Bodily Disease," *Bulletin of
the History of Medicine,* 4 (April 1967): 353. Rather notes that Fienus'
De Viribus Imaginationis Tractatus was published in Louvain in 1608,
though most bibliographies mention 1635 in Leyden.
6. Thomas Fienus, *De Viribus Imaginationis Tractatus,* conclusion 37,
quoted in Rather, "Dialectical Investigation," p. 361.
7. It is interesting that Fienus included the fetus in a special category: in
Park's words, that of the "internal alien body *(corpus alienum internum),*
matter contained within the body but not immediately dependent on
the governing soul" ("Imagination in Renaissance Psychology," p. 86).
8. Ambroise Paré, *Toutes les oeuvres* (1585), book 24, ch. 1, pp. 925–926,
quoted in Pierre Darmon, *Le mythe de la procréation à l'âge baroque*
(Paris: Seuil, 1981), p. 159.
9. Pietro Pomponazzi, *De Naturalium Effectuum Admirandorum Causis, sive
de Incantationibus* (Basel, 1556). I quote from *Les causes des merveilles de
la nature ou les enchantements,* trans. with an introduction by Henri Bus-
son (Paris: Rieder, 1930), p. 138, emphasis added. Pomponazzi was
born in Mantua on September 16, 1462. He taught medicine at the
University of Padua and became professor of natural philosophy in
1495. In 1511 he moved to Bologna, where he wrote and published
most of his works. Pomponazzi's work was later condemned by the
Church because it argued that many miracles could be attributed to
natural causes.
10. Fortunii Liceti, *De Monstrorum Caussis, Natura et Differentiis libri duo*
(Padua, 1616). I quote from *De la nature, des causes, et des différences des
monstres* (Leyden: Bastiaan Schouten, 1708), p. 228. A recent critical
edition by François Houssay offers a modern pathogeny of some of
the cases discussed by Liceti in *Traité des monstres* (Paris: Editions Hip-
pocrate, 1937). Liceti was an obstetrician and the son of a physician
from Rapallo, Italy. He taught natural philosophy at Pisa, Bologna,

and Padua, where he died in 1657. In the seventeenth century alone, his book had four editions (1616, 1634, 1665, 1666).

11. Paré, *On Monsters and Marvels*, pp. 41–42, translation modified.

12. On the role and importance of illustrations in Paré, see Céard's introduction to *Des monstres et prodiges*, pp. xxv–xxviii.

13. Paracelsus, *Traicté des vers, serpens, araignes, crapaux, cancres et signes, ou taches tirées du ventre de la mère*, trans. from Latin by Lazare Boet (Lyons: Jean Huguetan, 1593), p. 159. Philippus Aureolus Theophrastus Bombast von Hohenheim, or Paracelsus, was born in Switzerland in 1493 and died in Salzburg in 1541. He traveled extensively throughout Europe and was involved in a book-burning incident in Basel, where he threw into the flames the ancient works of Galen and Avicenna. The theme of the power of imagination, and particularly of women's imagination, is ever-present in his work. Paracelsus' cure for birthmarks implies a rigorous analogical principle but excludes the passion which might have moved the mother's imagination to cause the deformity. On Paracelsus' life and works, see Walter Pagel, *Paracelsus: An Introduction to Philosophical Medicine in the Era of the Renaissance* (New York: S. Karger, 1958). Paracelsus' ideas spread rapidly throughout Europe in spite of harsh criticism from the medical establishment. See Jacques Roger, *Les sciences de la vie dans la pensée française du XVIII siècle* (Paris: Armand Colin, 1963), pp. 19–25.

14. In *The Order of Things: An Archeology of the Human Sciences* (New York: Random House, 1970), Michel Foucault notes: "Up to the end of the sixteenth century, resemblance played a constructive role in the knowledge of Western culture. It was resemblance that largely guided exegesis and the interpretation of texts; it was resemblance that organized the play of symbols, made possible knowledge of things visible and invisible, and controlled the art of representing them" (p. 17). Foucault identifies four types of similitude: *convenentia, aemulatio, analogy,* and *sympathy.* Paracelsus' method brings together these four types of similitude, but most directly the principle of *analogy,* which is centered on the human body.

15. Nicolas Andry de Boisregard, *L'orthopédie ou l'art de prévenir et de corriger dans les enfants les difformités du corps, le tout par des moyens à la portée des pères et mères, et de toutes les personnes qui ont des enfants à élever,* 2 vol. (Paris: Laubert and Durand, 1741), vol. 2, pp. 191, 192–193 (first ed. Paris, 1700). In spite of the title, Andry does not suggest any cure for birthmarks, but insists that pregnant women should not be exposed to sights that might trouble their imagination.

16. See Introduction.

17. Empedocles' text is lost. Giambattista della Porta (1525?-1615), a natural philosopher, "quotes" Empedocles in Latin translation in his extraordinarily successful *Magia Naturalis, sive de Miraculis Rerum Naturalium Libri,* first published in Antwerp in 1558, translated into French and published at Lyons in 1612, reedited in 1621, 1650, and 1680; it was translated into English in 1669 and German in 1680. Empedocles' idea was probably disseminated during the Renaissance through Amyot's translation of Plutarch. Empedocles is regularly mentioned in essays on the power of imagination in pregnant women.

18. These texts are discussed in Jean Céard, *La nature et les prodiges, l'insolite au XVIe siècle, en France* (Geneva: Droz, 1977). See also Katharine Park and Lorraine J. Daston's "Unnatural Conceptions: The Study of Monsters in Sixteenth- and Seventeenth-Century France and England," *Past and Present,* 92 (August 1981): 20–54. Both essays provide an epistemological study of the monster as prodigy and prophecy.

19. Pierre Boaistuau, *Histoires prodigieuses* (Paris: Club Français du Livre, 1961), p. 24. Boaistuau was born in Nantes around 1515. He studied law in Avignon, traveled to Italy, where he met the most famous physicians of the time, and died in Paris in 1566. His *Histoires prodigieuses,* first published in Paris in 1560, became extremely popular. Paré plagiarized many passages from the text in his *Des monstres et prodiges.* It is often difficult to evaluate the specific pathology involved in most Renaissance accounts of monstrous births, though Houssay attempts to do so in his edition of Liceti. There is a certain degree of imagination involved, the author's mostly, and the illustrations are meant primarily to surprise readers and make them wonder at the prodigies of Nature. The case of the "hairy virgin," however, is recognizable and is discussed in some detail in a twentieth-century medical thesis by A. F. Le Double and François Houssay entitled *Les velus, contribution à l'étude des variations par excès du système pileux de l'homme et de leur signification au point de vue de l'anthropologie zoologique* (Paris: Vigot, 1912). The authors consider the case of the "hairy virgin" as well as the theory of the power of the imagination of pregnant women. They cite most of the classical examples and add a considerable number of modern instances in which mothers attributed the birth of a deformed progeny to an event that had deeply affected them during their pregnancy (see pp. 247–255). The authors' conclusions do not entirely repudiate the Renaissance belief in the maternal imagination. See also George M. Gould and Walter L. Pyle, *Anomalies and Curiosities of Medicine* (New York: The Julian Press, 1896), pp. 230–234.

20. Quoted in Pagel, *Paracelsus,* p. 124.

21. Although Renaissance treatises on monstrous births are not primarily

concerned with moral judgment, the ideal of moral opprobrium attached to the words "monster" and "monstrous" is not a new one. Examples can be found in the works of several Renaissance writers. Racine, of course, gave the word "monster" its most forceful moral connotation in his *Phèdre* (1677).

22. Ulysse Aldrovandus (1522–1607) was a physician who taught at Bologna. He was also known as an art lover and collector. His *Monstrorum Historia* was published in Bologna in 1642.

23. Paré, *On Monsters and Marvels,* pp. 38–39, translation modified. This theme became the subject of an early twentieth-century short story by Arthur Schniltzer, "Andreas Thameyer's Last Letter."

24. The question of whether a monster was a human being with a soul, and thus should be baptized, was the subject of lengthy debate from the Middle Ages to the eighteenth century. Practices varied and theologians disagreed. It seems, however, that unless the progeny was so severely deformed that it bore no resemblance at all to a human being, the monster was generally baptized. See Chapter 2.

25. *The Dialogues of Plato,* trans. Benjamin Jowett, 2 vol. (New York: Random House, 1937), vol. 2, p. 242. See also Rupert C. Lodge, *Plato's Theory of Art* (London: Routledge and Kegan Paul, 1953), pp. 167–191.

26. See Murray Wright Bundy, *The Theory of Imagination in Classical and Mediaeval Thought* (Urbana: *University of Illinois Studies in Language and Literature,* 12, 1927). On the difference between phantasia and imaginatio, see ch. 9, "Mediaeval Descriptive Psychology."

27. Ibid., p. 196.

28. Although Park and Daston briefly consider the role of the mother's imagination in monstrosity, they do not link the popularity of these tales to the Reformation. They note, however, that the question of monsters became a polemical tool in the religious wars: "Some writers, like Luther and Melanchthon, used monsters to argue a particular position in the Reformation debate; in their hands monsters became polemical weapons against Calvinism during the French wars of religion, against Rome in late sixteenth-century England, or against separatism during the English Civil War, and the familiar woodcuts appeared in altered form to serve the purpose at hand" ("Unnatural Conceptions," p. 32). They give as specific examples the engraving of the Pope-Ass, adapted for a Catholic audience, and a Protestant adaptation of Lycosthenes' *Prodigiorum et Ostentorum Chronicon.* Luther's famous pamphlet about two monsters, the "Pope-Ass" and the "monk-calf," *Deuttung der czwo grewlichen Figuren, Bapstesels czu Rom und Munchkalbs zu Freyberg ijnn Meijsszen funden,* was published in

1523. Luther "functioned as a mediator between more popular and learned culture" (p. 26). The pamphlet also politicized the question of monstrosity. Within that context, monsters born from the contemplation of sacred images would serve as a powerful iconoclast argument.

29. Carlos M. N. Eire, *War against the Idols: The Reformation of Worship from Erasmus to Calvin* (Cambridge: Cambridge University Press, 1986), pp. 20–21.

30. Jurgis Baltrusaitis, "Monstres et emblèmes, une survivance du moyenage au 16o et 17o siècles," *Médecine de France,* 39 (1953): 17–30. Baltrusaitis sees a clear connection between the development of Reformation thought and the renewed interest in theories of monstrosity. He believes that the dates of publication are significant and cites, in addition to the texts we mention, Luther's works and Joseph Grunpeck's *De Signis Portentis et Prodigiis,* published in 1502.

31. Martin Bucer (1491–1551) played an important role in Strasbourg during the Reformation. He is the author of *Basis and Reason for the Innovations,* published in 1524, and *That Any Kind of Images May Not Be Permitted,* published in 1530. According to Eire, the latter treatise marks "the repudiation of Lutheran influence. It is also a link in the theological chain leading up to Calvin" (*War against Idols,* p. 94).

32. Eire, *War against Idols,* p. 315. See also Carl Christensen, *Art and the Reformation in Germany* (Athens: Ohio University Press, 1979).

33. Calvin, *Institutes,* I.12.1. Quoted and discussed in Eire, *War against Idols,* p. 202.

34. See Voltaire, *Lettres philosophiques,* ed. Raymond Naves (Paris: Garnier, 1964), Letter II, "Sur les Quakers," p. 10.

35. This last point was an important argument in Pomponazzi's doctrine and one of the reasons the Catholic Church condemned his work.

36. Jean-Joseph Goux, *Les iconoclastes* (Paris: Seuil, 1978), pp. 12–13. In the perspective of Lacan's *Imaginary,* the exclusive relationship between child and mother is originally mediated neither by the figure of the father nor by way of words.

37. Another instance of the double rejection of images and the female role in religion can be found in the Cult of the Supreme Being during the French Revolution. See Marie-Hélène Huet, "Le sacre du printemps: Essai sur le sublime et la terreur," *Modern Language Notes,* 103, no. 4 (September 1988): 782–799.

38. Robert Robin and Simon Houdry, *Plaidoye de maistre Robin, advocat en la cour, avec l'ampliation du plaidoyé de maistre Simon Houdry, aussi advocat. Sur la question, sçavoir si un enfant, qu'on pretendoit avoit esté monstre: Et auquel, pour raison de ce, on luy avoit refusé le s. sacrement de baptesme,*

avoit esté capable de recueillir la succession de son pere, in vim eius testamenti: Et si par son decez il avoit donné lieu à la substitution pupillaire faicte au profit de sa mere (Paris: Villery, 1620).

39. Claude de Tesserant, *Histoires prodigieuses* (Paris, 1567). Discussed by Céard in *La nature et les prodiges*, p. 320.

Chapter 2

1. Jean Céard, *La nature et les prodiges* (Geneva: Droz, 1977), p. 81.
2. Katharine Park and Lorraine J. Daston, "Unnatural Conceptions: The Study of Monsters in Sixteenth- and Seventeenth-Century France and England," *Past and Present*, 92 (August 1981): 20–54. In their evaluation of the changes taking place around 1700, Park and Daston also note "more general prohibitions against mixing natural philosophy and theology." This last point, however, is less convincing if one considers the numerous contributions of theologians to the history of generation: following Honoratus Faber, a Jesuit, and Malebranche, a priest of the Oratory, Nicholas Stensen, who discovered the role of ovaries, joined the Church and became a bishop. Many treatises on sacred embryology were written in the eighteenth century.
3. On the general question of embryology in the seventeenth and eighteenth centuries, see Pierre Darmon, *Le mythe de la procréation à l'âge baroque* (Paris: Seuil, 1981); François Jacob, *The Logic of Life: A History of Heredity*, trans. Betty E. Spillmann (New York: Pantheon Books, 1973); Joseph Needham, *A History of Embryology*, 2nd ed., revised with the assistance of Arthur Hughes (New York: Abelard-Schuman, 1959); E. S. Russell, *Form and Function: A Contribution to the History of Animal Morphology* (London: Murray, 1916); and Jacques Roger's unsurpassed *Les sciences de la vie dans la pensée française du XVIIIe siècle* (Paris: Armand Colin, 1963). The frontispiece of William Harvey's *De Generatione Animalium* (1651) showed Zeus holding an egg inscribed with the words *Ex ovo omnia*. According to Needham, however, the saying *omne vivum ex ovo*, "often attributed to him, is only obliquely his" (p. 133).
4. The Aristotelian definition of "form" and "matter" was the subject of varied interpretations during the Middle Ages and the Renaissance. On the one hand, it was substantially challenged by the view that the maternal imagination influenced the form of the child, but only if one takes the word "form" at a literal level, that is, as a modification of visible "matter" rather than as the spiritual element suggested by Aristotle. On the other hand, the importance of the maternal imagination in the formation of monstrosities was also directly derived from

Aristotle's suggestion that the female and the monster are two examples of "deviations" from the norm. On Aristotle's influence as well
as "misinterpretations" of *Generation of Animals,* see A. L. Peck's introduction to Aristotle's *Generation of Animals* (Cambridge, Mass.: Harvard University Press), pp. v–xxxvii; Joseph Needham, *Biochemistry
and Morphogenesis* (Cambridge: Cambridge University Press, 1942),
and *A History of Embryology,* particularly pp. 37–60; Roger, *Les sciences
de la vie dans la pensée française au XVIIIe siècle,* pp. 64–74, 79–87.

5. Needham argues that Descartes did not write the posthumous *De la
   formation du foetus.* But Roger, who may be considered an authority on
   the subject, does not doubt Descartes's authorship and gives a striking
   illustration of the cogency of the Cartesian view of generation in *Les
   sciences de la vie,* pp. 140–154.

6. Quoted in Needham, *A History of Embryology,* p. 121. Needham comments on Gli Aromatari's preformationist theory as follows: "This
   suggestion did not begin to bear its malignant fruits till the time of
   Swammerdam."

7. Ibid., p. 139. Harvey had read Gli Aromatari's letter of 1625 in favor
   of preformation, and his own firm stand in defense of epigenesis may
   be viewed as a response to the writing of the Venetian scientist.

8. Ibid., p. 146. Harvey compares the mechanism of fertilization to specific contagious diseases such as leprosy, venereal diseases, the plague,
   and phthisis. See his *Exercitationes de Generatione Animalium,* 48, p. 138.
   See also Roger's analysis, in *Les sciences de la vie,* pp. 112–121. Roger
   underlines what he sees in Harvey as a markedly different belief from
   that of Aristotle—that both parents play an active role in procreation:
   "Contrairement à ce que pensait Aristote, les deux parents sont égale-
   ment causes efficientes du poulet" (p. 117).

9. Jean Rostand, *La formation de l'être, histoire des idées sur la génération*
   (Paris: Hachette, 1930), p. 58.

10. Rostand argues that the thesis of *emboîtement* and its "biological" ex-
    planation of original sin are due in part to the mystic influence of
    Antoinette Bourignon and to religious preoccupations, which ulti-
    mately led to Swammerdam's sinking into a somber melancholy (*La
    formation de l'être,* p. 71). This is one of many examples of the conver-
    gence of theological and biological inquiries in the seventeenth and
    eighteenth centuries. Roger also notes the similarity of views that ex-
    isted between Swammerdam and Malebranche's first book, *De la re-
    cherche de la vérité,* published between 1674 and 1678, a few years after
    the publication of Swammerdam's *Historia Insectorum Generalis* in
    Utrecht. Malebranche refers to Swammerdam's work and writes: "All
    the bodies of men and animals that will be born until the end of time

may have originated at the time of the creation of the world; by this, I mean to say that the females of the first animals may have been created with all those of the same species they engendered and will engender throughout the rest of time." In Roger, *Les sciences de la vie,* p. 337. As we shall see, this idea is somewhat difficult to reconcile with Malebranche's views on the role of the maternal imagination in the definition and continuation of species.

11. John Farley, *Gametes and Spores: Ideas about Sexual Reproduction, 1750–1914* (Baltimore: The John's Hopkins University Press, 1982), p. 20.

12. In Diderot's *Le rêve de d'Alembert,* d'Alembert, having ejaculated in his sleep, sighs: "If there is a planet where men multiply the way fish do, where a man's spawn is merely deposited on that of a woman . . . At least my own frustration would be easier to bear in that case . . . It's a shame to waste anything that could serve some useful purpose. Mademoiselle, if only this stuff could be gathered up and sent in a closed flask the first thing tomorrow morning to Needham." In *Rameau's Nephew and Other Works,* trans. Jacques Barzun and Ralph H. Bowen (Indianapolis: The Bobbs-Merrill Company, 1964), p. 118.

13. Quoted in Needham, *A History of Embryology,* pp. 198–199. A more detailed history of the debate and the ultimate downfall of epigenesis is given in Roger, *Les sciences de la vie,* pp. 364–441. Haller's engraving of a womb was later reproduced in Diderot's *Encyclopedia;* see Elizabeth de Fontenay's analysis in "Diderot gynéconome," *Digraphe,* 7 (1976): 29–50, and Chapter 4 of this book.

14. On Camille Dareste, see Chapter 5.

15. François Poulain de la Barre, *De l'excellence de l'homme* (Paris, 1675), p. 134. Quoted in Darmon, *Le mythe de la procréation,* pp. 45–46. Paradoxically, Poulain de la Barre (1647–1725) was also the author of a book entitled *De l'égalité des deux sexes,* published two years before in 1673, in which he argued from a Cartesian perspective that men and women are morally equals.

16. On Malebranche's contributions to the science of generation, see Roger, *Les sciences de la vie,* pp. 336–339, 397–418. See also Alain Grosrichard, "Le cas polyphème," *Ornicar?,* 11 and 12–13 (September and December 1977): 19–36, 45–57.

17. I quote from Nicolas Malebranche, *The Search after Truth,* trans. Thomas M. Lennon and Paul J. Olscamp (Columbus: Ohio State University Press, 1980), p. 87.

18. Malebranche's description of the effects of imagination and his description of compassion anticipate precisely Rousseau's later definition of pity in his *Discours sur l'origine de l'inégalité parmi les hommes* (1754).

19. Grosrichard, "Le cas polyphème," p. 53. The most common descriptions of birthmarks since the Middle Ages were descriptions of fruit-like spots on the skin.

20. Malebranche, *The Search after Truth,* p. 116. This text is also glossed by Grosrichard. It is interesting that Grosrichard studies the monstrous process from the point of view of the child, as if the mother did not act, but were rather a passive instrument allowing her progeny actively to seek a resemblance: *"What the child imitates,"* he writes, "is what strikes the eye and is imprinted on the mother's brain, that is, a flat representation which produces an effect of relief, distance, and depth through the artifice of perspective. A 'natural judgment,' joined to experience, allows us, adults, not to be taken in by the illusion of paintings. . . *But the child is mistaken"* ("Le cas polyphème," p. 34, emphasis added). Paradoxically, Grosrichard's reading ultimately erases the mother's active role in the shaping of progeny. On this story see also Marie-Hélène Huet, "Living Images: Monstrosity and Representation," *Representations,* 4 (Fall 1983): 73–87.

21. Grosrichard sees in this resemblance two different modes of identification: "A child resembles both parents through the maternal imagination, which allows a double imitation, or identification. But this identification is not the same in both cases. The child identifies himself with his mother in that he feels, he sees, he desires *like* her: she gives him her style. Identification with the father, on the contrary, is an identification with *what* the mother feels, sees, and desires" ("Le cas polyphème," p. 48). This seductive Lacanian interpretation is not immediately justified by Malebranche's text, if only because, for Malebranche, preformation accounted for most resemblances. Imagination is a *supplement* capable of modifying a shape already organized by nature. When Grosrichard associates resemblance and identification, he collapses a physically recognizable similarity on the one hand— one that will describe a child as normal or monstrous—and on the other hand, the mechanisms, both moral and physical, that account for this similarity.

22. On the "quarrel of true and false ideas" that opposed Malebranche and Antoine Arnauld, see Roger, *Les sciences de la vie,* pp. 400–418.

Chapter 3

1. René de Ceriziers, *Le philosophe français* (Rouen: A. Ferrand, 1654), p. 59 (first ed. Paris, 1643). Montaigne had noted in his *Essays:* "What we call monsters are not so to God, who sees in the immensity of his work the infinity of forms that he has comprised in it." *In The Complete*

Essays of Montaigne, trans. Donald Frame (Stanford: Stanford University Press, 1958), II, 31, p. 539.

2. See Danielle Jacquart and Claude Thomasset, *Sexuality and Medicine in the Middle Ages,* trans. Matthew Adamson (Princeton: Princeton University Press, 1988). For an examination of the way sexuality and monstrous conceptions were visualized in the eighteenth century, see Barbara Maria Stafford, *Body Criticism: Imaging the Unseen in Enlightenment Art and Medicine* (Cambridge, Mass.: MIT Press, 1991), particularly pp. 211–280.

3. Jean Palfyn, *Description anatomique des parties de la femme qui servent à la génération, avec un traité des monstres, de leurs causes, de leur nature et de leurs différences* (Leyden: Bastiaan Schouten, 1708). Palfyn was an avid reader of Fontenelle and reproduced as his own, in *Description anatomique,* Fontenelle's justification of ovism, first published in 1701. See Jacques Roger, *Les sciences de la vie dans la pensée française du XVIIIe siècle* (Paris: Armand Colin, 1963), pp. 268–269.

4. Pierre Darmon briefly explores the tradition that viewed the woman's reproductive organs as "porta inferni" (the gate of Hell), to use Augustine's words. See Darmon, *Le mythe de la procréation à l'âge baroque* (Paris: Seuil, 1981), pp. 9–17.

5. This line of thought may be read in light of Julia Kristeva's *Pouvoirs de l'horreur* (Paris: Seuil, 1980). See particularly her analysis of abjection of/in the mother's body, p. 66.

6. Lorenz Heister, *L'anatomie avec des essais de physique sur l'usage des parties du corps humain et sur le mécanisme de leurs mouvements* (Paris: Jacques Vincent, 1735), pp. 221–222, emphasis added (first ed. Altdorf, 1718). This text belongs to the tradition described by Pierre Darmon as "splendor and prestige of the penis." An interesting aspect of the tradition that praises the penis is the wealth of words used to designate it. In a text of 1612, the physician Jacques Duval mentions: "penis, veretrum, cauda, hasta, mulonis, vespa, mentulum, priapus, membrum virile . . . these significant words are so varied and in such quantity . . . that I cannot explain them all for fear of offending the reader" (Darmon, *Le mythe de la procréation,* pp. 9–10). One can once more observe the relationship between language and procreation. The penis gives birth to innumerable words, as its role as "father of mankind" requires.

7. In *L'anatomie de l'homme suivant la circulation du sang et les nouvelles découvertes démontrées au jardin du roi* (Paris: La Porte, 1780), Pierre Dionis, an ovist and a believer in epigenesis, took the view that monsters were caused by organic pressure on the fetus. He simultaneously expressed the view that women were not themselves monstrous: "I am

not among those who believe that the female is an imperfect animal and argue that nature always aims at producing males as its most accomplished work . . . Some philosophers sharing this belief considered women as monstrosities in nature" (p. 363, first ed. 1690).

8. Pierre-Sylvain Régis, *Système de philosophie, contenant la logique, la métaphysique, la physique et la morale* (Paris: Anisson, Posuel, and Rigaud, 1690), III, pp. 29–30. Quoted in Roger's *Les sciences de la vie,* p. 402. On this quarrel see Roger's very detailed analysis, pp. 397–418. This debate illustrates once more the interaction of theological and scientific inquiries. The most remarkable view is that the monster, which is hardly perceived as human, challenges a certain understanding of God. Regis' defense of the Jansenist point of view entails a specific definition of scientific knowledge: given the fact that our understanding of God is necessarily limited by the imperfection of our human nature, how can we attribute to Him a "mistake" such as a monster? Even if we were to attribute to God a general intention, whose scope would, of necessity, escape us, our deciphering of nature would remain limited by our fundamental incapacity to understand God or His intervention in the physical world.

9. Louis Lémery, *Sur les monstres, premier mémoire dans lequel on examine quelle est la cause immédiate des monstres,* in *Mémoires de l'académie des sciences,* 1738, p. 270, quoted in Roger, *Les sciences de la vie,* p. 410–411.

10. Louis Lémery, *Second mémoire sur les monstres,* 1738, p. 305, quoted in Roger, *Les sciences de la vie,* p. 415.

11. Nicolas Venette (1633–1698) studied at Bordeaux and practiced medicine in La Rochelle. For Roger, Venette is representative of the "provincial" practitioners, who were not only inactive in modern scientific debates, but who most often rejected all new theories or debates on the assumption that the Ancients had already foreseen everything from the circulation of blood to the importance of eggs. On these practicing skeptics, see Roger, *Les sciences de la vie,* p. 167. Venette's *Tableau de l'amour considéré dans l'état de mariage,* initially published in Amsterdam in 1687 (Jansson), was reedited many times throughout the eighteenth and nineteenth centuries under the title *De la génération de l'homme ou tableau de l'amour conjugal considéré dans l'état de mariage.* On Venette, see Darmon, *Le mythe de la procréation,* pp. 263–264 and Chapter 4 of this book.

12. Nicolas Venette, *De la génération de l'homme ou le tableau de l'amour considéré dans l'état de mariage* (London, 1751), p. 283. Roger lists the first edition as having been printed in Amsterdam in 1687 under the pseudonym M. Salocini.

13. James Blondel, *The Power of the Mother's Imagination over the Foetus, ex-*

amined in answer to Daniel Turner's book, intitled A Defence of the twelfth Chapter of the first part of a Treatise De Morbis Cutaneis (London: Brotherton, 1729).

14. Joseph Needham briefly discusses this "memorable dispute . . . whose polemics, written in an exceedingly witty manner, are still very pleasant to read. Blondel was the sceptic and Turner the defender of the numerous extraordinary stories which passed for evidence on this subject." In Needham, *A History of Embryology* (New York: Abelard-Schuman, 1959), pp. 215–216.

15. Isaac Bellet, *Lettre sur le pouvoir de l'imagination des femmes enceintes* (Paris: Guérin, 1745). I quote from this first edition. Very little is known about Isaac Bellet, who is rarely discussed in medical history, because he belonged to the category of brilliant commentators rather than to that of discoverers and scientists. He died in 1778.

16. Jean Varloot, Jacques Chouillet, and other Diderot scholars attribute the origin of Diderot's celebrated image of the body as harpsichord in *D'Alembert's Dream* to his 1748 study *Principes d'acoustique*. Bellet's text, however, was published three years earlier, the same year Shaftesbury wrote his *Inquiry Concerning Virtue* (later translated by Diderot), in which he too compares affections and passions with the cords or strings of a musical instrument. In 1748, La Mettrie published *L'homme-machine*, in which the human phonetic system is compared to the workings of a harpsichord. Jacques Chouillet comments upon the parallel between Shaftesbury's text and Diderot's metaphor in *Diderot poète de l'énergie* (Paris: Presses Universitaires de France, 1984), pp. 245–278. See also Herbert Dieckmann, "The Metaphoric Structure of the *Rêve de d'Alembert*," *Diderot Studies*, 17 (1973): 15–24. Although the comparison between the human body and a musical instrument was a fairly common one, Bellet is the only author to have given it extensive treatment before Diderot. Moreover, both authors use the image of the harpsichord while attempting to give a mechanical explanation of monstrosity—an element of *D'Alembert's Dream* too often seen as secondary. Both men may owe to Pascal the etymological link between *orgue* and *organe* (*organ* in its musical and physiological senses) noted by Varloot in his edition of Diderot's *Le rêve de d'Alembert* (Paris: Editions Sociales, 1971), p. 13. This link is made explicit in Bellet's text as well. Of course, a major difference of opinion separates the two writers: Bellet is a preformationist and Diderot is firmly opposed to the idea of the preexistence of germs. Their literary and philosophical strategies, however, are strikingly similar. On Diderot's theory of monstrosity, see Chapter 4.

17. Louis-Nicolas-Benjamin Bablot, *Dissertation sur le pouvoir de l'imagina-*

tion des femmes enceintes; dans laquelle on passe successivement en revue tous les grands hommes qui, depuis plus de deux mille ans, ont admis l'influence de cette faculté sur le FOETUS, et dans laquelle on répond aux objections de ceux qui combattent cette opinion (Paris: Croullebois and Royez, 1788). Bablot (1754–1802) has not been recognized by posterity, perhaps because his work belonged to a genre that has not yet been properly defined: medical commentary. Bablot studied at Reims and practiced medicine all his life at Châlons-sur-Marne, near Paris. He was a pioneer in the use of inoculation (still the object of much controversy) and served as doctor for several prisons. Darmon gives a short biographical note in *Le mythe de la procréation,* pp. 246–247 that fails to do justice to Bablot's remarkable erudition and intellectual honesty. Although not a brilliant scientist, he was a first-rate scholar.

18. Jean-Sylvain Bailly, *Exposé des expériences qui ont été faites pour l'examen du magnétisme animal* (Paris, 1784). Quoted in Bablot, *Dissertation,* pp. 40–42.

19. Jean-Baptiste Demangeon, *Considérations physiologiques sur le pouvoir de l'imagination maternelle durant la grossesse et sur les autres causes, prétendues ou réelles des difformités et variétés naturelles,* 2 vols. (Paris, 1807). Demangeon wrote another essay on generation, *Anthropogénésie ou génération de l'homme* (Paris, 1829).

20. Demangeon, *Considérations,* p. 16, emphasis added. P. Zacchias published *Quaestiones Medico-Legales* in Frankfurt in 1688. Zacchias is better known for his work on the nourishment of the fetus. See Needham, *A History of Embryology,* pp. 175, 180.

Chapter 4

1. Nicolas Venette, *La génération de l'homme ou tableau de l'amour conjugal considéré dans l'état de mariage* (London, 1751), for more on Nicolas Venette, see Chapter 3, note 11.

2. Benjamin Bablot wrote in 1788: "Venette . . . tolled the bell for the power of imagination." In *Dissertation sur le pouvoir de l'imagination des femmes enceintes* (Paris: Crouillebois and Royez, 1788), p. 70. In fact, Venette does not really argue against the power of the mother's imagination. One could say that he grants it such power that no resemblance can be trusted.

3. Venette, *La génération de l'homme,* p. 271, emphasis added.

4. Denis Diderot, *Eléments de physiologie,* in *Oeuvres Complètes* ed. J. Assézat (Paris: Garnier, 1875), vol. 9, p. 405.

5. I have kept the masculine pronoun applicable in French to the word

"enfant" in order to underline what I see in Diderot's text as a scene of reunion meant to duplicate and erase the pleasureless conception that made it possible.

6. Soranus was a second-century writer and the author of *Gynecology.*

7. Buffon, *Histoire naturelle des animaux* (Paris, 1749), II, p. 346. Quoted in Elizabeth de Fontenay, "Diderot gynéconome," *Digraphe,* 7 (1976): 29–50.

8. Fontenay, "Diderot gynéconome," p. 38.

9. Denis Diderot, *Le rêve de d'Alembert.* I quote from Ralph H. Bowen's translation in *Rameau's Nephew and Other Works* (Indianapolis: The Bobbs-Merrill Company, 1975), p. 135, translation modified.

10. Thomas Laqueur, *Making Sex: Body and Gender from the Greeks to Freud* (Cambridge, Mass.: Harvard University Press, 1990), p. 26.

11. Elizabeth de Fontenay, *Diderot ou le matérialisme enchanté* (Paris: Grasset, 1981), p. 120. Aram Vartanian gives an exhaustive examination of Diderot's scientific beliefs in *Diderot and Descartes: A Study of Scientific Naturalism in the Enlightenment* (Princeton: Princeton University Press, 1953).

12. There is a considerable amount of literature on hermaphrodism. Recent analyses by Michel Foucault and others have emphasized the question of sexual identity as *attribution,* a decision sometimes made by the medical body, as in the case of Herculine Barbin, and sometimes made by the hermaphrodite him- or herself. In the case reported by Diderot, any decision is preempted by the perfectly male organization of the pregnant soldier. Nothing remotely "feminine" in him attracts him to another man, either. There is no reconstruction of a fertile but flawed heterosexual relationship. Rather, the soldier's homosexuality is revealed and doomed by the monstrous and hidden femaleness of the womb he unknowingly carries within himself.

13. Jean Mayer, *Diderot, homme de science* (Rennes, 1959), quoted in French in Emita B. Hill, *The Role of "Le Monstre" in Diderot's Thought, Studies on Voltaire and the Eighteenth Century,* 97 (1972): 192, translation mine.

14. Hill, *The Role of "Le Monstre,"* p. 168.

15. Jay L. Caplan, *Framed Narratives: Diderot's Genealogy of the Beholder* (Minneapolis: University of Minnesota Press, 1985), pp. 65–66. Caplan further explores the link between the feminine and the monstrous in his analysis of *La religieuse,* pp. 71–75.

16. Hill, *The Role of "Le Monstre,"* p. 191.

17. Aristotle discusses the monster's complex "justification" on several occasions. In *Generation of Animals* he notes: "As for monstrosities, they are not necessary as far as the purposive or final cause is concerned, yet *per accidens* they are necessary, since we must take it that their ori-

gin at any rate is located here." *Generation of Animals,* trans. A. L. Peck (Cambridge, Mass.: Harvard University Press, 1963), IV, iii, p. 403. Later Aristotle adds: "A monstrosity, of course, belongs to the class of 'things contrary to Nature,' although it is contrary not to Nature in her entirety but only to Nature *in the generality of cases.* So far as concerns the Nature which is *always* and is *by necessity,* nothing occurs contrary to that; no; unnatural occurrences are found only among those things which occur as they do *in the generality of cases,* but which *may* occur otherwise" (IV, iv, p. 425).

18. See Georges May, "*Le rêve de d'Alembert,* selon Diderot," *Diderot Studies,* 17 (1973): 25–39; Jean Starobinski, "Le philosophe, le géomètre, l'hybride," *Poétique,* 21 (1975): 8–23; Jean Varloot, "La copie Naigeon: Prolégomènes philosophiques au *Rêve de d'Alembert,*" in *Essays on Diderot and the Enlightenment* (Geneva: Droz, 1974), pp. 302–324; Aram Vartanian, "La Mettrie, Diderot and Sexology in the Enlightenment," in *Essays on the Enlightenment* (Geneva: Droz, 1977), pp. 347–367; Wilda Anderson, *Diderot's Dream* (Baltimore: The Johns Hopkins University Press, 1990).

19. Bordeu, *Recherches anatomiques sur la fonction des glandes* (Paris, 1751). Quoted in Fontenay, "Diderot Gynéconome," p. 45.

20. Fontenay identifies the engraving as "a sick womb," but there is no statement in the *Encyclopédie* suggesting this.

21. It is worth noting that the *Encyclopédie's* article on imagination has a separate section considering the power of the pregnant woman's imagination over the fetus. The author argues that this power exists only in the beholder's imagination. *Encyclopédie* (1765), vol. 8, p. 563.

22. See Chapter 5.

23. Aristotle, *Generation of Animals,* IV, iii, p. 401.

24. Jacques-André Millot, *L'art de procréer les sexes à volonté ou système complet de la génération* (Paris, 1800), p. 288. Millot (1737–1811) was a famous obstetrician who personally assisted Marie-Antoinette's deliveries. The popularity of his book suggests that society under the Consulate and the Empire had preoccupations similar to those of the Old Regime, also preferring the birth of a son to that of a daughter.

25. François-Marie Pompée Colonna, *Les principes de la nature, ou de la génération des choses* (Paris, 1731), p. 166.

26. Denis Diderot, *Le neveu de Rameau,* in *Oeuvres,* ed. André Billy (Paris: Gallimard, 1969), p. 396. On this particular quotation, see Jay L. Caplan, *Framed Narratives,* pp. 3–14.

27. Charles Lebrun, *A Method to Learn to Design the Passions,* trans. John Williams (London, 1734), reproduced by the William Andrews Clark Memorial Library (Los Angeles: University of California Press, 1980),

p. 53. It is worth noting that Lebrun derives Physiognomy from *physis* (nature) and *nomos* (law), although the correct roots are *physis* and *gnomon* (one who knows). On the related change of etymology affecting the word *anomaly* see Georges Canguilheim, cited later in this Chapter.

28. The classical discourse on monstrosity had elicited the terror of a language entirely free of a stable origin, of a recognizable meaning. Perhaps there is more than a passing similarity between the epistemological system that can be inferred from theories of generation at the end of the eighteenth century and what is conceptually implied by the arbitrariness of the sign. Indeed, in another eighteenth-century text on generation, the author notes: "Readers should remember that words are but arbitrary signs, and the most modest writer is free to use them as art and create them at will." In Michel Procope-Couteau, *L'art de faire des garçons ou nouveau tableau de l'amour conjugal* (London, 1787), p. xi, (first ed. Montpellier, 1748). Like Millot, Procope-Couteau addressed the popular topic of choosing the sex of one's progeny. More specifically, he suggested an infallible way to have sons rather than daughters, arguing: "How many times a prince's birth, rather than a princess', would have spared the lives of millions, the desolation of the most illustrious dynasties and the ruin of states? . . . Although man is not worth more than [woman], the birth of a son flatters more than that of a daughter" (pp. ix–xi). Procope-Couteau reaffirms Buffon and Maupertuis' belief that "the father and the mother, participating equally in the creation of the fetus, one may conceive at least generally that the child may, one way or the other, resemble either parent and sometimes both" (p. 115). The "art" of making sons, or daughters, consists in removing the ovary or testicle that, according to Procope-Couteau, corresponds by its position—right or left—to the generation of a male or female.

29. Both articles are unsigned.

30. Charles Bonnet, *Oeuvres d'histoire naturelle et de philosophie* (Neuchâtel, 1779–1783), vol. 4, p. 152. Bonnet (1720–1793) is the first scientist said to have used the term "evolution" in its modern sense. Chapter 6 of his text is devoted to the question of imagination and memory, chapter 12 to the formation of monstrosities.

31. See Marcelle Bouteiller, *Médecine populaire d'hier et d'aujourd'hui* (Paris: Maisonneuve and Larose, 1966). Bouteiller notes a contemporary belief found in the area of Saumur (Loire Valley): "To make certain that the child will resemble one's husband—particularly if one has doubts as to the child's paternity—one should consider one's husband at length while he sleeps, holding a lighted candle in the hand" (p. 306).

32. Georges Canguilhem, *On the Normal and the Pathological,* trans. Carolyn Fawcett, with editorial collaboration of Robert S. Cohen, and an introduction by Michel Foucault (London: D. Reidel, 1978), p. 73. Translation modified.

33. Georges Canguilhem, *La connaissance de la vie* (Paris: Vrin, 1965), p. 177.

Chapter 5

1. Denis Diderot, *Eléments de physiologie, Oeuvres,* ed. J. Assézat (Paris: Garnier, 1875), vol. 9, p. 363.

2. Jean-Marie-Mathias-Philippe-Auguste, Comte Villiers de l'Isle-Adam (1838–1889), "Claire Lenoir," in *Contes fantastiques* (Paris: Flammarion, 1965), p. 93. On Villiers de l'Isle-Adam, see Chapter 9.

3. For our purpose, it may be said that one of the most important transformations in the field of embryology in the nineteenth century was the gradual acceptance of the fact that both parents contributed, with almost equal importance, to the production and the shape of progeny. Although this was not a new idea, since Aristotle medical thought had generally leaned toward either the father or the mother as the primary agent of reproduction, and the early part of the nineteenth century was still marked by great differences in opinion on the respective roles and natures of animalcules, sperm, and eggs. In 1850, François Lallemand, professor of medicine at the University of Montpellier, summarized the new medical belief that the two parents contributed equally to the formation of the progeny when he wrote in his *Traité de physiologie* (1850): "A fluid can obviously not transmit form and life that it does not possess. Fecundation is the union of two living parts that come together and develop in common." Obviously, growing acceptance of this principle marked the end of the concept of parental singularity, which had informed theories of generation in various ways since Antiquity. If both parents make vital contributions to the process of fecundation, the enormous responsibility for the child's form and appearance can no longer be attributed to the mother alone. Division of labor had now replaced parental singularity. In an article entitled "The Condition of Woman from a Zoological Point of View" William Brooks wrote: "The male is an organism specialized for the production of the variable element in the reproductive process, and the female an organism specialized for the production of the conservative element . . . if the female organism is the conservative organism, to which is intrusted the keeping of all that has been gained during the past history of the race, it must follow that the female mind

is a storehouse filled with the instincts, habits, intuitions, and laws of conduct which have been gained by past experience." Quoted in John Farley, *Gametes and Spores: Ideas about Sexual Reproduction, 1750–1914* (Baltimore: The Johns Hopkins University Press, 1982), pp. 113–114. Women reign over the past—the handing down of traditions and customs, instinctual history, memory; they are the archives of the past. That a woman's mind is first and foremost *memory*—instinctive memory, untouched by reason—can be traced to earlier theories linking the maternal imagination to memory. Imagination was thought capable of making imprints of the images that memory had preserved and of possibly transmitting them to the unborn.

4. Quoted in Farley, *Gametes and Spores,* p. 113.

5. In "L'elixir de longue vie," written in 1830, Balzac remarked: "God only knows the number of parricides committed in the mind! . . . European civilization rests entirely on HEREDITY as if on a pivot and it would be madness to do away with it; but couldn't we perfect this essential wheel as we have all these machines that are the pride of our time?" In *Contes philosophiques* (Paris: Dent, 1940), p. 82.

6. William Brooks, quoted in Farley, *Gametes and Spores,* p. 114. See also A. H. Sturtevant, *A History of Genetics* (New York: Harper and Row, 1965), pp. 1–50.

7. A. H. Sturtevant, *A History of Genetics,* pp. 19–20.

8. Jean Rostand, *La formation de l'être, histoire des idées sur la génération* (Paris: Hachette, 1930), p. 183.

9. Villiers de l'Isle-Adam, "Claire Lenoir," p. 17, emphasis added.

10. Duncan Crow, *The Victorian Woman* (London: George Allen, 1971), p. 25, quoted in Farley, *Gametes and Spores,* p. 116.

11. On teratology see Jean-Louis Fisher, "Comment est née la science des monstres," *La Recherche,* 162 (January 1985): 42–51; Etienne Wolff, *La science des monstres* (Paris: Gallimard, 1948).

12. Camille Dareste, *Recherches sur la production artificielle des monstruosités ou essais de tératogénie expérimentale* (Paris: Reinwald, 1877), p. 1.

13. Isidore Geoffroy Saint-Hilaire, *Histoire générale et particulière des anomalies de l'organisation chez l'homme et les animaux* (Paris, 1832), vol. 1, p. 18. Quoted in François Jacob, *The Logic of Life: A History of Heredity,* trans. Betty E. Spillmann (New York: Pantheon Books, 1973), p. 124.

14. Ernest Martin, *Histoire des monstres depuis l'antiquité jusqu'à nos jours* (Paris: Reinwald, 1880). An abbreviated history of theories of monstrosities with quantities of anecdotes, this work integrates recent scientific efforts to solve the question of anomalies.

15. Martin, *Histoire des monstres,* pp. 293–294.

16. For another contemporary examination of anomalies, see George G.

Gould and Walter L. Pyle, *Anomalies and Curiosities of Medicine* (New York: The Julian Press, 1896).

17. Etienne Geoffroy Saint-Hilaire, *Dictionnaire classique d'histoire naturelle,* vol. 11,, quoted in Martin, *Histoire des monstres,* p. 142.

18. Jean Riolan, *Mémoire sur un monstre né à Paris* (Paris, 1605), quoted in Martin, *Histoire des monstres,* pp. 158–159.

19. See Jean-Louis Fisher, "Le concept expérimental dans l'oeuvre tératogénique d'Etienne Geoffroy Saint-Hilaire," *Revue d'Histoire Scientifique,* 25 (1972): 347–364.

20. On Dareste, see Jean-Louis Fisher, "La vie et l'oeuvre d'un scientifique du XIXe siècle, Camille Dareste (1822–1899), fondateur de la tératologie expérimentale" (Ph.D. diss., University of Paris I, 1973).

21. Dareste, *Production artificielle des monstruosités,* pp. 20–21.

22. Ibid., pp. 22–23.

23. *Comptes rendus de l'académie des sciences* (1860), vol. 50, p. 249, quoted in Camille Dareste, *Production artificielle des monstruosités,* p. 46.

24. Gould and Pyle, *Anomalies,* p. 166.

25. "Hemiterata" designates a group of congenitally deformed beings not strictly classified as teratisms or monstrosities. "Heterotaxia" designates the anomalous placements or transpositions of viscera and parts.

26. "Autosite" describes a being capable of independent life but supplying nutrition to a parasitic monster. "Parasite" is an imperfect fetus incapable of autonomous existence, one which derives its nutrition from another, more developed fetus. "Omphalosite" is the underdeveloped member of allantoidoangiopagous twins, joined to the more developed member by the umbilical cord.

27. Following this tradition, the masculine uterus, also called "prostatic utricle," was described as a "vestigial vagina" in 1936 by Werner Laqueur. See Thomas Laqueur, *Making Sex: Body and Gender from the Greeks to Freud* (Cambridge, Mass.: Harvard University Press, 1990), p. 249.

28. Diderot had been similarly fascinated with the case of a young man who was found to have been carrying a fetus in a well-formed womb. See Chapter 4.

29. See Chapter 1.

30. Rauter, *Traité du droit criminel français* (Paris, 1826), vol. 2, p. 7. Quoted in Martin, *Histoire des monstres,* p. 178.

31. *The Letters of Virginia Woolf,* ed. Nigel Nicolson and Joanne Trautmann, vol. 2: 1912–1922 (New York: Brace Harcourt Jovanovich, 1976), October 9, 1919, to Katherine Arnold-Foster, p. 391.

Metaphors of Procreation

1. I take the word "Romanticism" in its broadest sense, as the movement that transformed the arts at the end of the eighteenth century and whose values dominated nineteenth-century culture. Strictly speaking, Villiers de l'Isle-Adam is more closely associated with the symbolists, and by the time Meyrink wrote *Der Golem,* 1906–1914, European culture was experiencing another important transformation. But in Villiers's and Meyrink's works, I am considering the continuation of the Romantic tradition that relied explicitly on metaphors of procreation to express its artistic beliefs.

2. In *Le corps-à-corps avec la mère* (Ottawa: Les éditions de la pleine lune, 1981), Luce Irigaray speculates that an "archaïc" murder, that of the mother, preceded that murder of the father posited by Freud as the origin of social order. The examples she discusses (that of Clytemnestra's murder by her son Orestes in Euripides' *Oresteia,* or Apollo's famous injunction to the Erinnyes in Aeschylus' *The Eumenides,* that "the mother of what is called her child is no parent to it, but nurse only to the young life that is sown in her") are, interestingly, the two standard literary references given in a number of modern histories of science and philosophical works to describe the changing appraisals of the roles of fathers and mothers in procreation as well as society. These examples are quoted and discussed by J. J.Bachofen, *Mutterrecht u. Urreligion* (Leipzig: Kröner, 1927); Pierre Darmon, *Le mythe de la procréation à l'âge baroque* (Paris: Seuil, 1981); Frederick Engels, *The Origin of the Family, Private Property and the State* (New York: International Publishers, 1942); Joseph Needham, *A History of Embryology* (New York: Abelard-Schuman, 1959); and Jean Rostand, *La formation de l'être, histoire des idées sur la génération* (Paris: Hachette, 1930), to mention just a few. See also Margaret Homans' discussion of these examples in *Bearing the Word: Language and Female Experience in Nineteenth-Century Women's Writing* (Chicago: The University of Chicago Press, 1986), p. 2. For historians of science, these much-quoted examples illustrate Antiquity's "physiological argument," to use Joseph Needham's words; that is, the strong view that the female was a purely passive element in procreation. From this perspective, far from being a constant element in the history of procreation or philosophical discourse, violence against the mother has erupted sporadically, in distinctive terms and at specific times in history, both in scientific and in artistic forms. I argue that, while superficially repressing the maternal body in favor of male generation, the Romantic meta-

phor of procreation continued to question all the distinctive elements traditionally involved in the idea of monstrous genesis.

Chapter 6

1. Lazzaro Spallanzani's work on frogs' embryos gained him lasting fame. He published the results of his work in *Saggio di osservazioni microscopiche concernenti il sistema della generazione dei signori di Needham e Buffon* (Modena, 1766) and *Expériences pour servir à l'histoire de la génération des animaux et des plantes* (Geneva, 1785). Professor Spalanzani in E. T. A. Hoffmann's famous tale of artificial generation, "The Sandman," was probably inspired by the Italian scientist.

2. Mary Wollstonecraft Shelley, *Frankenstein or the Modern Prometheus: The 1818 Text,* ed. with variant readings by James Rieger (Chicago: The University of Chicago Press, 1974), p. 229.

3. See Chapter 10.

4. Mary Jacobus, "Is There a Woman in This Text?" *New Literary History,* 14, 1 (Fall 1982): 131.

5. The name and story of Justine, the virtuous victim of the monster's evildoing, evokes D. A. F. de Sade's *Justine ou les infortunes de la vertu.* Critics have been quick to point to Rousseau as having had an obvious influence on the writing of *Frankenstein,* but it seems that Sade is being "quoted" as well in this brief but horrendous episode where virtue is systematically punished. Peter Brooks notes a more pervasive Sadian element in the novel: "The fact of monsterism suggests that nature in *Frankenstein* has something of the radical amorality described by Sade. For Sade, nature permits everything and authorizes nothing . . . There are perhaps parallels to be found in Victor Frankenstein's manic quest to push nature to a frontier where it becomes meta-nature, where it releases its own principle of being." Brooks, "'God-like Science/Unhallowed Arts': Language, Nature, and Monstrosity," in *The Endurance of Frankenstein: Essays on Mary Shelley's Novel,* ed. George Levine and U. C. Knoepflmacher (Berkeley: University of California Press, 1979), reprinted in *Mary Shelley (Modern Critical Views),* ed. with an introduction by Harold Bloom (New York: Chelsea House, 1985), p. 111.

6. Aristotle, *Generation of Animals,* trans. A. L. Peck (Cambridge, Mass.: Harvard University Press, 1963), IV, vii, pp. 465–467.

7. Barbara Johnson, "My Monster/My Self," *Diacritics,* 12 (1982): 6.

8. Marc A. Rubenstein notes the "Russian-doll" narrative structure of *Frankenstein,* a "book constructed like a pregnancy," in "'My Accurs'd Origin': The Search for the Mother in *Frankenstein*," *Studies in Roman-*

ticism, 15 (1976): 172. More generally, this structure replays a popular theory of generation and is also found in most of E. T. A. Hoffmann's tales, including "The Sandman."

9. Cardan, *De Subtilitate* (1550), quoted in Jean Céard, *La nature et les prodiges* (Geneva: Droz, 1977), p. 239.

10. *The Complete Works of Percy Bysshe Shelley,* ed. Roger Ingpen and Walter E. Peck, vol. 9, (New York: Charles Scribner's Sons, 1926), letter 330, p. 234.

11. *The Letters of Mary Wollstonecraft Shelley,* vol. 1, ed. Betty T. Bennett (Baltimore: The Johns Hopkins University Press, 1980), p. 47.

12. *The Quarterly Review,* 18 (London: John Murray, 1818): 379–385.

13. Percy Shelley read Plutarch and Rousseau in the summer of 1816, see *The Journals of Mary Shelley,* 1814–1844, vol. 1, ed. Paula R. Feldman and Diana Scott Kilvert (Oxford: Clarendon Press, 1987), p. 129.

14. *Frankenstein,* appendix A, "Mary Shelley's Introduction to the Third Edition" (1831), p. 229.

15. Critics have paid no attention to this obvious contradiction. Even Rieger describes the Preface as having been "written by Shelley from his wife's point of view" (*Frankenstein,* p. 6).

16. See Milton Milhauser, "The Noble Savage in Mary Shelley's *Frankenstein,*" *Notes and Queries,* 190 (June 15, 1946): 249; Mary Graham Lund, "Mary Godwin Shelley and the Monster," *University of Kansas Review,* 28 (1962): 254–255; David Marshall, *The Surprising Effects of Sympathy: Marivaux, Diderot, Rousseau and Mary Shelley* (Chicago: The University of Chicago Press, 1988); Judith Weissman, "A Reading of *Frankenstein* as the Complaint of a Political Wife," *Colby Library Quarterly,* 12 (1976): 177. These texts and the *Journals* are discussed by James O'Rourke in "Nothing More Unnatural: Mary Shelley's Revision of Rousseau" *ELH,* 56 (Fall 1989): 543–569. James O'Rourke considers *Frankenstein* as well as Mary Shelley's later essay on Rousseau. To sustain the assumption that Mary Shelley was influenced by Rousseau, much is made of the fact that Mary Shelley read the *Confessions* before the writing of *Frankenstein.* O'Rourke does not mention *Julie* or *Julie*'s obvious influence on the novel.

17. Many critics have commented on Julie's death scene, and Jean Starobinski, in *Jean-Jacques Rousseau, Transparency and Obstruction,* trans. Arthur Goldhammer (Chicago: The University of Chicago Press, 1988), argues that the theme of lifting the veil is emblematic of Rousseau's writings.

18. See E. B. Murray's important article, "Shelley's Contributions to Mary's *Frankenstein,*" *Keats-Shelley Memorial Bulletin,* 29 (1978): 50–68. Murray gives a thorough account of the passages written in Percy

Shelley's own hand in the two manuscripts on deposit at the Bodleian Library. However, since Mary Shelley regularly copied works for Percy Shelley, as well as for other writers such as Byron, an evaluation of Percy Shelley's contributions to *Frankenstein* should not be limited to his own handwritten lines.

19. Ibid., pp. 50–51.
20. Emily W. Sunstein, *Mary Shelley: Romance and Reality* (Boston: Little, Brown and Company, 1989), p. 260. Other biographical works include Jane Dunn, *Moon in Eclipse: A Life of Mary Shelley* (London: Weidenfeld and Nicolson, 1978); Elizabeth Nichie, *Mary Shelley, Author of Frankenstein* (New Brunswick: Rutgers University Press, 1953); Muriel Spark, *Mary Shelley* (New York: E. P. Dutton, 1987). See also Kenneth Neill Cameron and Donald H. Reiman, *Shelley and His Circle* (New York: The Carl H. Pforxheimer Library, 1961–1973).
21. Murray, "Shelley's Contributions," p. 65.
22. *Don Juan: With a Biographical Account of Lord Byron and His Family, Anecdotes of His Lordship's Travels and Residence in Greece, at Geneva, Etc. Including, Also, a Sketch of the Vampire Family* (London: William Wright, 1819).
23. Quoted by Sunstein in *Mary Shelley*, p. 436.
24. Margaret Homans, *Bearing the Word: Language and Female Experience in Nineteenth-Century Women's Writing* (Chicago: The University of Chicago Press, 1986), p. 109.
25. Hoffman, "The Sandman," *Tales of Hoffmann*, selected and trans. with an introduction by R. J. Hollingdale (London: Penguin Books, 1982), p. 120.
26. See Murray, "Shelley's Contributions," p. 59.
27. Ibid., p. 58.
28. Homans, *Bearing the Word*, pp. 105–108.
29. Mary Poovey underlines the significant differences between the 1818 text and the 1831 revised edition. She also sees the Preface as a justification of "the audacity of what now seems to her like blasphemy." In Poovey, *The Proper Lady and the Woman Writer* (Chicago: The University of Chicago Press, 1984), p. 137.
30. See James Rieger, "Dr. Polidori and the Genesis of *Frankenstein*," *Studies in English Literature*, 3 (1963): 461–472.
31. A recent example of this line of thought, a review-article by Robert Martin of Sunstein's biography of Mary Shelley, offers the following comments: "The novel . . . rings hollow and rhetorical, although it is a perfect vehicle for the kind of criticism that is more concerned with ideas tangential to the book than with the work itself." In Martin, "Ro-

mance Incarnate, *Mary Shelley: Romance and Reality* by Emily W. Sunstein," *New York Review of Books,* vol. 36, 11 (June 29, 1989): 13.

32. Robert Kiely, "Frankenstein," in Bloom, *Mary Shelley (Modern Critical Views),* p. 80.

33. Levine, *The Endurance of Frankenstein: Essays on Mary Shelley's Novel,* p. 3.

34. Bloom, *Mary Shelley (Modern Critical Views),* p. 4.

35. Ellen Moers, *Literary Women* (New York: Oxford University Press, 1963), pp. 92, 96.

36. Sandra M. Gilbert and Susan Gubar, *The Madwoman in the Attic: The Woman Writer and the Nineteenth-Century Imagination* (New Haven and London: Yale University Press, 1979), pp. 222, 242–243.

37. Chris Baldick, *In Frankenstein's Shadow: Myth, Monstrosity and Nineteenth-Century Writing* (Oxford: Clarendon Press; New York: Oxford University Press, 1987), p. 32. Fred Botting notes: "The distinctions between purely biographical and purely literary influence cannot, without great difficulty, be maintained in discussions of *Frankenstein's* many incorporations of and allusions to other texts." In Botting, *Making Monstrous, Frankenstein, Criticism, Theory* (Manchester: Manchester University Press, 1991), p. 78.

38. See in particular Homan's perceptive reading of *Frankenstein* as "the collision between androcentric and gynocentric theories of creation, a collision that results in the denigration of maternal childbearing through its circumvention by male creation" (*Bearing the Word,* p. 113). Were it not for the theoretical difficulty of associating the father's name with the monstrous child, such an analysis might have led to a reconsideration of Percy Shelley's co-authorship of the novel.

39. From a somewhat different perspective, Barbara Freeman considers the relationship between theory and monstrosity in "*Frankenstein* with Kant: A Theory of Monstrosity, or the Monstrosity of Theory," *Substance,* 52 (1987): 21–31.

Chapter 7

1. Nathaniel Hawthorne, *Note-Books,* 9, pp. 373–374 and 10, p. 300, quoted in Millicent Bell, *Hawthorne's View of the Artist* (New York: State University of New York Press, 1962), p. 51.

2. Nathaniel Hawthorne, "The Prophetic Pictures," *Selected Short Stories,* ed. Alfred Kazin (New York: Fawcett, 1966), p. 54.

3. Françoise Meltzer, *Salomé and the Dance of Writing: Portraits of Mimesis in Literature* (Chicago: The University of Chicago Press, 1987), p. 106.

Both Meltzer and Bell have extensively analyzed the question of portraiture in literary texts, and both offer in-depth readings of Hawthorne's tales and Poe's "The Oval Portrait." My own interpretation, although leading to a different conclusion, is much indebted to their provocative work.

4. Honoré de Balzac, "Le chef-d'oeuvre inconnu," *Contes philosophiques* (London and New York: Dent and Dutton, 1941). "The Unknown Masterpiece" has been translated by Ellen Marriage, *Tales from Balzac* (London: Eveleigh Nash and Grayson, 1927). Although page numbers refer to the translated text, all quotations have been modified for precision.

5. In "Hawthorne's Romanticism: The Artist of the Beautiful," Sheldon W. Liebman argues that after Annie's departure "Owen becomes the mirror-image of the infant who will eventually destroy his work." In *Nathaniel Hawthorne,* ed. with an introduction by Harold Bloom (New York: Chelsea House Publishers, 1986), p. 135.

6. Edgar Allan Poe, "The Oval Portrait," *Tales of Mystery and Imagination* (London: Dent, 1975), p. 189.

7. *The Collected Tales and Plays of Nikolai Gogol,* ed. with an introduction and notes by Leonard J. Kent (New York: Pantheon Press, 1964), p. 539.

8. See Chapter 4.

9. Bell offers an extensive analysis of "The Prophetic Pictures" in *Hawthorne's View of the Artist,* pp. 114–127. She views the painter's prophetic ability as a way of reading the future rather than creating it.

10. Bell sees the separation of the couple into individual portraits as "a peculiar circumstance," another instance of the painter's mark on their destiny.

11. François Marie Pompée Colonna, *Les principes de la nature, ou de la génération des choses* (Paris, 1731), p. 166.

12. Hawthorne, "The Birthmark," in Kazin, *Selected Short Stories,* p. 89.

13. Meltzer, *Salomé and the Dance of Writing,* p. 174.

14. Harry Levin, *The Power of Blackness: Hawthorne, Poe, Melville* (New York: Alfred Knopf, 1958), p. 58.

15. Frederick Crews, *The Sins of the Fathers: Hawthorne's Psychological Themes* (London: Oxford University Press, 1966), p. 111.

16. Ibid., p. 126.

17. Meltzer develops at length the role and metaphorical importance of the hand: "The hand of man wants to touch the untouchable—truth is here feminized, imagined as that which is to be unclothed, violated. Mother Nature, as she is often called in this story, will be grasped by the hand of man. It is not coincidental, given the gender difference

the story insists upon, that the love of a woman is rivaled by science; for science has its own woman as telos: Nature and her mysteries" (*Salomé and the Dance of Writing*, p. 172).

18. That the genesis of creation in Hawthorne is antithetical to the tradition of which *Frankenstein* is the most consummate expression is also illustrated in a parodic tale entitled "Feathertop: A Moralized Legend." Here Hawthorne simply admits: "Shall I confess the truth? At its present point of vivification, the scarecrow reminds me of some of the lukewarm and abortive characters, composed of heterogeneous materials, used for the thousandth time, and never worth using, with which romance-writers (and myself, no doubt, among the rest) have so overpeopled the world of fiction" (Bloom, *Nathaniel Hawthorne*, p. 10). The writer bows to the twofold model of the artist as painter and father. That failure is already inscribed in this image-obsessed iconoclast is also obvious from the title of "Ethan Brand: A Chapter from an Abortive Romance." "When [Hawthorne] portrays the artist as a detached observer, 'insulated from the mass of human kind,'" notes Harry Levin, "he seems clearly engaged in self-portraiture. The 'penetrative eye,' the diabolical insight of the painter in 'The Prophetic Pictures,' is dearly bought at the cost of an unfeeling heart. But it is morally justified by its 'pictorial fancy,' which foresees the tragic fate in store for the happy couple it contemplates" (*The Power of Blackness*, pp. 58–59).

19. Meltzer quotes James Frazer when he writes of "the fear that art can give or take life, just like a god" (*Salomé and the Dance of Writing*, p. 110).

20. Meltzer notes that "in the Judeo-Christian culture, the prohibition against image-making, unless explicitly commanded by God and carried out by his choice of artist, persists, even if at the subliminal level of consciousness" (*Salomé and the Dance of Writing*, p. 104).

21. See Chapter 1.

22. Jean-Joseph Goux, *Les iconoclastes* (Paris: Seuil, 1978), pp. 12–13. See the previous discussion of this text in Chapter 1.

23. Marie Bonaparte, *The Life and Works of Edgar Allan Poe: A Psycho-Analytic Interpretation*, trans. John Rodker, foreword by Sigmund Freud (London: Imago Publishing Co., 1949), p. 260. Poe's choice of a very young and sickly bride is also reminiscent of the crucial episode in *Frankenstein* when Victor's father decides to marry a child-bride found "in an agony of despair." See Chapter 6.

24. Michel Serres, *Genèse* (Paris: Grasset, 1982), p. 28. On "Le chef-d'oeuvre inconnu," see also Georges Didi-Huberman, *La peinture incarnée* (Paris: Minuit, 1985).

25. Didi-Huberman also suggests that Frenhofer's project implied a veil: "Catherine Lescaut had to fulfill a contradictory injunction: to be looked at (as a painting) and not be seen (as a lover). She is between (painted) canvas and veil (secret, hidden lover)" (*La peinture incarnée,* p. 64).

26. Didi-Huberman links Balzac's Frenhofer to the famous optician Fraunhofer, author of a theory on the decomposition of light and founder of spectroscopy. See *La peinture incarnée,* p. 35.

27. Josué Harari, unpublished essay on "Le chef-d'oeuvre inconnu."

28. Didi-Huberman writes in *La peinture incarnée:* "The foot lends itself to a fetishist structuration . . . as Lacan summarized the fetishistic object: it proceeds 'from an ambiguous feminine being which represents itself and incarnates, in a way, beyond the mother, the mother's missing phallus'" (pp. 94–95).

29. Honoré de Balzac, *Contes philosophiques,* p. 80, translation mine.

30. Edgar Allan Poe, "Imitation-Plagiarism," *Evening Mirror,* I (Feb. 15, 1845), quoted by Sidney P. Moss, *Poe's Literary Battles: The Critic in the Context of His Literary Milieu* (Durham: Duke University Press, 1963), p. 166.

31. The restriction implied in the traditional view of Fine Arts as pictorial representations underlines the primacy of images over words. This restriction reflects, as we have seen, a deeper meaning than a simple variation in media. It also explains why portraiture seemed to have been the preferred metaphor of artistic creation for Romantic writers, perhaps to be read as an appendix to declarations of authorship.

Chapter 8

1. John Theodore Tussaud, *The Romance of Madame Tussaud's,* with an introduction by Hilaire Belloc (New York: Doran, 1920), p. 27, emphasis added. The 1921 edition of Tussaud's book (London: Odhams Press) does not reproduce Belloc's introduction, and the text itself has been the object of numerous stylistic revisions. I will refer to the 1920 text, cited in this text as *Romance.*

2. *De l'enseignement du dessin, Revue des Deux-Mondes* (September 15, 1850), in *Oeuvres littéraires* (Paris: Crès, 1923), p. 17, emphasis added. See also Walter Benjamin, "Paris, Capital of the Nineteenth Century," in *Reflections,* trans. Edmund Jephcott (New York: Harcourt Brace Jovanovich, 1978) and his description of two concurrent events: Daguerre's invention of dioramas, technological replicas of some of the staging done in wax cabinets, and the ruin of the important group of miniaturists eclipsed by the progress of photography. Delacroix

echoes the general view among artists that photography cannot possibly match portraiture in artistic value.

3. George-Augustus Sala, *Madame Tussaud's Exhibition Guide* (1892), p. 6, emphasis added.

4. Madame Tussaud, *Memoirs and Reminiscences of the French Revolution,* ed. Francis Hervé (Philadelphia: Lea and Blanchard, 1839), pp. 23–24, cited in the text as *Memoirs.*

5. Pauline Chapman, *The French Revolution As Seen by Madame Tussaud, Witness Extraordinary* (London: Quiller Press, 1989), p. 11, cited in the text as *Witness.*

6. See Pauline Chapman, *Madame Tussaud's Chamber of Horrors: Two Hundred Years of Crime* (London: Constable, 1984), cited in the text as *Horrors,* and Pauline Chapman and Anita Leslie, *Madame Tussaud : Waxworker Extraordinary* (London: Hutchinson, 1978), cited in the text as *Waxworker.* Both works repeat the story of the role Madame Tussaud claimed to have played during the French Revolution, but they give no sources or verification other than Madame Tussaud's own "memoirs."

7. See Murray Wright Bundy, *The Theory of Imagination in Classical and Mediaeval Thought* (Urbana: The University of Illinois Press, 1927), p. 88.

8. Ibid., p. 196.

9. On the question of body snatching in Great Britain, see also Ruth Richardson, *Death, Dissection and the Destitute* (London: Routledge and Kegan Paul, 1987).

10. *Exhibition Catalogue,* 1892, p. 65.

11. *Exhibition Catalogue,* 1833, p. 3. Madame Tussaud's staging coincides with the renewal in England of the practice of royal coronation as public celebration of the king's glory.

12. Ibid., p. 27. I wish to thank Undine Concannon, archivist at *Madame Tussaud's,* for kindly making some of the older catalogues accessible to me.

13. Phrenology had been developed in the early 1800's by German physiologist Franz Joseph Gall.

14. *Exhibition Catalogue,* 1833, pp. 28–31.

15. Ibid., p. 30.

16. Michel Foucault, *Discipline and Punish: The Birth of the Prison,* trans. Alan Sheridan (New York: Vintage Books, 1979), pp. 28–29.

17. *Exhibition Catalogue,* 1833, p. 31.

18. It should be noted that the Chamber of Horrors, still extremely popular, has long since stopped being what J. T. Tussaud perceived as evidence of punishment. One of the most successful exhibits of recent

years is a reconstitution of the scene of Jack the Ripper's crimes. Jack the Ripper, of course, was never apprehended. The notion of "mystery" seems to have been substituted for the depiction of crime and punishment.

19. *Exhibition Catalogue*, 1892, p. 6.
20. Clearly, the meaning and "practice" of the Wax Museum have changed considerably since the early days of Madame Tussaud. Today's characters are no longer formed by the same technique, and they strike poses stressing an arrested movement. Further, as we are told, "the development of animated figures has continued apace and, with the use of advanced computer technology figures that can already 'move' and 'talk' will also 'walk' in future new exhibits at Madame Tussaud's" (*Souvenir Guide*, 1991, p. 7). The new characters belong to an epistemology of both "replicas" and "cyborgs."
21. Benjamin, "Paris: Capital of the Nineteenth Century," pp. 146–162.
22. Roland Barthes, *Camera Lucida: Reflections on Photography*, trans. Richard Howard (New York: Hill and Wang, 1981), p. 4.
23. Ibid., pp. 5–6.
24. Ibid., p. 9.
25. Ibid., pp. 30–31.
26. See Walter Benjamin, "The Work of Art in the Age of Mechanical Reproduction," in *Illuminations*, trans. Harry Zohn, ed. with a preface by Hannah Arendt (New York: Harcourt, Brace and World, 1968), pp. 219–253.
27. Ibid., p. 227.
28. On the theater and the guillotine, see Jules Michelet, *Histoire de la révolution française* (Paris: Gallimard, 1952), vol 2, books XX, XXI; Marie-Hélène Huet, *Rehearsing the Revolution: The Staging of Marat's Death, 1793–1797* (Berkeley: University of California Press, 1982); and "Le sacre du printemps: Essai sur le sublime et la terreur," *MLN* (Fall 1988): 782–799.
29. Barthes, *Camera Lucida*, p. 34.
30. Ibid., p. 36.
31. Madame Tussaud's exhibition moved to Baker Street on March 21, 1835. It moved to the present Marylebone address, in the same neighborhood, long after Madame Tussaud's death, in July 1884.

Chapter 9

1. Villiers de l'Isle-Adam, *Tomorrow's Eve*, trans. Robert M. Adams (Urbana: University of Illinois Press, 1982), p. 61. Villiers's text includes much emphasis: italics, capitals, and so forth. Unless otherwise indi-

cated, I have respected the author's emphasis. On Villiers de l'Isle-Adam, see A. W. Raitt, *The Life of Villiers de l'Isle-Adam* (Oxford: Clarendon Press, 1981).

2. The statue serving as an important model in the novel is fictitious. Most probably, Villiers combined several antique models of classical beauty, among them the Venus de Milo and the Victory of Samothrace, both in the Louvre Museum. Interestingly, in her article "Diderot gynéconome" Elizabeth de Fontenay compares Haller's drawing of a womb—which was reproduced in the *Encyclopédie*—to the Victory of Samothrace. In *Digraphe*, 7 (1976): 30. See Chapter 4.

3. Michael Wreen, "Is, Madam? Nay, It Seems!," in *The Forger's Art: Forgery and the Philosophy of Art*, ed. Denis Dutton (Berkeley: The University of California Press, 1983), p. 190, emphasis added.

4. Nelson Goodman, "Art and Authenticity," in Dutton, *The Forger's Art*, pp. 100, 110.

5. "The Unknown Masterpiece," *Tales from Balzac*, trans. Ellen Marriage (London: Eveleigh Nash and Grayson, 1927), p. 135, translation modified.

6. Sigmund Freud, "The Uncanny," *Studies in Parapsychology*, ed. Philip Rieff (New York: Collier Books, 1963), pp. 33–34. Much has been said on the question of doubles in the story. See Hélène Cixous, "La fiction et ses fantômes: Une lecture de l'Unheimliche de Freud," *Poétique*, 3 (1972); Sarah Kofman, "Le double e(s)t le diable," in *Quatre Romans analytiques* (Paris: Galilée, 1973); Françoise Meltzer, "The Uncanny Rendered Canny: Freud's Blind Spot in Reading Hoffman's 'Sandman,'" in *Introducing Psychoanalytic Theory*, ed. Sander L. Gilman (New York: Brunner Mazel, 1982).

7. Freud, "The Uncanny," pp. 38–39.

8. Ibid., p. 36.

9. Villiers, *Tomorrow's Eve*, author's foreword.

10. Here again, as with theories on the reproduction of the species, there are several schools of thought. One maintains that monsters are not sterile and that their issue is "normal." Diderot mentions this in *Entretien entre d'Alembert et Diderot*, not excluding the possibility that certain anomalies might be inherited. Another theory contends that monstrous deformity dooms the creature to an early death and in any case precludes fecundity.

11. Stéphane Mallarmé, *Oeuvres complètes*, ed. Henri Mondor and G. Jean-Aubry (Paris: Gallimard, 1945), p. 1439. Villiers wrote a letter to Mallarmé about the *Don du poème* in January 1866 (*Oeuvres*, p. 1437). This can also be read in light of Leo Bersani's comments on "L'après-midi d'un faune" as artistic sublimation that does not transcend sexual de-

sire, but rather "extends" it: "Mallarmé encourages us to view sublimation not as a mechanism by which desire is denied, but rather as a
self-reflexive activity by which desire multiplies and diversifies its representations. There is, to be sure, a certain purification of the desiring
impulse, but purification should be understood here as an abstracting
process which is not necessarily desexualizing." In Bersani, *The Freudian Body: Psychoanalysis and Art* (New York: Columbia University Press,
1986), p. 49. Artistic creation, as translated by Villiers in terms of Edison's automaton, can be said to repress superficially the need for the
other sex in order to procreate, a repression that will guarantee access
to what is termed the IDEAL, while suggesting a feminization of Edison
as *image* of the artist. Edison's image (or Edison as image), Hadaly
herself, although always temporarily repudiated, is ultimately puri-
fied by fire; Edison, like Mallarmé's faun, "narcissistically indulges a
self already burned away" (ibid., p. 50).

12. In his analysis of Freud's text on "The Sandman," Neil Hertz emphasizes that the instance of repetition whose model has just been bril-
liantly exposed by Freud generates its own discourse: "Freud is about
to move from his discussion of the compulsion to repeat to a concept
he hopes will explain its relation to the rest of his theory, the concept
of the death instinct, and he begins his paragraph with a question:
'But how is the predicate of being instinctual related to the compulsion to repeat?' He then produces, italicized for emphasis, a preliminary statement: 'It seems that an instinct is an urge inherent in organic life to restore an earlier state of things,' a sentence to which he
appends the following footnote: 'I have no doubt that similar notions
as to the nature of instincts have already been put forward repeatedly.' It is the word 'repeatedly' that is striking." In Hertz, "Freud and
the Sandman," *Textual Strategies: Perspectives in Post-Structuralist Criticism,* ed. Josué Harari (Ithaca: Cornell University Press, 1979), p. 319.
On sterility in "The Sandman," see also Kofman, "Le double e(s)t le
diable," p. 164.

13. In *Zig-Zag* (Paris: Flammarion, 1981), Jean-Claude Lebenztejn comments at length on the position and meaning of the signature in pictorial space: "Le nom signé désigne le haut, le ciel, c'est-à-dire Dieu,
le Nom (Père créateur) absolu" ("the signed name designates the
high, the heavens, that is, God, the absolute [father-creator] Name").
See pp. 68–75.

Chapter 10

1. See Susan Niditch, "The Cosmic Adam: Man as Mediator in Rabbinic
Literature," *Journal of Jewish Studies,* 35, 2 (1983): 137–146; Emily D.

Bilski and Moshe Idel, "The Golem: An Historical Overview," in *Golem! Danger, Deliverance and Art,* ed. Emily D. Bilski (New York: The Jewish Museum, 1988), pp. 10–14.

2. Gershom G. Scholem, *On the Kabbalah and Its Symbolism,* trans. Ralph Manheim (New York: Schocken Books, 1965), p. 161.

3. Sanhedrin 38b. Quoted in Scholem, *On the Kabbalah,* p. 161.

4. Bilski and Idel, "The Golem," p. 11.

5. Quoted in Moshe Idel, *Golem: Jewish Magical and Mystical Traditions on the Artificial Anthropoid* (New York: State University of New York Press, 1990), p. 100. This is the most exhaustive study on the question of the golem. Although Idel is mostly preoccupied with a close examination of the texts that compose the tradition, the last chapters are extremely suggestive in their views of the golem in relation to other traditions. Cited in the text as *Golem: Jewish Magical and Mystical Traditions.*

6. Bilski and Idel, "The Golem," p. 13.

7. Quoted in Scholem, *On the Kabbalah,* p. 159. See also Beate Rosenfeld, *Die Golemsage und irhe Verwertung in deutschen Literatur* (Breslau, 1934).

8. Bilski and Idel, "The Golem," p. 14.

9. Isaac Bashevis Singer, "Foreword," in Bilsky, *Golem! Danger, Deliverance and Art,* p. 7. Singer's story "The Golem" was first published in the *Jewish Daily Forward* in 1969 and translated in 1982 (New York: Farrar, Straus, Giroux).

10. Emily D. Bilski, "The Art of the Golem," *Golem! Danger, Deliverance and Art,* p. 48.

11. Singer, "The Golem," p. 84.

12. Jacques Lacan's distinction between the *imaginary* and the *symbolic* provides a key to a modern understanding of the creation of the golem. Conversely, it might be said that Lacan's categories are the result, or rather the latest manifestation, of a two-thousand-year-old tradition that conceived of a subject born through and to language in a process that would involve an all-powerful father. In that perspective, the emergence of the *symbolic* would be Lacan's own version of the golem story, a birth of the subject that follows and supplants the initial birth and the *imaginary* dominated by the maternal in a pre-verbal environment. The tradition attributing the responsibility for unnatural births to the sole power of the mother's imagination and the legend giving a lone father the power to animate an artificial creature through the use of linguistic structures are strangely echoed in Lacan's genealogy of the subject.

13. I wish to thank Madeleine Joret-Meisel for providing me with important documentation on Gustav Meyrink and *The Golem.* Jacques Meisel, who wrote an essay on Meyrink and Flaubert (partially reproduced in the special edition of *Cahiers de l'Herne* on Gustav Meyrink)

also gave me some valuable insights into the meaning of Meyrink's work.

14. See the special issue of *Cahiers de l'Herne* (Paris: Editions de l'Herne, 1976) dedicated to Gustav Meyrink, which contains a particularly hate-filled article by Manfred Turkeim. In his article, Turkeim argues that Meyrink's illegitimate birth and his mother's Jewish blood predestined him to expose the decadence of the decomposing Austro-Hungarian empire.

15. Scholem, *On the Kabbalah*, p. 158.

16. E. F. Bleiler, introduction to Gustav Meyrink, *The Golem* (New York: Dover, 1976), p. v.

17. Gustav Meyrink, *The Golem*, trans. Madge Pemberton and E. F. Bleiler, ed. with an introduction by E. F. Bleiler (New York: Dover, 1976), pp. 73–74. Antoine Court de Gébelin had argued in his *Monde primitif analisé et comparé avec le monde moderne* (1781) that the game of tarot was of Egyptian origin, comparing it with the Book of Thoth. Many scholars of the occult also associated the twenty-two major arcana of the tarot with the twenty-two letters of the Hebrew alphabet. See Stuart R. Kaplan, *The Encyclopedia of Tarot* (New York: U.S. Games Systems Publishers, 1978).

18. Marius Lepage sees in the golem's name the symbol of an infinite unfolding: *ATH*-ANASIUS PERN-*ATH*. "The name is 'the sign' of this work. An infinite folding, accompanied by an infinite unfolding. A sort of monstrous Ouroboros, the snake that bites its tail, a symbol of eternity. There was no beginning, there will be no end. I believe this is the key to the *golem*." In *Le Symbolisme*, 358 (October–December 1962): 96.

19. The blinding of women was also a theme in Hoffmann's tale "The Sandman," particularly in the violent scene where the two fathers, Spalanzani and Coppola, fight over their creature, Olympia. See Chapter 6 and E. T. A. Hoffmann, *Tales of Hoffmann,* selected and trans. with an introduction by R. J. Hollingdale (London: Penguin Books, 1982), p. 120.

20. Scholem, *On the Kabbalah*, p. 179.

21. Jean-Jacques Pollet, "En marge de l'expressionisme allemand," in *Cahiers de l'Herne*, p. 82.

22. Manfred Lube, "La genèse du golem," in *Cahiers de l'Herne*, pp. 66–72.

23. Jorge Luis Borges, "Les serres magiques de la culture juive," in *Cahiers de l'Herne*, pp. 106–107.

24. Jorge Luis Borges, *Ficciones,* ed. with an introduction by Anthony Kerrigan (New York: Grove Press, 1962), p. 58. Cited in text as *Ficciones*.

25. Jorge Luis Borges, *The Aleph and Other Stories, 1933–1969,* ed. and trans. Norman Thomas di Giovanni in collaboration with the author (New York: E. P. Dutton, 1970), p. 16.

26. *A Dictionary of Christian Biography: Literature, Sects and Doctrines,* ed. William Smith and Henry Wace (Boston: Little, Brown and Co., 1880), vol. 2, p. 126.

27. *Invasion of the Body Snatchers,* directed by Philip Kaufman, produced by Robert H. Solo, screenplay by W. D. Ritcher (MGM), 1978. The first *Invasion of the Body Snatchers* was directed by Don Siegel, produced by Walter Wanger, with a screenplay by Daniel Mainwaring from the *Collier's* serial by Jack Finney (Republic Pictures Corporation), 1956.

28. See *Invasion of the Body Snatchers,* ed. Al LaValley, Don Siegel, director (New Brunswick: Rutgers University Press, 1989). The book contains the script of the movie, interviews with the director, and a collection of essays. See in particular Nancy Steffen-Fluhr, "Women and the Inner Game of Don Siegel's *Invasion of the Body Snatchers,*" pp. 206–221.

29. *Frankenstein or the Modern Prometheus,* ed. with variant readings by James Rieger (Chicago: The University of Chicago Press, 1982), p. 53.

30. The ending was imposed on Siegel by the studio. Siegel had planned a more radical epilogue: "I wanted to end it with McCarthy on the highway turning to the camera and saying: 'You're next!'" See Stuart M. Kaminski, "Don Siegel on the Pod Society," in La Valley, *Invasion,* p. 153.

Index